GEOLOGY
MADE SIMPLE

Revised Edition

GEOLOGY
MADE SIMPLE

Revised Edition

WILLIAM H. MATTHEWS III

Regents' Professor of Geology
Lamar University, Beaumont, Texas

MADE SIMPLE BOOKS

Doubleday & Company, Inc.

Garden City, New York

Library of Congress Cataloging in Publication Data
Matthews, William Henry, 1919–
Geology made simple.
(Made simple books)
Bibliography: p. 207
Includes index.
1. Geology. I. Title. II. Series.
QE28.M38   1982   550
AACR2
ISBN: 0-385-17142-0
Library of Congress Catalog Card Number 67–10378

In Memory of My Parents,
Douglass Fain, and Will H. Matthews, Jr.

About the Revised Edition

Since the publication of the first edition of GEOLOGY MADE SIMPLE there has been a revolution in the geosciences: geology, geophysics, and related earth sciences. New information has been gathered from satellite imagery, lunar exploration, deep-sea drilling, and laboratory investigations.

Moreover, the theory of plate tectonics, with its major concepts of continental drift and sea-floor spreading, has revolutionized geological thinking with respect to ancient climates, prehistoric life, and the locations of the oceans and landmasses throughout earth history. The role of global tectonics in understanding volcanoes (such as Mount St. Helens), earthquakes, and earthquake prediction has been especially important. These recent developments—and much more—have been included in this edition in order that the reader might better appreciate the role of geology in aiding our understanding of our planetary home and the importance of conserving its rapidly dwindling, nonrenewable mineral resources.

William H. Matthews III
Beaumont, Texas
February 9, 1981

Contents

PART I—PHYSICAL GEOLOGY

CHAPTER 1

THIS EARTH OF OURS

This earth we live on—what could be more important to us? Yet, how little most of us really know about the composition and history of the planet that is our home. We enjoy the products of soils which have been formed by weathered rock, oil formed from the remains of prehistoric plants and animals, and the beauty of precious stones. But these are only a fraction of the useful and valuable materials with which the earth provides us.

Think also of the importance of earth products in the development of modern industry. Our vast mineral resources such as lead, iron, coal, and petroleum are derived from the earth, and these products have been made more readily available through the application of basic geology and geological engineering.

The earth has also provided us with areas of exceptional beauty. Who does not marvel at the breath-taking vastness of the Grand Canyon, the mystery of a great cavern, or the natural wonders of Yellowstone or Yosemite? All of these, and many more, are the results of geologic processes that are still at work within and on the earth today. They are the same processes which began to shape the earth soon after its birth—more than 4 billion 600 million years ago!

THE NATURE AND SCOPE OF GEOLOGY

What is geology?

Derived from the Greek *geo*, "earth," plus *logos*, "discourse," geology is the science which deals with the origin, structure, and history of the earth and its inhabitants as recorded in the rocks.

To the geologist, the earth is not simply the globe upon which we live—it is an ever present challenge to learn more about such things as earthquakes, volcanoes, glaciers, drifting continents, and the meaning of fossils. How old is the earth? Where did it come from? Of what is it made? To answer these questions, earth scientists must study the evidence of events that occurred millions of years ago. They must then relate their findings to the results of similar events that are happening today. Geologists attempt, for example, to determine the location and extent of ancient oceans and mountain ranges, and to trace the evolution of life as recorded in rocks of different ages. They also study the composition of the rocks and minerals forming the earth's crust in an attempt to locate and exploit the valuable economic products that are to be found there.

In pursuing the study of the earth geologists rely heavily upon other basic sciences. For example, **astronomy** (the study of the nature and movements of planets, stars, and other heavenly bodies) tells us where the earth fits into the universe and has also developed several theories as to the origin of our planet. **Chemistry** (the study of the composition of substances and the changes which they undergo) is used to analyze and study the rocks and minerals of the earth's crust. The science of **physics** (the study of matter and motion) helps explain the various physical forces affecting our earth, and the reaction of earth materials to these forces.

To understand the nature of prehistoric plants and animals we turn to **biology,** the study of all living forms. **Zoology** provides us with information about the animals, and **botany** gives us some insight into the nature of ancient plants. By using these sciences, as well as others, the geologist is better able to cope with the many complex problems that are inherent in the study of the earth and its history.

The scope of geology is so broad that it has been divided into two major divisions: **physical geology** and **historical geology.** For convenience in study, each of these divisions has been subdivided into a number of more specialized branches or subsciences.

The term **earth science** is commonly used in conjunction with the study of the earth. Although earth science includes the study of geology, it also encompasses the sciences of **meteorology** (the study of the atmosphere), **oceanography** (the study of the oceans), and **astronomy.**

PHYSICAL GEOLOGY

Physical geology deals with the earth's composition, its structure, the movements within and upon the earth's crust, and the geologic processes by which the earth's surface is, or has been, changed.

This broad division of geology includes such basic geologic subsciences as **mineralogy,** the study of minerals, and **petrology,** the study of rocks. These two branches of geology provide much-needed information about the composition of the earth. In addition, there is **structural geology** to explain the arrangement of the rocks within the earth, and **geomorphology** to explain the origin of its surface features. Another important branch of physical geology is **economic geology,** the study of the economic products of the earth's crust and their application for commercial and industrial purposes. Included here, for example, are the more important fields of mining and petroleum geology. (There are several other branches of physical geology, but they will be considered elsewhere in this book.)

These branches of physical geology enable the geologist to make detailed studies of all phases of earth science. The knowledge gained from such research brings about a better understanding of

the physical nature of planet Earth. Information from each of these geological subsciences has also helped in developing the theory of plate tectonics and in relating Earth to other bodies in the solar system.

HISTORICAL GEOLOGY

Historical geology is the study of the origin and evolution of the earth and its inhabitants. Like physical geology, historical geology covers such a variety of fields that it has been subdivided into several branches. Each of these branches is actually a science within itself, and one may devote a lifetime of study to specializing in any one of them.

In working out the geologic history of an area, the geologist utilizes **stratigraphy,** which is concerned with the origin, composition, proper sequence, and correlation of the rock strata. **Paleontology** (the study of ancient organisms as revealed by their fossils) provides a background of the development of life on earth, and **paleogeography** affords a means of studying geographic conditions of past times. It is thus possible to reconstruct the relations of ancient lands and seas and the organisms that inhabited them.

The major branches of historical geology, like those of physical geology, overlap in some areas and are interdependent. The physical geologist uses mineralogy and petrology to determine what types of rocks are present and from what they were derived. The historical geologist studies the same rocks to ascertain what kinds of animals or plants were living at the time the rocks were deposited, the environment they lived in, and the kind of climate that was present. Thus, the unification of physical and historical geology leads ultimately to a better understanding of the composition and history of the earth.

THE GEOLOGY AROUND US

How can we learn more about this fascinating earth and the stories to be read from its rocks? Actually it is very simple, for geology is all around us. The geologist's laboratory is the great outdoors, and each walk through the fields or drive down the highway brings us in contact with the processes and materials of geology.

For example, pick up a piece of common limestone. There may be fossils in it. And these fossils may well represent the remains of animals that lived in some prehistoric sea which once covered the area.

Or maybe you are walking along a river bank. Notice the silt left on the bank after the last high-water stage. This illustrates the ability of running water to deposit **sediments**—sediments that may later be transformed into rocks. Notice, too, how swift currents have scoured the river banks. The soil has been removed by **erosion,** the geologic process which is so important in the shaping of the earth's surface features.

Perhaps you see a field of black fertile soil supporting a fine crop of cotton or corn. It may surprise you to learn that this dark rich soil may have been derived from an underlying chalky white limestone—still another reminder of the importance of earth materials in our everyday life.

Within recent years there has been a notable increase in interest in earth science. This is not surprising, for people have become more aware of the importance of geology in their everyday lives. Geology will become even more important in the future as energy-producing mineral resources and world supplies of industrial and metallic minerals become increasingly scarce.

Meanwhile, more people are visiting museums, joining rock and mineral clubs, taking field trips with various museum and nature groups, or taking earth science courses in high schools, colleges, or universities. They are learning that even a passing acquaintance with geology can make this earth we live on a more interesting place.

THE PLANET EARTH

The earth, its relation to the stars and planets, and speculations as to its origin attracted human curiosity long before the birth of the geological sciences. Although such studies fall more properly within the realm of astronomy,[1] a brief sur-

[1] For a more complete presentation of astronomy, see *Astronomy Made Simple,* new revised edition, by Meir H. Degani, Made Simple Books, Doubleday & Company, Inc., Garden City, New York, 1976.

vey of the earth and its planetary relations will provide the reader with some understanding of Earth's place in the universe.

THE EARTH IN SPACE

Galaxies, disc-shaped clusters containing millions or billions of stars, are the major constituents of the universe. Astronomers estimate that there are large numbers of galaxies in outer space. However, only one, the **Milky Way,** the galaxy in which Earth is located, will be discussed here. This galaxy, which contains every star that we can see with the naked eye, is lens-shaped and contains billions of stars, including the sun.

A great mass of gaseous material like the other stars, our sun has a diameter of about 865,000 miles and is located about halfway between the center and the edge of the Milky Way. The sun is important to man, for it is the center of the solar system. The solar system is composed of the sun, nine planets (all of which revolve around the sun), thousands of asteroids or planetoids (small planets), comets, and meteors.

The **planets,** the largest of the solid bodies in the solar system, all move on essentially the same plane around the sun. Nine in number, they are (in order from the sun), Mercury, Venus, Earth, Mars, Jupiter, Saturn, Uranus, Neptune, and Pluto.

Associated with most of the planets are smaller bodies called **satellites** or **moons,** which revolve around each planet. The moon, Earth's satellite, revolves around our planet approximately once every month. Some planets (Mercury, Venus, and Pluto) have no known satellites. However, Jupiter, the largest planet, has fourteen.

Located between the orbits of Mars and Jupiter are thousands of small planet-like bodies called **asteroids** (or **planetoids).** They revolve about the sun in much the same manner as the planets.

Meteors, rocklike objects traveling through space, become highly heated when they enter the earth's atmosphere. These so-called "shooting stars" are usually consumed by heat before they reach the earth's surface. Some, however, strike the earth as **meteorites.**

The solar system also contains large, self-luminous, celestial bodies called **comets.** When comets come near the sun they can be seen from the earth. Unfortunately, because of their eccentric (off-center) orbits, comets are visible only at long intervals.

SHAPE, SIZE, AND MOTIONS OF THE EARTH

As mentioned above, the earth is one of nine planets comprising the solar system. It is the largest of the four planets of the inner group (Mercury, Venus, Earth, and Mars) and is third closest to the sun (Fig. 1).

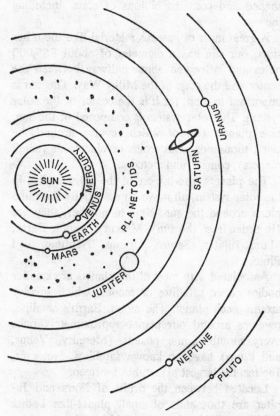

Fig. 1. Planets of the solar system and their relation to the sun.

Shape of the Earth. The earth has the form of an **oblate spheroid.** That is, it is almost ball-shaped, or spherical, except for a slight flattening at the poles. This flattening, and an accompanying bulge at the equator, are produced by the centrifugal force of rotation.

Size of the Earth. Although the earth is of great size, Jupiter, Saturn, Uranus, and Neptune all have greater equatorial diameters. Earth has a polar diameter of about 7900 miles (the equatorial diameter is approximately 27 miles greater because of the bulge described above). The circumference of the earth is about 24,874 miles, and the surface area comprises roughly 197 million square miles, of which only about 51 million square miles (29 percent) are surface lands. The remaining 71 percent of the earth's surface is covered by water.

Earth Motions. We have already learned that each of the planets revolves around the sun within its own orbit and period of revolution. In addition to its trip around the sun, the earth also rotates.

Rotation of the Earth. The earth turns on its **axis** (the shortest diameter connecting the poles), and this turning motion is called **rotation.** The earth rotates from west to east and makes one complete rotation each day. It is this rotating motion that gives us the alternating periods of daylight and darkness which we know as day and night.

Precession of the Earth. As the earth rotates it precesses, or "wobbles." This single wobble has to do with the fact that the earth's axis is tilted at an angle of 23½ degrees. However, this wobbling motion is so slow that it takes approximately 26,000 years to complete a single wobble. The tilting of the earth's axis is also responsible for the seasons.

Revolution of the Earth. The earth revolves around the sun in a slightly elliptical **orbit** approximately once every 365¼ days. During this time (a solar year), the earth travels at a speed of more than 60,000 miles per hour, and on the average it remains about 93 million miles from the sun.

In addition to rotation, revolution, and precession, our entire solar system is heading in the general direction of the star Vega at a speed of about 400 million miles per year.

PRINCIPAL DIVISIONS OF THE EARTH

The earth consists of air, water, and land. We recognize these more technically as the **atmosphere,** a gaseous envelope surrounding the earth; the **hydrosphere,** the waters filling the depressions and covering almost 71 percent of the earth; and the **lithosphere,** the solid part of the earth which underlies the atmosphere and hydrosphere.

The Atmosphere. The atmosphere, or gaseous portion of the earth, extends upward for hundreds of miles above sea level. It is a mixture of nitrogen, oxygen, carbon dioxide, water vapor, and other gases (see Table 1).

GAS	PERCENT BY VOLUME
Nitrogen	78.084
Oxygen	20.946
Argon	.934
Carbon dioxide	.033
Neon	.001818
Helium	.000524
Methane	.0002
Krypton	.000114
Hydrogen	.00005
Nitrous oxide	.00005
Xenon	.0000087

TABLE 1. Analysis of gases present in pure dry air. Notice that nitrogen and oxygen comprise 99 percent of the total volume of atmospheric gases.

Of great importance to humans, the elements of the atmosphere make life possible on our planet. Moreover, the atmosphere acts as an insulating agent to protect us from the heat of the sun and to shield us from the bombardment of meteorites, and it makes possible the evaporation and precipitation of moisture. The atmosphere is an important geologic agent (see Chapter 8) and is responsible for the processes of weathering which are continually at work on the earth's surface.

The Hydrosphere. The **hydrosphere** includes all the waters of the oceans, lakes, and rivers, as well as **ground water**—which exists within the lithosphere. As noted earlier, most of this water is contained in the oceans, which cover 70.8 percent of the earth's surface to an average depth of about two and a half miles.

The waters of the earth are essential to the existence of life and they are also of considerable geologic importance. Running streams and oceans are actively engaged in eroding, transporting, and depositing sediment. Indeed, running water, working in conjunction with atmospheric agents, has been the major force in forming the earth's surface features throughout geologic time. The geologic work of the hydrosphere is discussed in some detail in later chapters of this book.

The Lithosphere. Of prime importance to the geologist is the **lithosphere.** This, the solid portion of the earth, is composed of rocks and minerals which, in turn, comprise the continental masses and ocean basins (see Chapter 13). The rocks of the lithosphere are of three basic types, **igneous, sedimentary,** and **metamorphic.** Igneous rocks were originally in a molten state but have since cooled and solidified to form rocks such as granite and basalt. Sedimentary rocks are formed from sediments (fragments of pre-existing rocks) deposited by wind, water, or ice. Limestone, sandstone, and clay are typical of this group. The metamorphic rocks have been formed from rocks that were originally sedimentary or igneous in origin. This transformation takes place as the rock is subjected to great physical and chemical change. Marble, which in its original form was limestone, is an example of a metamorphic rock.

Most of what we know about the lithosphere has been learned through the study of the surface materials of the earth. However, by means of deep bore holes and seismological studies, geologists have gathered much valuable information about the interior of the earth. Additional geologic data are derived from rocks which were originally buried many miles beneath the ground but have been brought to or near the surface by violent earth movements and later exposed by erosion.

The Biosphere. Thanks to the life-giving qualities of air and water, Earth is populated by countless species of plants and animals. This horde of organisms comprises the **biosphere**—an organic realm of the earth that is intricately interrelated with the atmosphere, hydrosphere, and lithosphere.

Plants and animals are involved in a number of earth processes. Moreover, such valuable economic products as coal and petroleum have been formed from the remains of prehistoric organisms. Many rocks, especially certain limestones, are also of organic origin. In addition, there are bacteria that play a key role in the development of certain types of iron ore, and perhaps in the formation of petroleum.

Our interest in the biosphere reaches far back into the past. Geologists study the record of prehistoric life as revealed by fossils in an attempt to learn more about the history of the earth. They have also used these millions-of-years-old plant and animal remains to trace the development of life on earth.

The spheres of the earth are rather clearly defined and each has its own special role in the overall composition of the planet. However, the boundaries between them are not always as distinct. Instead, they are continually intermingling as air touches rock, rock comes in contact with water, and water mixes with air. There is constant interaction between Earth's spheres of matter, and important changes occur at the **interface**, or boundary, between them. These changes have been taking place for billions of years and will probably continue for billions more.

MAJOR PHYSICAL FEATURES OF THE EARTH

The major relief features of the earth are the **continental masses** and the **ocean basins.** These are the portions of the earth which apparently remained stable throughout all of known geologic time.

The Continental Masses. The continents are rocky platforms which cover approximately 29 percent of the earth's surface. Composed largely of granite, they have an average elevation of about three miles above the floors of the surrounding ocean basins and rise an average of one-half mile above sea level. The seaward edges of the continental masses are submerged and

these are called the **continental shelves.** The seaward edges of these shelves extend downward to form the **continental slopes** (Fig. 2).

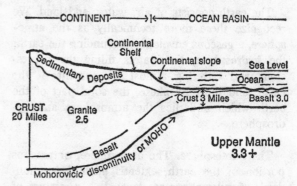

Fig. 2. This cross section through the earth's crust is about 400 miles in length. Note the relative thickness and density (indicated by numbers) of the continental and oceanic crust.

Although the continental surfaces appear to be very irregular to man, the difference in elevation between the highest mountain (Mount Everest—more than 29,000 feet above sea level) and the deepest part of the ocean (more than 35,000 feet deep, south of the Mariana Islands in the Pacific) is inconsequential when considered in relation to the size of the earth. The landforms responsible for the earth's surface irregularities are discussed in Chapter 16.

The Ocean Basins. The ocean basins contain the greatest part of the hydrosphere and cover almost 71 percent of the earth's surface. The floors of the oceans were originally believed to be quite flat and featureless, but recent oceanographic studies indicate that this is not so. The surface of the ocean floor possesses as many irregularities as the land and includes deep trenches, canyons, and submarine mountain ranges.

Of the five oceans, Arctic, Antarctic, Atlantic, Indian, and Pacific, the latter is deepest (about 35,000 feet) and largest, covering almost half of the earth. The bottoms of the deepest parts of the oceans are composed of basalt, a rather dense, dark, igneous rock. In many places the basaltic bottom is covered by layers of marine sediments.

The origin of the continents and ocean basins and their relationship to each other are discussed in later chapters.

GEOLOGIC PROCESSES

Geologic investigation of almost any part of the earth's surface will reveal some indication of great changes which the earth has undergone. These changes are of many kinds and most have taken place over millions of years. They are, in general, brought about by the processes of **erosion, tectonism,** and **volcanism.**

Erosion. The surface rocks of the earth are constantly being affected by erosion. For example, the atmosphere attacks the rocks, weathering them both physically and chemically. In addition, the rivers and oceans of the hydrosphere are continually wearing away rock fragments and transporting them to other areas where they are deposited.

Tectonism. This term encompasses all the movements of the solid parts of the earth with respect to each other. Tectonic movements, which are indicative of crustal instability, produce **fault-** ing (fracture and displacement), **folding, subsidence,** and **uplift** of rock formations. Known also as **diastrophism,** tectonism is responsible for the formation of many of our great mountain ranges and for most of the structural deformation that has occurred in the earth's crust. However, these tectonic features (such as folds and faults) are not usually seen until they have been exposed by the process of erosion.

In addition, widespread tectonic movements are responsible for certain types of metamorphism (see Chapter 6). The intrusion of **magma,** more closely associated with volcanism (see below), may also bring about rock deformation by folding.

Tectonic activity is also closely associated with continental drift and sea-floor spreading, as well as certain other geologic phenomena that are now being explained by the theory of plate tectonics (see Chapter 2).

Volcanism. This term, known also as **vulcanism,** refers to the movement of molten rock materials within the earth or upon the surface of the earth. Volcanic processes produce the lavas,

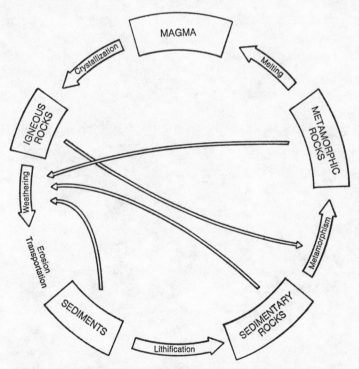

Fig. 3. The rock cycle, if uninterrupted, will continue completely around the outer margin of the diagram. However, as shown by the arrows, the cycle may be interrupted or "short-circuited" at various points in its course.

ashes, and cinders which are ejected from volcanoes. Volcanism is also responsible for the rocks, once molten, which solidified at great depth within the earth (see Chapter 4).

THE ROCK CYCLE

With time and changing conditions, the igneous, sedimentary, and metamorphic rocks of the lithosphere are subject to alteration by the processes of erosion, volcanism, and tectonism. Any of these rock types can be changed from one kind to another in a variety of ways. For example, an igneous rock can be worn away by erosion and reduced to fragments which may eventually end up as a deposit of sediments. In time these sediments may become consolidated into sedimentary rock. The sedimentary rock may later be subjected to forces that would transform it into a metamorphic rock. If the metamorphic rock continues to undergo increased heat and pressure, it may eventually melt to form magma. When this magma cools and solidifies, an igneous rock will be formed. Thus, we have a cycle that began with the erosion of igneous rock and ended with the formation of new igneous rock.

Known as the **rock cycle,** this series of events represents a response of earth materials to various forms of energy. Note that the outer circle of Figure 3 represents the complete, uninterrupted cycle. But the cycle is not always completed, for there can be many "short circuits" along the way. Some of the shortcuts that bypass parts of the cycle are indicated by the arrows within the circle. Notice that the starting point in the rock cycle is magma. This subterranean molten rock is a key link in an endless chain that connects present-day rocks with the igneous rocks of the earth's first crust.

CHAPTER 2

PLATE TECTONICS

Within the past fifteen or twenty years geologists have made some startling discoveries about the structure and behavior of the earth's solid outer shell. Their findings have led to the theory of plate tectonics—a theory so important that it has revolutionized the way earth scientists now study our planet. What is this revolutionary concept? The theory of plate tectonics deals with the formation, destruction, and motion of great segments of the earth's crust, called **plates** (Fig. 4). This theory relies heavily on the now generally accepted concepts of continental drift and seafloor spreading to help explain the cause of earthquakes and volcanic eruptions, and the origin of fold mountain systems—linear mountain ranges produced by bending and buckling of the earth's crust.

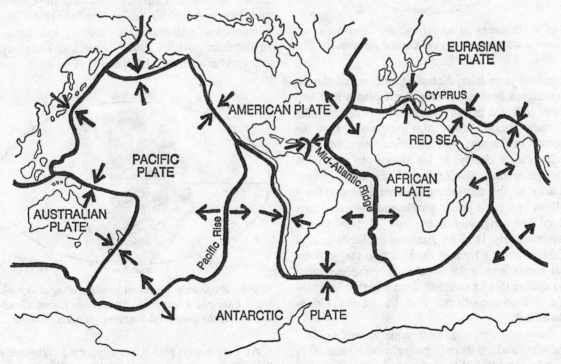

Fig. 4. World map of plates (arrows show direction of movement) and oceanic ridges.

CONTINENTAL DRIFT

Early geologists quite naturally assumed that our continents were both stable and stationary. But as long ago as 1620, Sir Francis Bacon, the famous English philosopher, noted the remarkable similarity of the Atlantic coastlines of Africa and South America (Fig. 5). More than two

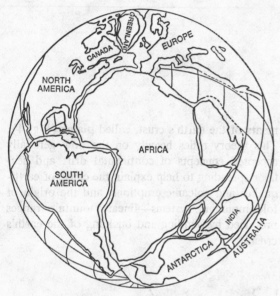

Fig. 5. Proposed fit of Africa, the Americas, and other continents prior to continental drifting.

hundred years later, Antonio Snider noted the resemblance between certain fossil plants that had been collected in both Europe and America. Like Francis Bacon, Snider also recognized that the coasts of Europe and America matched each other rather closely. In his attempt to determine the geographic distribution of his fossil plants, Snider fit the continents together like matching pieces in a giant jigsaw puzzle and theorized that they had originally been part of one master landmass. By 1885 an Austrian geologist named Eduard Suess advanced the idea that the geological formations in the Southern Hemisphere were so similar that he could fit them together in a single, massive continent that he named **Gondwanaland.**

Bacon, Snider, and Suess made valuable observations and gathered geologic evidence that clearly suggested the continents have not always

been where they are today. It remained, however, for Alfred Wegener (a German meteorologist) to attempt an explanation of this usual phenomenon. His solution—the **theory of continental drift** —was proposed in 1912 and triggered a scientific controversy that raged for decades.

Briefly stated, Wegener, like Suess, proposed the earlier existence of a single ancestral continent which he named **Pangaea** (Pan-gee'-uh), derived from Greek words meaning "all earth." Wegener assumed that his "mother" continent broke apart some 200 million years ago and the fragments slowly drifted to their present locations. In addition to earlier evidence, he used rocks, fossils, and other geologic clues to support his controversial idea. Despite great differences today, Wegener contended that worldwide climates, global geography, and the distribution of life forms had once been similar in different parts of the globe. Consequently, he assumed that the continents originally had been much closer together, or even connected.

Although the presence of Pangaea is still supported by some, more recent evidence favors the concept of two original landmasses: **Laurasia** in the Northern Hemisphere and **Gondwanaland** in the Southern. Supporters of the two-continent theory hold that Laurasia consisted of Eurasia and North America, while Gondwanaland was composed of Australia, Antarctica, the Indian subcontinent, Africa, South America, Malagasy, and various submerged fragments (Fig. 6).

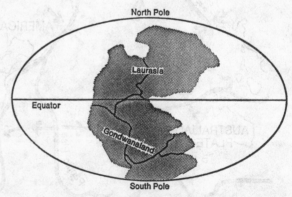

Fig. 6. Wegener's ancestral continent of Pangaea. Note Laurasia (north of the equator) and Gondwanaland, the proposed southern "supercontinent."

At first many geologists supported Wegener's idea. But as time passed a host of objections were leveled at continental drift and the theory was eventually cast aside and ignored or ridiculed by most earth scientists. But no more. After being in disrepute for years, continental drift is in vogue once again and is a keystone of plate tectonics.

EVIDENCE FOR CONTINENTAL DRIFT

Many earth scientists now find this once revolutionary theory quite logical in the light of recent scientific discoveries. These show that the continents have not only shifted in the past but are drifting even now. It has been learned, for example, that Iceland is being separated by the same forces that are thought to drift continents. An English scientist has found that parts of Iceland are being pulled apart at the rate of one-third of an inch per year. Additional support for continental drift has come from the study of the ocean floor, the distribution of fossils, evidence of ancient climates, and radiometric dating.

The Continental "Jigsaw Puzzle." As noted earlier, if we examine the outlines of certain continents, it almost seems as if they would fit together like the pieces in a giant jigsaw puzzle. The match of the eastern coast of South America with the western margin of Africa is especially striking (Fig. 5). At first glance the outlines of the other continents do not fit as neatly as do those of Africa and South America. But if we fit the other continents together at the continental slope (about 2950 feet below sea level), they fit together remarkably well.

Sea-floor Spreading. Some of the strongest evidence in favor of drifting land has been found on the bottom of the sea. Marine geologists studying the oceanic ridges have found this 40,000-mile-long submarine mountain chain (Fig. 4) to be the source of much valuable scientific information. This is especially true of the **Mid-Atlantic Ridge.** This 10,000-mile undersea range begins at the southern tip of Africa and snakes its way across the ocean floor to Iceland. It averages 20 miles in width and rises as much as a mile above the ocean floor.

The rocks on and near the Mid-Atlantic Ridge tell us much about the crust and how the continents may have drifted. Investigations reveal that the ocean floor near the ridge is not stationary; like the continents, it is spreading apart (Fig. 7). A deep **rift**, or trench, runs along the crest of the Mid-Atlantic Ridge. The expansion of the sea bottom appears to be associated with volcanic activity that originates beneath the ridge. Molten rock periodically boils out of the ridge's central rift and lava pours down the flanks of the submarine range. Each time there is an eruption, the pressure of the outpouring lava pushes the sides of the trench progressively farther apart. The newer lava hardens in and adjacent to the central rift. Consequently, the flows of lava become increasingly older on each side of the trench. The result is a series of progressively older parallel bands of lava away from the ridge.

Rift in Mid-Ocean Ridge

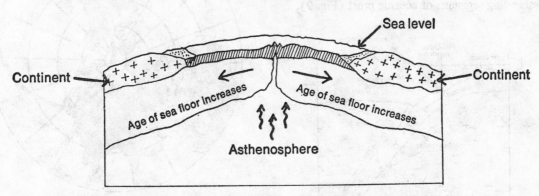

Fig. 7. A spreading center at a mid-ocean ridge. New sea floor is formed as lava is extruded from the rift in the oceanic ridge. As the rift widens, the sea floor moves and becomes increasingly older in the directions of the arrows.

As the sea floor expands, countless fractures develop in the relatively thin, brittle rocks of the oceanic crust. Many of these fractures have a lateral (sideways) movement and are called **transform faults** (Fig. 8). The lava flows and the transform faults suggest that the sea floor is continually tearing apart and being repaired by lava flowing from the central trench.

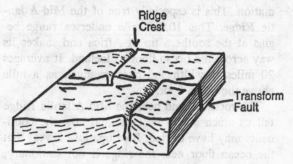

Fig. 8. Transform fault showing offset of an oceanic ridge.

Some scientists have suggested that the expanding sea bottom is somewhat like a great conveyor belt. In other words, as the ocean bottom spreads, it may be carrying the continents along with it.

The concept of sea-floor spreading suggests that the Atlantic Ocean basin is becoming wider as the continents are being pushed away from the Mid-Atlantic Ridge. This means, in turn, that the Pacific Ocean basin is presumably becoming smaller. The excess material in the shrinking Pacific basin is believed to be forced downward through **subduction zones,** a series of oceanic trenches, where it is pulled into the mantle by the descending segments of oceanic crust (Fig. 9).

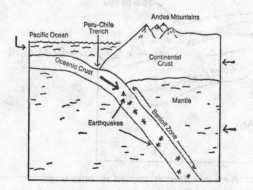

Fig. 9. Subduction zone and oceanic trench off west coast of South America.

Paleomagnetism. How do we know that the rocks become increasingly older on each side of the Mid-Atlantic Ridge? The clues are found in tiny "fossil" magnets embedded in the lava flows. Most of us have seen how the earth's magnetic poles cause the needle of a compass to line up in a north-south direction. When rocks containing tiny particles of magnetic iron minerals were formed, the flecks of iron tended to line up with the earth's magnetic field as it was when the rocks were formed. Equally important, these tiny "compass needles" retain their magnetic properties for hundreds of millions of years. This rock characteristic is called **paleomagnetism,** a word that literally means "ancient magnetism."

In rocks of any given age, the "fossil compasses" are in line with the magnetic poles as they were at the time of the rock's origin. But in older or younger rocks, the telltale "needles" may point in quite different directions—evidence that the poles had changed. In both instances, however, paleomagnetism might indicate polar directions unlike the north the south of today. Paleomagnetic studies suggest that there have been many changes in the earth's magnetic field. Indeed, they reveal that the poles have done quite a bit of wandering (Fig. 10) and that the earth's magnetic field may have been completely reversed at least 9 times in the last 3½ billion years!

Fig. 10. As indicated by the numbers, Earth's magnetic pole has been at different places during different intervals of geologic time.

Scientists have plotted curves to indicate the position of the poles during various chapters in earth history. They consider these to be evidence of continental drift, because their studies yield different polar curves for different continents. If the continents have *not* drifted, it is assumed that the polar curves for all continents would remain the same.

The "fossil magnets" in the lava flows on either side of the Mid-Atlantic Ridge are of interest to students of sea-floor spreading and continental drift. They indicate that one flow will have normal polarity while the next shows that the poles have been reversed. This suggests that one outpouring of lava occurred when our magnetic

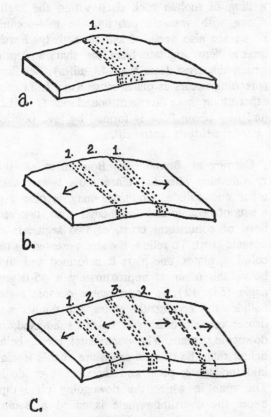

Fig. 11. Section of spreading sea floor showing bands of rock forming along an oceanic ridge crest. (a) The rocks at 1 (shaded area) have normal polarity. (b) The rocks have split apart and moved away from the ridge crest. New rock is now forming at the crest (2) and has reversed polarity (as indicated by shading). (c) The rocks at 2 have moved apart and the new rock forming at the ridge crest (3) has normal polarity.

poles were much as they are today. However, the next band of lava was laid down many thousands of years later when the poles were reversed. As a result of continuing lava flows and changing poles, the growth of the ocean floor has been recorded in a series of magnetized bands of normal and reversed polarity (Fig. 11).

The stripelike pattern of these alternating bands records the development of the sea bottom much as the rings in a tree trunk reveal the growth pattern of a tree.

Paleoclimatology. Paleoclimatologists reconstruct ancient climates in order to better interpret the record of life on earth. An understanding of prehistoric climates also helps confirm continental drift. For example, the distribution of glacial deposits in South America, Africa, Australia, and India suggests that parts of these continents were once covered by a huge ice sheet. Moreover, the direction of ice flow leads to the assumption that the ice of Africa and South America were part of the same glacier when these two continents were still joined. This indicates that the south pole might have been somewhere in the vicinity of South Africa during late Paleozoic time. In addition, the apparent continuity of the glacier's flow pattern strongly suggests a single southern continent called Gondwanaland.

Other ancient climatic indicators are coral reefs (suggesting warm, shallow seas) and beds of coal formed from plants that inhabited warm, moist climates. Fossil coral reefs and coal deposits are now found in parts of the world that are much too cold and/or dry to support either corals or swamp-loving vegetation.

Paleontology. The occurrence of fossils of identical land-dwelling plants and animals further supports continental drift. Consider *Glossopteris,* a fern, and *Mesosaurus,* a meat-eating reptile. The *Glossopteris,* or "tongue fern," is commonly found associated with widespread glacial deposits that blanket much of central and southern Africa, Australia, New Zealand, parts of South America, and peninsular India. Regardless of how these plants were dispersed, botanists agree that the "tongue ferns" could not possibly have spread across the broad expanse of open sea that now separates these areas.

Geochronology. Scientists who have studied the physical and chemical characteristics of rocks on the ocean floor and opposing continents find significant similarities between them. By means of radiometric dating, they also know that rocks in such widely separated locations as India, Australia, South America, and Africa can be closely related to each other on the basis of their geologic age. The implication is, of course, that the matching rock sections in these widely separated areas were formed at the same time and thus were once connected.

CRUSTAL PLATES

Crustal plates are great slabs of rock which make up the **lithosphere**—the rigid, outer part of the earth. Each plate measures from about 43 to 70 miles in thickness and may cover many thousands of square miles. Thus, the plates are tabular in shape, for they are thin in comparison to their length and width.

Some plates consist largely of **oceanic crust,** the part of the lithosphere that underlies the oceans. The oceanic crust is composed of dense, dark-colored rocks that are rich in iron and magnesium. Other plates are made up of **continental crust,** which consists of less dense, lighter-colored rocks that contain much silica and alumina. Such rocks are characteristic of the earth's landmasses. Some plates are composed of both types of crust, for plate boundaries do not always closely coincide with continental margins. For example, many of the major plates, including the American plate, are composed of both oceanic and continental crustal material.

Most geologists recognize at least six major plates and numerous smaller ones. These include the American, Antarctic, African, Eurasian, Pacific, and Australian plates (Fig. 4). Other investigators have recognized as many as ten major plates. Among the more generally agreed-upon smaller plates are the Nazca, Philippine, Caribbean, and Cocos plates.

PLATE BOUNDARIES

Boundaries between plates are typically associated with mid-oceanic ridges, deep-sea trenches, large faults, or linear fold mountain ranges. The motion of plates with respect to other adjacent plates results in three principal types of boundaries: (1) where plates move away from each other; (2) where plates move toward each other; and (3) where plates slide past each other in a more-or-less parallel fashion.

Divergent Boundaries. This type of boundary occurs along the mid-oceanic ridges, which form a nearly continuous submarine mountain range dividing the ocean basins. The ridges are zones of tension within the lithosphere, where tensional forces create fractures along the axis of the ridge, causing the adjacent plates to be pulled apart. New crust is formed along the fracture by the upwelling of molten rock deep within the earth. Along with volcanic activity, the mid-oceanic ridges are also areas of seismic activity. Earthquakes here originate from the shallow depths within the crust (less than 43 miles). Sea-floor spreading occurs as plates move away from each other along these divergent boundaries (Fig. 12) and new ocean floor is formed by lava pouring out of the ridge's central rift.

Convergent Boundaries. Boundaries of this type develop when two plates move toward each other and collide. Collisions may involve segments of oceanic and continental crust, two sections of continental crust, or two segments of oceanic crust. To relieve the stress created by the colliding plates, one plate is deformed and slips below the other at approximately a 45-degree angle (Fig. 12). In areas where oceanic plates collide with continental plates, the thinner and denser oceanic crust will be the subducted, or downgoing, plate. The continental rocks, being lighter than the oceanic crust, are unable to sink into the denser plate and therefore override it. The zone in which the downgoing plate dips under the overriding plate is called a **Benioff zone** or **subduction zone** (Fig. 9).

Physiographic features associated with subduction zones are deep ocean trenches and volcanic island arc systems such as those found around the western edge of the Pacific Ocean. As the downgoing plate continues to be overridden, earthquakes are produced. These quakes can occur in shallow regions or deep within the earth's interior (down to 435 miles). Earthquakes

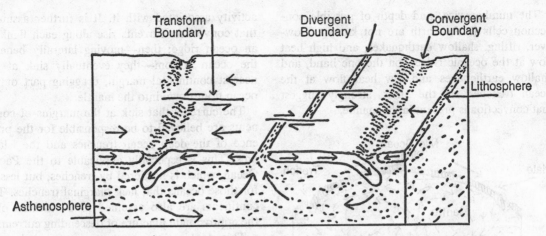

Fig. 12. Principal types of plate boundaries showing their relation to the lithosphere and asthenosphere.

associated with subduction zones are produced in two ways. Shallow-focus earthquakes originate as the downgoing plate breaks as it bends to move under the leading edge of the overriding plate. Farther down on the subsiding plate, deeper earthquakes are generated by slippage between the downgoing oceanic crust and the overriding plate. The formation of fold mountains is another feature associated with colliding plates. These form on the overriding plate and are caused by the buckling and crumpling of the leading edge of the overriding plate. Magma is generated when the downgoing plate melts, and this molten material rises forcefully into fractures in the continental plate. Thus, oceanic crust—which is destroyed at convergent margins—may be recycled and returned to the crust as lava.

Transform, or Shear, Boundaries. In this type of boundary plates do not separate or collide; rather, they slide past each other with a shearing motion (Fig. 12). Such boundaries consist of fractures which are essentially perpendicular to the ridge system; they are known as **transform faults** (Fig. 12). The San Andreas fault in California is now considered by many earth scientists to be a transform fault which is associated with the mid-ocean ridge located on the eastern edge of the Pacific Ocean. Along these boundaries plates are able to slip past each other without being greatly deformed.

Triple Junctions. At some places three plates may meet at a common point to form a triple junction. The three parts of the junction may involve three different types of plate margin features such as divergent, convergent, or transform boundaries.

PLATE MOVEMENTS

It is generally assumed that the plates ride on the partially molten, plastic asthenosphere. This part of the earth is composed of the upper part of the mantle that lies directly beneath the lithosphere (Fig. 13). The movement of the plates is now well established, but the driving force that propels the continents and causes the ocean floor to spread is still something of a mystery.

Convection. Many geoscientists believe that sea-floor spreading and continental drift are caused by thermal convection currents within the mantle of the earth (Fig. 13). It is known that convection currents are generated when gases and liquids are heated, for when heat is applied the cooler portion of a liquid sinks because it is more dense than the heated portion. The sinking cooler material pushes up the heated part, and as the rising liquid reaches the surface it loses its heat, becomes more dense, and then moves down again. This continual exchange of heat results in circulating currents or **convection cells** that churn through the liquid as long as heat is applied.

The number, size, and depth of possible convection cells in the earth are not known. However, rifting, shallow earthquakes, and high heat flow at the oceanic ridges, on the one hand, and shallow earthquakes and low heat flow at the ocean trenches, on the other, strongly suggest that convection is present in the mantle.

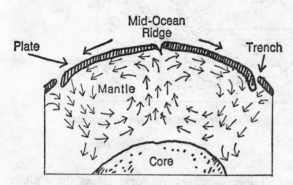

Fig. 13. Schematic diagram of convection cells in mantle (circulation of mantle material indicated by arrows). Note relation of circulation to mid-ocean ridge and trench.

But where do Earth's proposed convection cells get their energy? It is generally agreed that the heat responsible for convection cells in the mantle is caused by the steady disintegration of radioactive elements such as uranium. This nuclear heat is contained in the mantle because the overlying rocks conduct heat very slowly and act as an insulating "blanket." This permits the buildup of heat, which produces energy, causing the mantle to expand and convect upward. In time, some of this molten rock material will reach the surface by means of rifts in the oceanic ridges. As the lava pours out on the ocean floor, it moves the earlier formed rock along the crust and away from the ridge.

This would explain the spreading of the ocean floors, but what causes continental drift? A growing number of geologists are convinced that the portions of the convection cells that move parallel to the surface have caused the surface of the sea bottom to move. By combining the mechanism of drift with that of convection in the mantle, it is assumed that mid-ocean ridges are located above the junctions of upwelling currents that tend to spread the oceanic crust apart. This has produced the broad arch of the ridge, the rift along its crest, and the volcanic and earthquake

activity associated with it. It is further assumed that convection currents rise along each flank of an ocean ridge; then—moving laterally beneath the ocean bottom—they eventually sink at the nearest continental margin, dragging part of the ocean floor down into the mantle.

The currents that sink at the margins of continents are believed to be responsible for the presence of the deep ocean trenches and the island arcs. This is especially applicable to the Pacific Ocean, which is bordered by trenches, but less so for those oceans that lack marginal trenches. The continents are also assumed to be located over the approximate juncture of descending currents.

This explanation of plate movement is supported by paleomagnetism, for the magnetic lineations of the ocean floor (Fig. 12) might be compared to "footprints" left by the continents as they moved to their present positions.

Plumes. In Chapter 4 we learn that all volcanism is not confined to the plate boundaries or major volcanic belts. Some volcanoes (for example, those in Hawaii) and thermal areas (Yellowstone National Park) are said to be **intraplate** features because they are located over plumes, or **hot spots,** far from continental margins. Consisting of hypothetical jets of hot, rising, solid mantle some several hundred miles in diameter, these hot spots create rather localized areas of volcanic activity.

According to the plume theory, columns of hot mantle rock rise vertically and then spread out horizontally in the asthenosphere. Meanwhile, the mantle material surrounding the plume moves slowly downward to balance the upward movement in the hot spot. It is assumed that plate movement is caused by several forces. These include pressure exerted by the upward flow in the plume, the outward radial flow of plume material into the asthenosphere, and the returning downward flow of the mantle surrounding the hot spot.

Plumes are believed to be fixed in the mantle and hence do not move with the plates. Consequently, as a crustal plate moves over a hot spot, the plumes may periodically burn their way through the plate, merging as centers of volcanic activity. The Hawaiian Islands are thought to have been formed when active volcanoes originated over a stationary plume. As the plate moves, the plume breaks through the crust in a

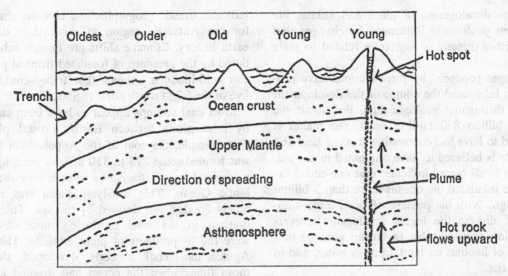

Fig. 14. Age relationships of volcanoes produced as lithospheric plate passes over a "hot spot" during sea-floor spreading.

new place, forming a new volcano. The former volcano, deprived of its magma reservoir, becomes extinct. Thus, the hot spot leaves a string of extinct volcanoes which become increasingly older away from the most recent active volcano. In addition to the Hawaiian and Yellowstone hot spots, some eighteen other major plumes are believed to exist in other parts of the world.

PLATE TECTONICS AND HUMANS

Volcanoes and Earthquakes. The concept of plate tectonics has not only revolutionized geological thinking, it also explains many phenomena which have serious human implications. For example, most volcanoes are associated with plate margins (Fig. 31). Magma generated as the result of plate motions may reach the surface as lava, which may cause much property damage and loss of life. Moreover, most of the world's earthquakes are spawned in areas where crustal plates are colliding and grinding past each other (Fig. 9).

But the human implications of plate tectonics are not all negative. The movement of certain plates has had much to do with the origin and distribution of many of the earth's more valuable mineral resources.

Plate Tectonics and Mineral Deposits. The origin of many mineral deposits can now be ex-

plained by plate tectonics. Metallic minerals such as copper, tungsten, gold, molybdenum, silver, and lead appear to have formed from magmas originating above subduction zones at convergent plate boundaries. In western North America, for example, this apparently occurred from 100 to 15 million years ago when Pacific Ocean crust was rapidly subducted beneath North America. This created great volcanic belts. In the subsurface, granites crystallized from the huge volumes of magma located beneath the volcanoes. After crystallization of the silicate minerals in the magma, the metals were concentrated in the liquids that remained in the magma chamber. In those magmas where conditions were favorable, mineral-enriched fluids altered or replaced the adjacent wall rocks to form valuable ores.

Other mineral deposits—most associated with hot liquids or solutions that have passed through crustal rocks—occur along spreading margins. New crust is created at divergent boundaries, such as the oceanic ridges, and the newly created rocks often contain concentrations of valuable minerals. Unfortunately, most such deposits are difficult, if not impossible, to recover.

Plate Tectonics and Fossil Fuels. The formation and distribution of fossil fuels—coal, oil, and natural gas—is intricately linked with the development of life throughout geologic time.

And the development of plant and animal life has been profoundly influenced by changes that were either directly or indirectly related to plate motions.

Changes produced by plate motions have profoundly influenced the course of the development of life throughout geologic time. For about the past 3 billion 800 million years, our planet is believed to have had contrasting areas of land and sea. Life is believed to have originated in the sea, and the fossil record indicates that one-celled organisms inhabited the oceans more than 3 billion years ago. With the passage of time, large numbers of diverse life forms developed. In ever-increasing numbers these organisms adapted to a variety of habitats on land, in fresh water, and in the oceans.

As the landmasses changed position on the face of the globe, they were also subject to changes in climate. These geographic changes—and the sometimes dramatic climatic changes they produced—had a profound effect on the plants and animals of that time. This, in turn, has greatly influenced the way geologists search for fossil fuels.

Coal. Coal, like virtually all fossil fuels, is found largely in sedimentary rocks. In fact, lignite and bituminous coal *are* sedimentary rocks. Anthracite coal, however, has been greatly altered and is considered to be a metamorphic rock.

Regardless of type, coal consists of the carbonized remains of prehistoric tropical and subtropical plants that once flourished in vast "coal swamps." Such swamps and marshes were present on several continents during the Mississippian and Pennsylvanian periods (see Geologic Time Scale, Fig. 119). Similar conditions conducive to coal formation existed in the western United States some 50 to 80 million years ago.

The prehistoric wetlands responsible for most of our nation's coal were characterized by very warm, moist climates. Moreover, like modern swamps they were situated in areas of low elevation and little relief. But today most of our coal is located in inland areas of very high relief, where climates are far from tropical in nature. Indeed, deposits of coal have even been found in Antarctica. The coal, which is assumed to have formed under tropical to semitropical conditions,

indicates drastic geographic and climatic changes for the Antarctic region at some time during earth history. Climatic shifts are further substantiated by the presence of fossilized tropical plants and cold-blooded animals that today could not live in the frigid north polar regions.

Most coal swamps appear to have been caused by interactions between Earth's crustal plates. For example, the coal of the Appalachian fields was formed some 275 to 310 million years ago in a foreland basin adjacent to what is now the Atlantic Ocean. This low-lying basin was alternately flooded and drained by the sea. The fluctuations in sea level producing these changes were the by-products of plate motions. The old Appalachian coal swamps developed during those times when the ocean had drained away, thereby exposing the coastal lowlands and encouraging the development of lush vegetation.

The lignite and bituminous coal of the Great Plains and western interior of the United States are considerably younger than Appalachian coal. They originated in Early Tertiary and Cretaceous times. The oldest western coal developed in a broad foreland basin. Characterized by coastal swamps, this basin paralleled the west side of a shallow inland sea. The development of this interior sea may have been due to rapid sea-floor spreading.

Although the coals in the Rocky Mountain region are much younger than those in the Appalachians, their origin is also related to plate motions. Rocky Mountain coals developed in extensive swamps located in more localized basins than those associated with Appalachian coal. The local basins appear to have been produced by plate movements resulting from oblique (or sidelong) compression of the continental crust of the western interior. These massive beds of younger (Cretaceous) coals constitute one of the world's greatest energy reserves.

Oil and Natural Gas. Like coal, oil and natural gas are found in sedimentary rocks. However, whereas coal is typically associated with sedimentary strata representing terrestrial sediments, oil and gas are generally found in beds of porous and permeable marine sedimentary rock. These oil-bearing strata commonly occur in wedges and basins that are largely the results of the motions of certain crustal plates.

Although the exact process is not thoroughly understood, crude oil and natural gas are produced by the breakdown of organic matter. The oil-forming process as well as the maturation, migration, and entrapment of these hydrocarbons will be discussed in Chapter 17.

Plate tectonics also has a role in determining where—or whether—crude oil and natural gas will be formed. Therefore an understanding of the processes and products of plate tectonics can be of inestimable value in petroleum exploration.

Most of the world's oil, including the vast reserves of the Persian Gulf, is locked up in strata associated with continental shelves. These sedimentary rocks have formed from marine sediments deposited on continental margins that are **rifted,** or split apart. When a continent first begins to rift, the pieces separate and the ocean spreads between them. Meanwhile, the edge of the continental shelf slowly spreads seaward, thins, and gradually subsides. As sedimentation continues, the strata on top of the subsiding shelf assume a subhorizontal position. But the deeper beds tend to dip (or slope) more steeply toward the sea. Even so, the slope of the oceanward-dipping strata is still relatively gentle.

Excellent conditions for oil formation may occur in such rifted areas with tilted rocks. Hydrocarbons formed in such places will typically migrate updip (up the slope of the beds) toward the continent. Most oil found on the Gulf Coast of the United States formed in such a tectonic setting. In addition, the exploration of the offshore Atlantic Outer Continental Shelf of the eastern United States assumes that there may be commercial quantities of hydrocarbons to be found in a similar tectonic environment.

Oil may also accumulate in strata formed in a foreland basin developed on the landward side of subduction systems (see page 14). Certain small fields in western Wyoming seem to have formed in such areas. More important, the huge Prudhoe Bay field of northern Alaska appears to owe part of its petroleum to this setting.

Elsewhere oil is found in broad basins located well within the continents. Some of these basins appear to be caused by the wrenching of continental plates as they collided with adjacent crustal segments. Other basins do not now appear to be directly related to interaction between plates. Rather, they may have formed as surface rocks subsided because of cooling at the base of the crustal plate.

CHAPTER 3

MINERALS

We now know that the geologist is primarily interested in the earth's rocky crust, but before one can study rocks it is necessary to know something about minerals, for these are the building blocks of the earth's crust. Although geologists differ when defining the term mineral, the following definition is generally accepted: **Minerals are chemical elements or compounds which occur naturally within the crust of the earth.** They are **inorganic** (not derived from living things), have a definite chemical composition or range of composition, an orderly internal arrangement of atoms (crystalline structure), and certain other distinct physical properties. It should be noted, however, that the chemical and physical properties of some minerals may vary within definite limits.

Rocks are aggregates or mixtures of minerals, the composition of which may vary greatly. Limestone, for example, is composed primarily of one mineral—calcite. Granite, on the other hand, typically contains three minerals—feldspar, mica, and quartz.

Certain minerals, such as calcite, quartz, and feldspar, are so commonly found in rocks that they are called the **rock-forming** minerals. Other minerals, like gold, diamond, uranium minerals, and silver, are found in relatively few rocks.

Minerals vary greatly in their chemical composition and physical properties. Let us now become acquainted with the more important physical and chemical characteristics that enable us to distinguish one mineral from the other.

CHEMICAL COMPOSITION OF MINERALS

Although a detailed discussion of chemistry is not within the scope of this book,[1] an introduction to chemical terminology is necessary if we are to understand the chemical composition of minerals.

All matter, including minerals, is composed of one or more **elements.** An element is a substance that cannot be broken down into simpler substances by ordinary chemical means. Theoretically, if you were to take a quantity of any element and cut it into smaller and smaller pieces, eventually you would obtain the smallest pieces that still retained the characteristics of the element. These minute particles are **atoms.** Although atoms are so small that they cannot be seen with the most powerful microscope (it would take 100 million of them to make a line one inch long) we know a great deal about them. We know, for instance, that the nucleus of an atom is composed of **protons,** positively charged particles, and **neutrons,** or uncharged particles. Outside the nucleus and revolving rapidly around it are negatively charged particles called **electrons.** It is now known, of course, that certain elements have been broken down by atomic fission or "atom-smashing," but these are not considered to be "ordinary chemical means." Although there

[1] For an easy-to-understand introduction to general chemistry, read *Chemistry Made Simple*, by Fred C. Hess, Made Simple Books, Doubleday & Company, Inc., Garden City, New York, 1955.

are only ninety-two elements occurring in nature, several more have been created artificially.

Some minerals, such as gold or silver, are composed of only one element. More often, however, minerals consist of two or more elements united to form a **compound.** For example, calcite is a chemical compound known as calcium carbonate. The chemical composition of a compound may be expressed by means of a chemical formula ($CaCO_3$ in the case of calcite) in which each element is represented by a symbol. The symbol is derived from an abbreviation of the Latin or English name of the element it represents. For many elements, the first letter of the element's name is used as its symbol—thus H for an atom of hydrogen, and C for an atom of carbon. If the names of two elements start with the same letter, two letters may be used for one of them to distinguish between their symbols. For example, an atom of helium may be represented as He, an atom of calcium as Ca. Some symbols have been derived from an abbreviation of the Latin name of the elements: Cu (from *cuprum*) represents an atom of copper, and Fe (from *ferrum*) an atom of iron. The small numerals used in a chemical formula represent the proportion in which each element is present. Hence, the formula for water, H_2O, indicates that there are two atoms of hydrogen for each atom of oxygen present in water.

Although more than one hundred elements are known, eight of these elements are so abundant that they constitute more than 98 percent (by weight) and almost 100 percent, by volume, of the earth's solid crust. These elements, their symbols, and relative percentages in the crust include:

ELEMENT	SYMBOL	% OF WEIGHT	% OF VOLUME
oxygen	O	46.71	94.24
silicon	Si	27.69	0.51
aluminum	Al	8.07	0.44
iron	Fe	5.05	0.37
calcium	Ca	3.65	1.04
sodium	Na	2.75	1.21
potassium	K	2.58	1.85
magnesium	Mg	2.08	0.27
		98.58	99.93

As indicated in the above table, two elements, oxygen and silicon, make up approximately three-fourths of the weight of the rocks. Both these elements are **nonmetals,** but the remaining six are **metals.** Metals are characterized by their capacity for conducting heat and electricity, their ability to be hammered into thin sheets (malleability) or to be drawn into wire (ductility), and their luster (the way light is reflected from the mineral's surface). Such minerals as gold, silver, copper, and iron are included in the metals. The nonmetallic, or industrial, minerals do not have the properties mentioned above. Some typical nonmetallic minerals are sulfur, diamond, and calcite.

CRYSTALS

When crystalline minerals solidify and grow without interference, they will normally adopt smooth angular shapes known as crystals. The planes that form the outside of the crystals are known as **faces.** These are related directly to the internal atomic structure of the mineral, and the size of the faces is dependent upon the frequency of the atoms in the different planes. The shape of the crystals and the angles between related sets of crystal faces are important in mineral identification.

Crystal Systems. Each mineral has been assigned to one of six crystal systems. These systems have been established on the basis of the number, position, and relative lengths of the crystal **axes**—imaginary lines extending through the center of the crystal (Figs. 15 and 16). Crystal axes are used to orient the crystal when it is studied. For example, crystals assigned to the te-

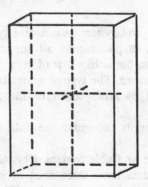

Fig. 15. Crystal axes. (Shown as intersecting dash-dot lines.)

tragonal system (see below) have three axes: two of equal length called the horizontal axes; the third (vertical) axis, which may be longer or shorter than the other two, is always placed vertically when the crystal is properly oriented (see Fig. 16b). Thus, the vertical axis of a crystal will always be perpendicular to the horizontal axes when the crystal is properly oriented.

characterized by having all three axes at right angles. The lateral (horizontal) axes (see below) are of equal length but are longer or shorter than the vertical axis (Fig. 16b).

Hexagonal System. This system has crystals marked by three horizontal axes of equal length which intersect at angles of 120 degrees, and a vertical axis at right angles to these. The vertical

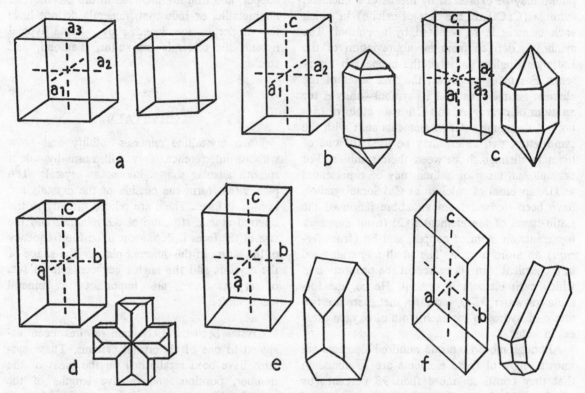

Fig. 16. Examples of the six crystal systems and a typical crystal from each. (Crystal axes are shown as broken lines and are lettered a, b, c.)

a–Isometric (halite)   b–Tetragonal (zircon)
c–Hexagonal (quartz)   d–Orthorhombic (staurolite)
e–Monoclinic (orthoclase)   f–Triclinic (albite)

Every crystal system possesses a type of symmetry that is peculiar to all members of any given system but unlike that of crystals belonging to other systems. The type of symmetry present is determined by arrangement of the axes of the crystal.

Mineralogists recognize the following crystal systems:

Isometric or Cubic System. Crystals belonging to this system have three axes of equal length and at right angles to one another (Fig. 16a).

Tetragonal System. Tetragonal crystals are

axis is either longer or shorter than the horizontal axes (Fig. 16c).

Orthorhombic System. Crystals assigned to this class have three axes all at right angles and each of a different length (Fig. 16d).

Monoclinic System. Monoclinic crystals have three unequal axes, two of which intersect at right angles. The third axis is oblique to one of the others (Fig. 16e).

Triclinic System. The triclinic system has crystals characterized by three axes of unequal length and all oblique to one another (Fig. 16f).

Crystal Habits. Any given mineral crystal will grow or develop in such a way as to form certain typical shapes. These forms are called their habits. Crystal habits are useful in the identification of minerals because they indicate what forms or combination of forms a mineral is likely to assume. For example, tourmaline has a **columnar** habit (Fig. 17b), galena a **cubic** habit (Fig. 17a), and barite a **tabular** habit (Fig. 17c). Because crystals of a specific mineral will develop only in the crystal system of that mineral, it follows that a cubic system crystal will show only cubic system characteristics. However, when crystals are formed at different temperatures, they may assume different habits within their system. Thus, fluorite crystals formed at low temperatures have a cubic form while those formed at high temperatures have an octahedral form. In some instances a mineral crystal may show a combination of two forms.

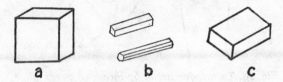

Fig. 17. Types of crystal habits.
a—Cubic b—Columnar c—Tabular

In addition to temperature, such factors as pressure, composition of the solutions from which the minerals crystallize, and variation in mineral composition may affect crystal forms. The presence of impurities in a mineral may also modify the habit of a crystal.

PHYSICAL PROPERTIES OF MINERALS

Each mineral possesses certain physical properties or characteristics by which it may be recognized or identified. Although some may be identified by visual examination, others must be subjected to certain simple tests.

Physical properties especially useful in mineral identification are (1) hardness, (2) color, (3) streak, (4) luster, (5) specific gravity, (6) cleavage, (7) fracture, (8) shape or form, (9) tenacity or elasticity, and (10) certain miscellaneous properties. The geologist must know how to test a mineral specimen for the above properties in order to identify it. Many of these tests do not require expensive laboratory equipment and may be done in the field. Some of them may be made by using such commonplace articles as a knife or a hardened steel file, a copper penny, a small magnet, an inexpensive pocket lens with a magnification of six to ten times, a piece of glass, a piece of unglazed porcelain tile, and a fingernail.

Hardness. One of the easiest ways to distinguish one mineral from another is by testing for hardness. The hardness of a mineral is determined by what materials it will scratch, and what materials will scratch it. The hardness or scratch test may be done with simple testing materials carried in the field. For great accuracy, one may use the scale of hardness called the **Mohs scale.** This scale, named for the German mineralogist Friedrich Mohs, was devised more than one hundred years ago. In studying his mineral collection, Mohs noticed that certain minerals were much harder than others. He believed that this variation could be of some value in mineral identification, so he selected ten common minerals to be used as standards in testing other minerals for hardness. In establishing this scale, Mohs assigned each of the reference minerals a number. He designated talc, the softest in the series, as having a hardness of 1. The hardest mineral, diamond, was assigned a hardness of 10.

The Mohs scale, composed of the ten reference minerals arranged in order of increasing hardness, is as follows:

No. 1—Talc (softest)
No. 2—Gypsum
No. 3—Calcite
No. 4—Fluorite
No. 5—Apatite
No. 6—Feldspar
No. 7—Quartz
No. 8—Topaz
No. 9—Corundum
No. 10—Diamond (hardest)

Most of the minerals in the Mohs scale are common ones, which can be obtained in inexpensive collections. Diamond chips are more expensive, but not beyond reason. Note that the Mohs scale is so arranged that each mineral will be scratched by those having higher numbers, and will scratch those having lower numbers.

It is also possible to test for hardness by using the following common objects:

ITEM	HARDNESS
Fingernail	About 2½
Copper penny	About 3
Glass	5–5½
Knife blade	5½–6
Steel file	6½–7

Each of the above items will scratch a mineral of the indicated hardness. For example: the fingernail will scratch talc (hardness of 1) and gypsum (hardness of 2), but would not scratch calcite, which has a hardness of 3.

In testing for hardness, first use the more common materials. Start with the fingernail; if that will not scratch the specimen, use the knife blade. If the knife blade produces a scratch, this indicates that the specimen has a hardness of between 2½ and 6 (see scale above). Referring to the Mohs scale, it is found that there are three minerals of known hardness within this range. These are: apatite (5); fluorite (4); and calcite (3). If the calcite will not scratch the specimen but the fluorite will, its hardness is further limited as between 3 and 4. Next, try to scratch the fluorite with the specimen. If this can be done, even with difficulty, the hardness is established as 4; if not, then it is between 3 and 4.

Color. Probably one of the first things that is noticed about a mineral is its color. However, the same mineral may vary greatly in color from one specimen to another, and with certain exceptions, color is of limited use in mineral identification. Certain minerals, for example, azurite, which is always blue, malachite, which is green, and pyrite, which is yellow, have relatively constant colors. Others, such as quartz or tourmaline, occur in a wide variety of colors; hence, color may be of little use in identifying these two minerals. Color variations of this sort are primarily due to minor chemical impurities within the mineral.

When using color in mineral identification, it is necessary to take into consideration such factors as (1) whether the specimen is being examined in natural or artificial light, (2) whether the sur-face being examined is fresh or weathered, and (3) whether the mineral is wet or dry. Each of these may cause color variations in a mineral. In addition, certain of the metallic minerals will tarnish and the true color will not be revealed except on a fresh surface.

Streak. When a mineral is rubbed across a piece of unglazed tile, it may leave a line similar to a pencil or crayon mark. This line is composed of the powdered minerals. The color of this powdered material is known as the streak of the mineral, and the unglazed tile used in such a test is called a **streak plate** (Fig. 18).

Fig. 18. Testing for streak by means of streak plate.

The streak in some minerals will not be the same as the color of the specimen. For example, a piece of black hematite will leave a reddish brown streak, and an extremely hard mineral such as topaz or corundum will leave no streak. This is because the streak plate has a hardness of about 7, and both topaz (8) and corundum (9) are harder than the streak plate, hence the mineral will not be powdered.

Luster. The appearance of the surface of a mineral as seen in reflected light is called luster. Some minerals shine like metals, for example, silver or gold. These are said to have metallic luster. Other lusters are called nonmetallic. The more important nonmetallic lusters and some common examples are shown below:

Adamantine—brilliant glossy luster: typical of diamond

Vitreous—glassy, looks like glass: quartz or topaz

Resinous—the luster of resin: sphalerite

Greasy—like an oily surface: nepheline

Pearly—like mother-of-pearl: talc
Silky—the luster of silk or rayon: asbestos or sat-
in-spar gypsum
Dull—as the name implies: chalk or clay

Submetallic luster is intermediate between metallic and nonmetallic luster. The mineral wol-
framite displays typical submetallic luster.

Terms such as **shining** (bright by reflected
light), **glistening** (a sparkling brightness), **splen-
dent** (glossy brilliance), and **dull** (lacking brilliance or luster) are commonly used to indicate
the degree of luster present. Here too, one must
take into consideration such factors as tarnish,
type of lighting, and general condition of the
mineral specimen being examined.

Specific Gravity. The relative weights of minerals are also useful in identification, for some
minerals, such as galena (an ore of lead), are
much heavier than others. The relative weight of
a mineral is called its **specific gravity.** Specific
gravity is determined by comparing the weight of
the mineral specimen with the weight of an equal
volume of fresh water. Thus, a specimen of
galena (specific gravity about 7.5) would be
about 7½ times as heavy as the same volume of
water.

In order to determine the specific gravity of a
given specimen, the specimen is weighed in air
on a spring scale (sometimes called a Jolly-
Kraus balance); then lowered into a container of
fresh water and weighed in the water. The
specific gravity (Sp. Gr.) equals the weight in air
divided by the loss of weight in water. When the
specific gravity has been determined, it may then
be compared with the known weight of other
minerals in order to identify the specimen.

Cleavage and Fracture. Mineral crystals will
break if they are strained beyond their plastic
and elastic limits. If the crystal breaks irregularly
it is said to exhibit **fracture,** but if it should break
along surfaces related to the crystal structure it is
said to show **cleavage** (Fig. 19). Each break or
cleavage plane is closely related to the atomic
structure of the mineral and designates planes of
weakness within the crystal. Because the number
of cleavage planes present and the angles between them are constant for any given mineral,
cleavage is a very useful aid in mineral identification.

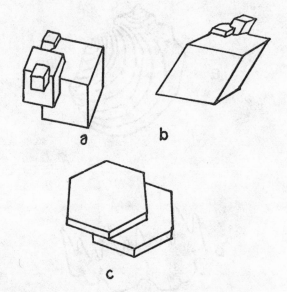

Fig. 19. Three types of cleavage.
a–Cubic   b–Rhombic   c–Perfect basal

Minerals may have one, two, three, four, or six
directions of cleavage. The mineral galena, for
example, cleaves in three planes (directions) at
right angles to one another. Thus, if galena is
struck a quick, sharp blow with a hammer, the
specimen will break up into a number of small
cubes. Calcite, on the other hand, has three
cleavage planes that are not at right angles to one
another. Therefore it will always produce a number of rhombohedral cleavage fragments. Hence,
galena is said to have **cubic** cleavage, calcite
rhombohedral cleavage.

Many minerals break or fracture in a distinctive way, and for this reason their broken surfaces (Fig. 20) may be of value in identifying
minerals.

There are several types of fractures; some of
the more common types (with example) are:

Conchoidal—the broken surface of the specimen shows a fracture resembling the smooth
curved surface of a shell. This type of fracture is typical of chipped glass: quartz and
obsidian.

Splintery or Fibrous—fibers or splinters are
revealed along the fracture surface: pecto-
lite.

Hackly—fracture surface marked by rough
jagged edges: copper, silver, and certain
other metals.

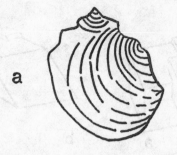

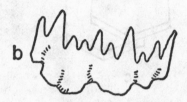

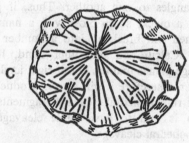

Fig. 20. Some Types of Fracture.
a–Conchoidal   b–Hackly   c–Splintery

Uneven—rough irregular fracture of surface. This type of fracture is common in many minerals and is, therefore, of limited use in identification: jasper, a variety of quartz.

Even—as the name implies: magnesite.

Earthy—as the name implies: kaolinite.

Tenacity. The tenacity of a mineral may be defined as the resistance that it offers to tearing, crushing, bending, or breaking. Some terms used to describe the different kinds of tenacity are:

Brittle—the mineral can be broken or powdered easily. The degree of brittleness may be qualified by such terms as tough, fragile, etc.: galena or sulfur.

Elastic—the mineral, after being bent, will return to its original form or position: mica.

Flexible—the mineral will bend but will not return to its original shape upon release of pressure: talc.

Sectile—the mineral can be cut with a knife to produce shavings: selenite gypsum and talc.

Malleable—the mineral can be hammered into thin sheets: gold and copper.

Ductile—the mineral can be drawn out into wire: gold, silver, and copper.

Other Physical Properties. In addition to those properties discussed above, the mineral characteristics below may also aid greatly in identification. Examples of minerals exhibiting these properties are given.

Play of Colors. Some minerals show variations in color when viewed from different angles: labradorite.

Asterism. This may be observed if the mineral exhibits a starlike effect when viewed either by reflected or transmitted light: certain specimens of phlogopite or the star-sapphire.

Diaphaneity or Transparency. This property refers to the ability of a mineral to transmit light. The varying degrees of diaphaneity are:

Opaque—no light passes through the mineral: galena, pyrite, and magnetite.

Translucent—light passes through the mineral but an object cannot be seen through it: chalcedony and certain other varieties of quartz.

Transparent—light passes through the mineral and the outline of objects can be clearly seen through it: halite, calcite, clear crystalline quartz.

Magnetism. A mineral is said to be magnetic if, in its natural state, it will be attracted to an iron magnet: magnetite, or lodestone, and pyrrhotite.

Luminescence. When a mineral glows or emits light that is not the direct result of incandescence, it is said to be luminescent. This phenomenon is usually produced by exposure to ultraviolet rays. Exposure to X rays, cathode rays, or radiation from radioactive substances can also cause luminescence. If the mineral is luminous only during the period of exposure to the ultraviolet rays or other stimulus, the material is said to be **fluorescent** (scheelite and willemite are fluorescent). A mineral exhibiting **phosphorescence** will continue to glow after the cause of excitation has been removed.

MINERALOIDS

Although most substances accepted as minerals are crystalline, some lack the ability to crystallize and occur instead as a hardened gel. Substances of this type are commonly referred to as mineraloids. They are also said to be **amorphous** —that is, without form, for example, opals.

ROCK-FORMING MINERALS

Of some two thousand different minerals that are known to be present in the earth's crust, relatively few are major constituents of the more common rocks. Those minerals that do make up a large part of the more common types of rocks are called the rock-forming minerals. Most of the rock-forming minerals are **silicates,** that is, they consist of a metal combined with silicon and oxygen. Because they are among the most common and abundant of all minerals, some of the more important rock-making minerals are briefly discussed below.

FELDSPARS

Minerals belonging to the feldspar group constitute the most important group of rock-forming minerals. They are so very abundant, in fact, that they have been estimated to make up as much as 60 percent of the earth's crust. Feldspars are found in almost all igneous rocks as well as in many sedimentary and metamorphic rocks. (Later chapters will explain the three types of rocks.)

The feldspars all have similar physical properties; crystals may be monoclinic or triclinic; cleavage is in two directions at right angles, or nearly so; average specific gravity is 2.6; hardness is 6 (or slightly more); and they display a vitreous to pearly luster. Varying greatly in color, they range from white through pink, yellow, red, gray, or green; streak is white or uncolored.

Chemically, the feldspars are silicates of aluminum and one or two other metals. These may be either potassium, sodium, and calcium, or, more rarely, barium. Orthoclase and plagioclase, the two principal groups of feldspars, are discussed below.

Orthoclase. This is a rather common potash feldspar. The chemical formula is $KAlSi_3O_8$ (showing potassium, aluminum, silicon, and oxygen), although some forms may contain sodium or barium. Orthoclase is transparent to translucent and in color may range from colorless to white, gray, flesh-red, yellow, or pink. It has a vitreous luster, hardness of 6, and specific gravity of 2.5 to 2.6. It crystallizes in the monoclinic system and has two easy cleavages making an angle of 90 degrees. Fracture is uneven to somewhat conchoidal; streak is white or uncolored. Orthoclase can usually be distinguished from plagioclase feldspar (see below) by absence of striations (stripes). Microcline is another potassium aluminum silicate of the same chemical composition ($KAlSi_3O_8$) as orthoclase. However, they crystallize in different crystal systems and differ in certain other physical characteristics.

Plagioclase. Feldspars of the plagioclase series, known also as soda-lime feldspars, are common in many igneous rocks and in certain metamorphic rocks. Colors are white, yellow, reddish gray to black; luster vitreous; hardness 6; specific gravity 2.6 to 2.8; transparent to translucent; two good cleavages at almost 90 degrees to each other and two poor prismatic cleavages. Two varieties of plagioclase, albite moonstone and labradorite, are characterized by white to bluish internal flashes (a play of colors called opalescence).

The feldspars are of considerable economic importance. Orthoclase is used in the manufacture of china, porcelain, and scouring powders. Feldspars are also used in making paints, enamels, and glass. Plagioclase feldspars are less commonly used than potash feldspars, but some are used in the ceramics industry.

QUARTZ

Quartz is one of the most widely distributed of all minerals; it forms an important part of many igneous rocks and is common in many sedimentary and metamorphic rocks. Quartz may occur in combination with other minerals, or, as in the case of pure sandstones and quartzites, may be the only one present.

Pure quartz is composed of silicon dioxide (SiO_2), but certain varieties contain impurities such as iron or manganese. These impurities are responsible for the varied colors of certain types of quartz. Quartz occurs in crystalline aggregates or in irregular grains or masses. The term **cryptocrystalline** (literally "hidden crystals") is used to describe quartz varieties in which crystals are not evident.

Crystallizing in the hexagonal system, quartz commonly forms six-sided crystals with pyramidal ends (Fig. 21). It may be colorless, white, rose, violet, smoky, gray, or a wide variety of other colors. It has a vitreous to greasy luster, a hardness of 7, specific gravity of 2.65, and conchoidal to uneven fracture. Quartz may be transparent to opaque and leaves a white or very pale colored streak.

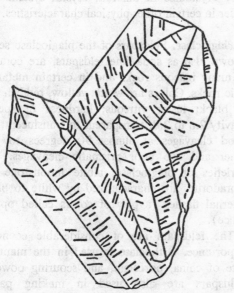

Fig. 21. Well-developed hexagonal quartz crystals with pyramidal ends.

Some of the more common crystalline varieties of quartz are amethyst, milky quartz, rose quartz, rock crystal quartz (Fig. 22) and smoky quartz. Massive or cryptocrystalline varieties include agate, chalcedony, chert, flint, and jasper.

Quartz is apt to occur almost anywhere, and most sands are composed largely of quartz fragments. Quartz is used in the manufacture of electronic equipment such as radios, televisions, and radar, and some quartz varieties are used in making lenses and prisms. Other types of quartz are valuable as semiprecious stones or gems. Sandstone is used as building stone, and quartz sands are used as abrasives and in making concrete and glass.

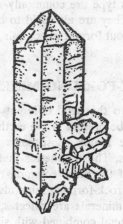

Fig. 22. Rock crystal quartz.

MICA

Minerals of the mica group are characterized by perfect basal cleavage (commonly called micaceous cleavage). Micas are usually easily identified, as they typically occur in paper-thin, shiny, elastic cleavage plates.

The micas, like the feldspars, are aluminum silicates that are characterized by very complex chemical formulas. The more important physical characteristics of the group are: crystal system: monoclinic; hardness: 2 to 3; cleavage: perfect basal; color: colorless to black; streak: white to gray; luster: pearly to vitreous; specific gravity: 2.7 to 3.4; transparency: transparent to opaque.

Only two varieties of mica, muscovite and biotite, are especially important as rock-forming minerals. However, phlogopite and lepidolite are fairly common in some rocks.

Muscovite. This mineral, known also as white mica or "isinglass," is usually transparent. It is colorless, gray, or light brown, has a hardness of 2 to 2.5, specific gravity of 2.8 to 3.1, and a pearly to vitreous luster. Occurring typically in thin, elastic, scalelike crystals, muscovite is a common constituent of certain granites and pegmatites (see Chapter 4). It also occurs in certain metamorphic and sedimentary rocks. Muscovite is found in many parts of the country including New England, North Carolina, South Dakota, and Colorado.

Commercially, muscovite is used in manufacturing electrical equipment, insulating cloth and tape, lamp chimneys, lubricants, paints, and Christmas tree "snow."

Biotite. Biotite, or black mica, is a very common mica and commonly occurs in association with muscovite. It is found in many igneous and metamorphic rocks, where it is seen as thin, platy, shiny black sheets or scales. Biotite is typically dark brown to black (sometimes green), and is a complex silicate of aluminum, calcium, magnesium, and iron. With the exception of the black color, the physical properties of biotite are essentially the same as those of muscovite. Unlike muscovite, biotite mica has very little commercial value.

PYROXENES

The pyroxene group is composed of complex silicates, and is among the most common of all rock-forming minerals. Physical properties of the group are: crystal system: monoclinic or orthorhombic (they may crystallize in either system); color: green, brown, or black; hardness: 5 to 6; specific gravity: 3.2 to 3.6; luster: vitreous, resinous, or dull; streak: white to grayish green; cleavage: two at nearly right angles.

The most widespread pyroxene is **augite,** a common constituent of many of the dark-colored igneous rcoks. Pyroxenes are also commonly found in certain metamorphic rocks.

AMPHIBOLES

The amphiboles, another group of common rock-forming minerals, are closely related to the pyroxenes. Because of their great similarity, these two groups are often confused. Chemically, they are complex silicates containing magnesium, calcium, and iron.

Amphiboles crystallize in either the orthorhombic or monoclinic system; have a hardness of 5 to 6; specific gravity of 2.9 to 3.3; display highly vitreous luster on cleavage faces; leave an uncolored or pale streak; and have two good cleavages meeting at angles of 56 degrees and 124 degrees.

Hornblende, the most common amphibole, is a common constituent of igneous and metamorphic rocks. Its physical properties are: crystals: monoclinic prisms; color: black to dark green; hardness: 5 to 6; specific gravity: 2.9 to 3.3; luster: vitreous (fibrous varieties have silky luster); cleavage: perfect prismatic with angles of 56 degrees and 124 degrees.

Actinolite and **tremolite** are other interesting amphiboles. Some mineralogists consider these as separate and distinct minerals. Others treat them as a single mineral or refer to them as the tremolite-actinolite series. They commonly occur in long prismatic, bladed crystals, or as fibrous or asbestiform (resembling asbestos) masses. Fibrous tremolite is used to some extent as asbestos in fireproofing and insulation. (Tremolite asbestos should not be confused with serpentine or chrysotile asbestos. The latter are more commonly used in industry.)

CALCITE

The mineral calcite is composed of calcium carbonate ($CaCO_3$) and is the most common member of the calcite group. It occurs in many sedimentary and metamorphic rocks, and is the primary constituent of most limestones (see Chapter 5). Calcite occurs in crystalline, granular, or chalky masses, as a vein mineral, in cave and spring deposits, and in the shells of certain animals (corals, snails, clams, and others).

Perfect rhombohedral crystals, forming in the hexagonal system, are common. Calcite is typically colorless, white, or yellowish, but the presence of impurities may bring about a wide variety of colors. Other properties: hardness: 3; specific gravity: 2.72; luster: vitreous to dull; streak: white to grayish; cleavage: perfect rhombohedral in three directions at oblique angles. Moreover, calcite will **effervesce** or "fizz" in cold dilute acids; some forms are fluorescent; and certain clear calcite crystals have the property of **double refraction.** That is, an object when viewed through such a crystal will appear double (see Fig. 23).

Some of the more common varieties of calcite are Iceland spar, dogtooth spar, chalk, travertine (including the calcareous tufa deposited by

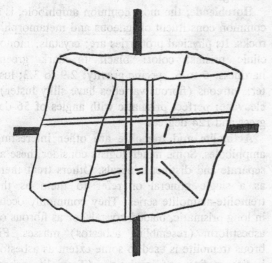

Fig. 23. Rhombohedral calcite crystal exhibiting double refraction.

springs and stalactites and stalagmites formed in caves), and limestone.

Calcite, as the chief component of limestones and marbles, is used in making cement, lime, and plaster, as a flux in the smelting of iron ores, and as building or ornamental stone. Calcite is also used in the manufacture of glass, paint, and fertilizer. Certain transparent varieties of calcite are used in making optical instruments—especially as polarizing prisms.

DOLOMITE

Dolomite, calcium magnesium carbonate [$CaMg(CO_3)_2$], is common in sedimentary rock, where it is often mixed with calcite. It may also occur in association with many ore deposits and in veins or cavities in some igneous rocks. Dolomite differs from calcite in that it is slightly harder (3½), is only mildly affected by cold dilute acids, and may include crystals with curved faces. Its major uses are for building stone

(much "marble" consists of dolomite), in the manufacture of cement, and as a source of magnesium.

ARAGONITE

Aragonite, like calcite, is composed of calcium carbonate, but it differs from calcite in that it is less stable and crystallizes in the orthorhombic system. Furthermore, aragonite has a higher specific gravity (2.9) and is somewhat harder (3½) than calcite. It occurs as a secondary mineral in cavities of limestone, as a deposit around hot springs and geysers, in cave deposits, and in the shells of certain animals, such as clams or corals. Although not as common as calcite, aragonite is used for the same purposes.

GYPSUM

Gypsum, calcium sulfate ($CaSO_4 \cdot 2H_2O$), is a very common mineral. A product of evaporation, it occurs in thick-bedded deposits in Texas, New Mexico, New York, California, Michigan, Ohio, Kentucky, and Kansas.

Gypsum is colorless or white (but may be a variety of colors if impurities are present), has a hardness of 2, a specific gravity of 2.3, is vitreous to pearly or silky in luster, has a white streak, and is transparent to opaque. It crystallizes in the monoclinic system and has one perfect micaceous cleavage, yielding thin leaves or plates. There are two other less perfect cleavages. Among the more common varieties of gypsum are selenite, satin spar, alabaster, and rock gypsum.

A mineral of great economic importance, gypsum is extensively used in the manufacture of plaster board (sheet rock), plaster of Paris, and as land plaster for fertilizer. It is also used in the manufacture of Portland cement, paint, glass, porcelain, and crayons. The alabaster variety of gypsum is used in statuary and as an oranmental stone.

ANHYDRITE

Anhydrite ($CaSO_4$), although chemically similar to gypsum, does not contain water and is harder and heavier than gypsum. This mineral typically occurs in massive, fine- to medium-grained, colorless, white, or grayish masses, has a hardness of 3 to 3½, a specific gravity of 2.9, a vitreous, pearly, or greasy luster, and leaves a white streak. Commonly found in the cap rock of certain salt domes in Texas and Louisiana, anhydrite may fluoresce pink, yellow-green, or blue-white upon heating.

Anhydrite is used in the manufacture of Portland cement and fertilizer, and to a lesser degree as an ornamental stone.

HALITE

Commonly called rock salt, halite is composed of sodium chloride ($NaCl$). It occurs in cubic crystals as well as in massive granular forms. It is colorless to white and sometimes reddish or blue to violet, depending upon impurities. Halite has a hardness of 2 to 2½, specific gravity of 2.1 to 2.3, vitreous luster, white streak, and a salty taste. It is characterized by perfect cubic cleavage, conchoidal fracture, and is soluble in water.

Large occurrences of halite have been formed as a result of the evaporation of prehistoric seas, and in some areas (such as New York, Michigan, and New Mexico) the salt occurs in thick beds. In the Gulf Coast region of Texas and Louisiana, the salt occurs in salt plugs or salt domes which have been squeezed up through weak places in the earth's crust.

KAOLINITE

Kaolinite ($H_4Al_2Si_2O_9$) is typical of the three or four minerals that are commonly found in clay. Kaolin, formed primarily by the decomposition of rocks containing large amounts of feldspar, is an impure mixture of a variety of clay minerals.

Occurring in soft, compact, earthy masses, kaolinite is characterized by its dull earthy luster, greasy feel, and rather distinctive property of adhering to the tongue. It becomes plastic when wet and has an earthy or claylike odor when breathed upon. Hardness ranges from 1 to 2½; specific gravity from 2.2 to 2.6. It is an impor-

tant constituent of clay and soil, and is widely used in the ceramics industries.

SERPENTINE

The serpentines, a complex group of hydrous magnesium silicates ($H_4Mg_3Si_2O_9$), commonly occur in compact masses which feel smooth or greasy. Common, or massive, serpentine is generally dark (blackish green), has a greasy or resinous luster, hardness of 2½ to 4, specific gravity of 2.5 to 2.8, a white streak, and a conchoidal to splintery fracture.

Chrysotile, a fibrous variety of serpentine, is the principal mineral used as asbestos. Verde antique or serpentine marble is a massive serpentine mixed irregularly with white minerals such as calcite or dolomite. Because it can be highly polished, this stone is commonly used for small carvings and as an ornamental stone.

CHLORITE

The chlorite group is composed of minerals which are complex silicates of aluminum, magnesium, and iron in combination with water. These minerals resemble the micas and commonly occur in foliated or scaly masses, although tabular six-sided crystals may occur. The chlorite minerals are typically green, have one perfect cleavage, a hardness of 1 to 2½, specific gravity of 2.6 to 3, and leave a greenish streak. They are common constituents of many igneous and metamorphic rocks.

METALLIC OR ORE MINERALS

Metals are among the most valuable products known, and for this reason the metallic or ore minerals are of great interest to the geologist. These minerals are found in ore deposits—rock masses from which metals may be obtained commercially. Usually occurring with the valuable ore minerals are certain worthless minerals called gangue minerals. These, of course, must be separated from the more valuable ore minerals.

Because of their great importance and commercial value, some of the more important metals and their ores are briefly discussed below.

ALUMINUM

Aluminum, one of the more important metals of industry, is derived primarily from **bauxite**. A hydrous aluminum oxide ($Al_2O_3 \cdot 2H_2O$), bauxite is actually a mixture of minerals. It occurs in earthy, claylike masses, or in a **pisolitic** form as rounded concretions in a claylike matrix. Physical properties are: color: white, yellow, brown, red; hardness: 1 to 3; specific gravity: 2.0 to 2.5; streak: like the color.

Because it is light, resists corrosion, and is relatively strong, aluminum is especially useful in the construction of airplane frames, household utensils, and ornamental objects. It is also used in the manufacture of artificial abrasives. Most bauxite produced in the United States comes from Arkansas, but Surinam and Guyana are considered to be the world's major producers.

COPPER

Copper, one of the most useful of all metals, has contributed much to the development of civilization. It is found principally in igenous rocks or in vein deposits and is widely distributed over much of the world. Although there are many different copper minerals—about 165 have been described—only those of major economic importance will be discussed below.

Native copper (Cu) occurs in irregular masses, or plates, in northern Michigan, New Jersey, New Mexico, Arizona, Mexico, and Bolivia. Native copper has a hardness of 2½ to 3 and a density of 8.9.

Chalcopyrite ($CuFeS_2$), known also as copper pyrite, is widely distributed in many rocks and is the principal ore of copper. It typically occurs in massive forms and is found in many parts of the world. Its physical properties are: color: brass-yellow or gold (may tarnish green or black); hardness: 3½ to 4; specific gravity: 4.2; luster: metallic; streak: greenish black; very brittle. Chalcopyrite differs from pyrite in that it is slightly darker and much softer. The extreme brittleness of chalcopyrite serves to distinguish it

from gold, which is always malleable. However, in some localities chalcopyrite may carry gold and also silver.

Chalcocite (Cu_2S), one of the most important of the copper ore minerals, commonly occurs scattered throughout the enclosing rock, and because of this it has been called copper porphyry. It occurs also as vein deposits. Although typically a low-grade ore, chalcocite is usually easily and economically extracted. Chalcocite occurs in commercial quantities in such western copper-mining states as Montana, Arizona, Utah, and Nevada. It is mined also in the Kennecott region of Alaska. Its physical properties are: color: lead gray to black (may tarnish dull black); hardness: 2½ to 3; specific gravity: 5.5 to 5.8; luster: metallic; streak: grayish black; fracture: conchoidal; brittle.

Azurite [$Cu_3(CO_3)_2(OH)_2$] is characterized by its blue color and the tendency to effervesce in acid. A copper carbonate, it usually occurs in smooth or irregular masses and is commonly found associated with malachite (see below). Short, tabular, azure blue monoclinic crystals may be developed. Azurite is a rather important copper ore and is commonly found associated with other copper ores. Its physical properties are: color: azure blue; hardness: 3½ to 4; specific gravity: 3.8; luster: vitreous; streak: light blue; fracture: conchoidal; brittle.

Malachite, although of the same chemical composition as azurite, is easily distinguished from the latter by its bright green color and pale green streak. Malachite is more abundant than azurite and commonly occurs in veins in limestone. Malachite is an important copper ore and has been used to a limited extent in table tops, vases, and other ornamental art objects. It has been mined in Arizona and New Mexico, Siberia, Africa, France, and Australia. Its physical properties are: color: bright green; hardness: 3½ to 4; specific gravity: 3.9 to 4.03; luster: silky, velvety, or dull; fracture: uneven.

GOLD

Because of its great beauty and the fact that it is soft enough to be easily fashioned into coins, jewelry, and other valuable objects, gold has been prized since the dawn of history. Its value is further enhanced by the fact that most of the world's gold is found in the native state and does not, therefore, have to be extracted from the ore by complicated and expensive metallurgical processes. This metal occurs as native gold (Au) and is typically found in quartz veins and in association with the mineral pyrite. Physical properties: color: pale to golden yellow; hardness: 2½ to 3; specific gravity: 19.3 (when pure); luster: metallic; streak: yellow to white (depending on impurities); fracture: hackly; very malleable and ductile.

LEAD

Galena (PbS), the most important source of lead, occurs in a wide variety of rocks, including igneous, sedimentary, and metamorphic. A sulfide of lead, it may be found as a replacement in limestone, in veins, or in localized concentrated "pockets." Copper, zinc, and silver ores are often found associated with galena, and some of these ores occur in sufficient amounts to make them valuable commercially. Galena has perfect cubic cleavage and its crystals are usually cubic or octahedral. It may also occur in massive, granular, or compact masses. Physical properties: color: lead gray; hardness: 2½; specific gravity: 7.4 to 7.6; luster: bright metallic; streak: same as color; fracture: subconchoidal.

Most of the galena in the United States is mined in the so-called Tri-State Area (Missouri, Kansas, and Oklahoma). There are also commercial quantities in Australia, South America, and Europe.

Lead is used in the manufacture of paints (in the form of white lead), as type metal, pipe, shot, solder, metal alloys, and as shielding materials to protect against radioactivity and X rays.

MERCURY

The most abundant ore of mercury (known also as quicksilver) is cinnabar, or mercuric sulfide (HgS). Although found in relatively few places, cinnabar occurs in both volcanic and sedimentary rocks, and near hot springs. It occurs most typically in fine-granular or earthy masses.

Physical properties: color: bright to brownish red; hardness: 2 to 2½; specific gravity: 8.1; luster: adamantine to dull; streak: scarlet; fracture: subconchoidal to uneven.

Native (or free) mercury may also be found in small silvery droplets in certain cinnabar deposits.

The world's leading producer of mercury is Spain, but Italy is also a relatively large producer. There are also important cinnabar deposits in the Big Bend area of Texas, in California, Washington, Nevada, and certain other western states.

Mercury is used in the amalgamation process of recovering gold and silver from their ores, in the manufacture of explosives, and the manufacture of such scientific instruments as thermometers and barometers.

SILVER

Silver, another metal that is highly prized by man, may occur as native silver (Ag) or in one of several silver ore minerals. When found in nature it is usually tarnished. It may occur in veins or may be disseminated throughout the rocks. Physical properties: color: silver-white (may be tarnished gray or black); hardness: 2½ to 3; specific gravity: 10.5 (when pure); luster: metallic; streak: silver-white; fracture: hackly; very malleable and ductile.

Argentite, a silver sulfide (Ag₂S), is one of the more important silver ores. Found in veins, where it may be associated with free silver and a number of other metallic minerals, it is usually massive or encrusting, but cubic crystals may be formed. Physical properties: color: blackish gray; hardness: 2 to 2½; specific gravity: 7.3; luster: metallic; streak: lead-gray shining; fracture: subconchoidal; very sectile.

Mexico is the largest producer of silver, with the United States second, and Canada third; Idaho, Montana, Utah, and Arizona are responsible for most of our domestic production.

Used in making coins, jewelry, and tableware, silver is also used in plating metals, and in the photographic, chemical, and electronic industries.

TIN

The only important tin ore is **cassiterite** (SnO_2), or tin oxide. Although widely distributed in small amounts, it occurs in commercial quantities in igneous rocks, where it is commonly associated with quartz, topaz, galena, and tourmaline. Its physical properties are: color: various shades of green, brown, yellow, red, or gray; hardness: 6 to 7; specific gravity: 6.8 to 7.1; luster: adamantine to submetallic and dull; streak: white to gray; fracture: conchoidal to uneven.

Little tin ore is produced in the United States (small amounts are found in Alaska), the world's most important suppliers being Malaya, Bolivia, and the Dutch East Indies.

Tin is used for tin plating (the lining of tin cans is one of its major uses), type metal, tinfoil, and—mixed with copper—to make bronze.

ZINC

Another metal of considerable economic importance is zinc.

Sphalerite (ZnS), the primary ore of zinc, is a rather common mineral and its origin and occurrence are similar to that of galena, with which it is commonly associated. It is found in veins in igneous, sedimentary, and metamorphic rocks, and as replacement deposits in limestone. Physical properties: color: yellow, brown, or black; hardness: 3½ to 4; specific gravity: 4.1; luster: resinous to adamantine; streak: light to brownish yellow; fracture: conchoidal cleavage in six directions. About eighteen different states produce zinc, and it is also produced in Canada, Mexico, Peru, and Australia.

Zinc is used in galvanizing steel, and in the manufacture of paint, cosmetics, type metal, dry cell batteries, and for a multitude of other purposes.

IRON

Iron, a particularly useful metal, is obtained from a variety of iron minerals. Among these are hematite, magnetite, and limonite.

Hematite, the most important ore of iron, is ferric iron oxide (Fe_2O_3). One of the world's most common minerals, it occurs in massive black beds and in scaly schistose rocks. Hematite is sedimentary in origin, and most deposits have been altered and enriched by subsequent solutions. Physical properties: color: gray, reddish brown to iron black; hardness: 5 to 6½; specific gravity: 4.9 to 5.3; luster: metallic to earthy; streak: red (regardless of color); fracture: splintery to uneven. In the United States large deposits of hematite are found in Minnesota (the famed Mesabi Range), Alabama, and Michigan.

Magnetite (Fe_3O_4) is a combination of ferric and ferrous oxides. Magnetite is strongly attracted by a magnet. A variety of magnetite that acts as a magnet is known as lodestone. Physical properties: color: black; hardness: 5½ to 6½; specific gravity: 5.0 to 5.2; luster: metallic to submetallic; streak: black; fracture: conchoidal to uneven.

Limonite is a term used to refer to several comingled hydrous iron oxides (the chemical formula is roughly $Fe_2O_3 \cdot H_2O$). It occurs in compact or earthy masses and is a relatively common iron ore. Physical properties: color: yellow, brown, or black; hardness: 1 to 5½; specific gravity: 3.4 to 4.0; luster: dull earthy; streak: yellow-brown; fracture: uneven.

Pyrite, or "fool's gold," is an iron mineral that is little used as a source of iron. It is an iron sulfide (Fe_2S) and is commonly associated with a number of different ores, including copper and gold. Pyrite is a valuable source of sulfur in the manufacture of sulfuric acid. Physical properties: color: brass yellow; hardness: 6 to 6½; specific gravity: 4.9 to 5.2; luster: metallic; streak: greenish or brownish black; fracture: uneven; commonly found in well-formed cubic crystals with striated faces.

RADIOACTIVE MINERALS

In this so-called "atomic age," radioactive minerals have come to play an ever-increasing part in modern technology. Certain of these minerals are widely used as sources of energy for nuclear power plants, in nuclear or isotope medicine, and in modern weapon systems. Although there are a number of radioactive minerals, only two of the more important ones will be considered here.

Uraninite, known also as **pitchblende,** is the most important source of uranium and radium. A complex oxide of uranium (UO_2), uraninite also contains minor amounts of thorium, lead, helium, and certain other relatively rare elements. Physical properties: color: black to brownish black; hardness: $5\frac{1}{2}$; specific gravity: 9.0 to 9.7; luster: pitchy to submetallic; streak: brownish black; fracture: uneven to conchoidal.

Uraninite may be found as a primary constituent in certain granites and pegmatites. It is also known to occur as a secondary mineral with ores of lead, copper, and silver.

Carnotite, or potassium uranyl vanadate $[K_2(UO_2)_2(VO_4)_2 \cdot 3H_2O]$, is an earthy, powdery mineral which is an ore of uranium and vanadium. Carnotite commonly occurs disseminated throughout weathered sedimentary rocks, especially sandstone. It may, however, occur in earthy masses. Physical properties: color: brilliant canary yellow; hardness: very soft; specific gravity: 4.0; luster: earthy; streak: pale yellow; fracture: uneven.

There has been considerable carnotite production in Montrose County, California; other productive localities have been reported in Arizona, New Mexico, and Utah.

NONMETALLIC OR INDUSTRIAL MINERALS

Included here are those minerals that do not contain metals or that are not used as metals. It is in this vast category that such valuable and varied materials as coal, petroleum, sulfur, fertilizer, building stones, and gemstones are placed. Some of these products and the minerals from which they come are described below.

Abrasives. Materials used to polish, abrade, or cut other materials are called abrasives. Minerals commonly used for this purpose are garnet, diamond, corundum, and varieties of quartz.

Asbestos. Certain of the fibrous silicate minerals are useful in insulating, fireproofing, the manufacture of plastic, and in brake linings, etc. The most important of these are chrysotile, crocid-

olite, and actinolite-tremolite. Unfortunately, this very useful mineral now appears to be a cancer-producing agent and will be much less utilized in the future.

Cements, Lime, and Plasters. Limestone (see Chapter 5), composed primarily of calcium carbonate, is used in the manufacture of Portland cement, lime, steel, and as a building stone.

Gypsum, composed of calcium sulfate, is used in making plaster, wallboard (sheet rock), paints, and plaster of Paris.

Clays. Clay minerals, in combination with certain other minerals, provide the basic raw materials for the ceramics industries. Products thus made are brick, tile, pottery, china. Clay minerals are also used in making paper, linoleum, cement, and in foundry work. Certain types of clays are also used as refractory brick to line kilns, furnaces, and the like.

Mineral Fertilizers. The three most essential elements for promoting plant growth are potassium, nitrogen, and phosphorus. Phosphate rock is a valuable source of phosphorus because it contains a large amount of the mineral apatite. **Sylvite** is an important source of potassium, and natural nitrates are used to provide nitrogen to mineral fertilizers. Most of the latter are produced in Chile.

Ground limestone, glauconite, gypsum, and borax are also used in certain mineral fertilizers.

Salt. Halite, common rock salt, is much used in the chemical industry as an important source of sodium and chlorine. It is also employed in the tanning of leather, food preparation, and in certain refrigerants. These are but a few uses of this all-important mineral which has long been so valuable to humans.

Sulfur. This yellow, nonmetallic mineral is found in volcanic rocks, around hot springs, and associated with salt domes. Much of the United States production is from the "cap rock" of certain salt domes in the Gulf Coast region of Texas and Louisiana. Its physical properties are: color: yellow (may vary through different shades of yellow according to presence of impurities);

hardness: 1½ to 2½; specific gravity: 2.1; luster: resinous to greasy; streak: white; fracture: conchoidal to uneven.

Sulfur is used as a bleaching agent, in making paper, sulfuric acid, gunpowder, matches, insecticides, and medicines. It is also used in the process of vulcanizing rubber.

MINERAL RESOURCES AND HUMAN NEEDS

Metallic and nonmetallic minerals are among our most important resources. And, like such other natural resources as coal, oil, and natural gas, they are **nonrenewable resources.** That is, once Earth's supply of these minerals has been exhausted, they will not be replaced or renewed. Moreover, the earth's mineral wealth is not evenly distributed and no one country can claim self-sufficiency in mineral resources.

Two of the more important metals, iron and aluminum, are especially important in an industrial society. Only a few countries have these relatively abundant resources in adequate amounts. The imbalance of supplies of these and other mineral resources not only has a profound effect on the world's economy but is also related to many social and political problems. In short, the interdependence of people everywhere in regard to mineral resources means that there must be a free exchange of goods among nations if there is to be any prospect of equal sharing by all.

CHAPTER 4

IGNEOUS ROCKS AND VOLCANISM

Igneous rocks are those rocks that have solidified from an original molten state. The word igneous is derived from the Latin word *ignis,* meaning "fire." We have already learned that temperatures deep within the earth are exceedingly hot and that many rocks and minerals exist in a molten condition called **magma.** These magmas are large bodies of molten rock deeply buried within the earth. Sometimes magmatic materials are poured out upon the surface of the earth as, for example, when lava flows from a volcano. These molten materials which spill out upon the surface are known as **eruptive, extrusive,** or **volcanic** rocks. Under certain other conditions, magmas do not come to the surface but may force their way or intrude into other rocks where they solidify. These intruding rock materials harden and form **intrusive** or **plutonic** rocks.

Igneous rocks may be distinguished from sedimentary and metamorphic rocks by their texture and structure, their composing minerals, and their complete lack of fossils. They have been classified according to (1) their origin, (2) texture, and (3) chemical composition.

ORIGIN OF IGNEOUS ROCKS

This classification is based upon the position of the magma with reference to the earth's surface.

INTRUSIVE OR PLUTONIC ROCKS

These are rocks that have solidified from molten mineral mixtures beneath the surface of the earth. The more deeply buried intrusive rocks tend to cool slowly and develop a coarse texture composed of relatively large mineral crystals (Fig. 24). On the other hand, those that cooled more quickly (because they were near the surface) are finer textured. The texture of an igneous rock depends largely upon the shape, size, and arrangement of the grains comprising it. As a result of the crowded conditions under which mineral particles are formed, they are usually angular and irregular in outline. Some typical intrusive rocks, granite, gabbro, peridotite, and syenite, are described below.

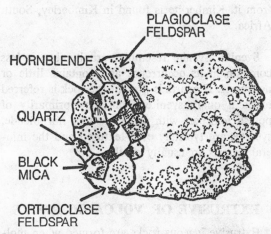

Fig. 24. Granite, a coarse-textured intrusive igneous rock.

Granite. Granite (Fig. 24) is the most common and best-known of the coarse-textured intrusive rocks. Usually cooling and solidifying at great depths within the earth, it is characterized by crystals which are all about the same size (from $\frac{1}{16}$ inch to $\frac{1}{2}$ inch or more). Granite always contains quartz and feldspar, usually intermixed with mica or hornblende. **Aplite** is a type of granite containing a great deal of orthoclase feldspar mixed with quartz.

Granites are typically light in color and may be white, gray, pink, or yellowish brown. The individual mineral grains are usually easily distinguished, but are so well joined together that they form a hard, long-lasting rock. Because it is durable and can take a high polish, granite is especially useful as a building and monumental stone. Commercial granites are quarried in Colorado, Minnesota, Massachusetts, Texas, Vermont, and elsewhere. Granites are commonly found in stocks, laccoliths, and batholiths.

Gabbro. Gabbro is a heavy, dark-colored igneous rock consisting of coarse grains of plagioclase feldspar and augite. Quartz is absent, and the mineral crystals are usually dark gray, dark green, or black.

Peridotite. A rock in which the dark minerals are predominant is called a peridotite or pyroxenite. Kimberlite, a peridotite composed of a pyroxene-olivine mixture, is famous for the large numbers of diamonds that have been extracted from it. Kimberlite is found in Kimberley, South Africa.

Syenite. Syenite resembles granite, but is less common in its occurrence and contains little or no quartz. If quartz is present the rock is referred to as a quartz-syenite. Consisting primarily of potash feldspars with some mica or hornblende, syenites are typically even-textured and the mineral crystals are usually small.

EXTRUSIVE OR VOLCANIC ROCKS

Extrusive igneous rocks are formed when molten rock solidifies after forcing its way out to the surface of the earth. Such rocks may pour out of the craters of volcanoes or from great fissures or cracks in the earth's crust. In addition to the liquid lava, solid particles such as volcanic ash or volcanic bombs may also be thrown out during volcanic eruptions.

As the magma reaches the surface, it loses its gases and undergoes relatively rapid cooling. This prevents slow crystal growth and results in a microcrystalline texture in which the crystals cannot be seen with the unaided eye. Some cool so rapidly that no crystallization occurs and this produces volcanic glass (see below).

Some of the more common extrusive rocks are felsite, basalt, pumice, and obsidian.

Felsite. Felsite is a general term applied to igneous rocks of very fine texture—so fine that the individual grains, which are light in color, cannot be seen through an ordinary magnifying glass. Felsites may range in color from white, light to medium gray, or shades of pink, red, green, purple, or yellow. Felsite commonly contains quartz, orthoclase feldspar, and biotite mica. These are the same minerals found in granite, a typical intrusive rock. Granites, however, are coarsely crystalline in texture, and the felsites are typically fine-grained. We see, then, that the same magma (containing quartz, orthoclase feldspar, and biotite mica) cooling at different distances from the surface may form rocks of similar chemical composition, although their physical appearance is quite different.

Basalt. This is one of the world's most abundant extrusive rocks. Basalts are typically dark gray, dark green, brown, or black in color and are normally quite heavy. They are fine-grained in texture and consist primarily of pyroxene, plagioclase feldspar, and, in some cases, olivine. Some basalts are characterized by a large number of open spaces or pores which mark the site of former gas bubbles. This porous rock, called **scoria,** is common in many hardened lava flows. With the passage of time these pores, or **vesicles,** may become filled with minerals such as quartz or calcite. Such mineral-filled vesicles, usually almond-shaped, are known as **amygdules.** Basalts characterized by large numbers of amygdules are called amygdaloidal basalts, and often yield fine mineral crystals.

Basaltic rocks commonly display columnar jointing. This comes about as the rocks cool and shrink and split into vertical columns (Fig. 25). Striking examples of this may be seen in the basaltic columns on the Yellowstone River near Tower Fall in Yellowstone National Park and at Devils Tower National Monument, Wyoming.

Basaltic rocks may also be seen in the great lava flows of Hawaii and in the western and southwestern parts of the United States. In some areas of India and the northwestern United States there are large basalt flows covering about 200,000 square miles to depths of thousands of feet.

Fig. 25. Columnar jointing in basalt.

Because of their hardness, basalts are valuable as trap rock for road building and other construction purposes. In addition, large deposits of copper have been found in amygdaloidal deposits in northern Michigan.

Pumice. Lava that solidified while steam and other gases were still bubbling out of it is called pumice. It is formed from a rapidly cooling volcanic froth and is characterized by the presence of large numbers of fine holes which give the rock a spongelike appearance (Fig. 26). This rock is very light in weight and because many of the air spaces are sealed, pumice can float on water. Blocks of pumice thrown into the sea during eruptions of island volcanoes have been known to float for great distances from their site of origin. Pumice is typically light in color and, though differing greatly in appearance, has the same chemical composition as obsidian and granite.

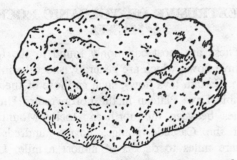

Fig. 26. Pumice, a type of extrusive igneous rock.

It is used as an abrasive, in soap, cleansers, and some rubber erasers. Most of the pumice found in the United States comes from California, Kansas, New Mexico, and Oregon.

Obsidian. Known also as volcanic glass, obsidian is a glassy extrusive rock which cooled so rapidly that there was no formation of separate mineral crystals. It is a lustrous, glassy, black or reddish brown igneous rock (Fig. 27). Obsidian exhibits a conchoidal fracture which leaves sharp edges; consequently this stone was commonly used to make arrowheads, spear points, knives, and other implements. Formed by the rapid cooling of surface lava flows, obsidian occurs in parts of California, New Mexico, Oregon, and Utah. One of the better-known occurrences of obsidian, the Obsidian Cliffs of Yellowstone National Park, attracted into that area Indians who used the rock to fashion spear points and arrowheads.

Fig. 27. Obsidian, or volcanic glass.

TEXTURE OF IGNEOUS ROCKS

Texture is a physical characteristic of igneous rock that is influenced by the rate of cooling or crystallization of a magma. Commonly used to refer to the general appearance of any rock, it refers more specifically to the shape, size, and arrangement of silicate minerals in the igneous rocks. A rock with mineral grains large enough to be seen and identified with the unaided eye is said to have a **granular,** or **granitic,** texture. If the individual mineral grains in a rock are too small to be seen with the naked eye, the texture of the rock is said to be **aphanitic.** Glassy textured rocks such as obsidian appear to be composed of glass. Some igneous rocks appear to have a mixed texture. This type of texture is called **porphyritic** and is characterized by relatively large crystals, called **phenocrysts,** surrounded by a groundmass (or background) of smaller crystals (Fig. 28). Porphyries, as such rocks are called, are believed to represent two distinct phases of cooling and solidification.

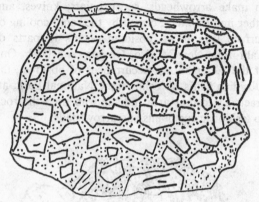

Fig. 28. Porphyry showing light-colored phenocrysts in the darker groundmass.

Intrusive rocks which cool at a very slow rate may form crystals ranging from several inches to several feet in length. Such coarse-grained rocks are called **pegmatites** and are especially characteristic of certain types of granite.

MINERAL COMPOSITION OF IGNEOUS ROCKS

The type of igneous rock that is formed by a magma or lava is primarily dependent upon the chemical composition of the original molten rock material.

Sialic or Light-colored Igneous Rocks. Those igneous rocks that have a high silica content are known as acidic or sialic rocks. The term **sialic** is derived from the chemical symbols for silicon and aluminum. Such rocks have a high content of silica and sodium-potassium feldspar. They typically contain relatively low percentages of iron, magnesium, and calcium. Acidic igneous rocks are usually light in color and have a low specific gravity, that is, they are light in weight. They are the predominant rocks of the continents and are represented by such common igneous rocks as granite, rhyolite, and pumice.

Simatic or Dark-colored Igneous Rocks. These are dark-colored, relatively heavy igneous rocks. They are known as basic or **simatic** rocks because of their low silica content and proportionately higher content of such iron-magnesium minerals as biotite, olivine, pyroxene, and hornblende. Basic rocks underlie the acidic rocks of the earth's crust and are believed to make up most volcanic islands and form large parts of the deep ocean floor. Gabbro and basalt are typical basic igneous rocks.

It should be noted that there are numerous gradations between acidic and basic rocks, and many specimens fall into an intermediate or transitional category.

Intermediate Igneous Rocks. These rocks are of intermediate chemical composition and their rock compositions blend continuously from one to another. They also range from light to dark in color. Typical examples are andesite and diorite.

THE OCCURRENCE OF IGNEOUS ROCKS

As previously mentioned, igneous rocks are formed in the earth's crust in two ways: they may harden on the surface as extrusive rocks or solidify beneath the surface as intrusive or plutonic rocks.

EXTRUSIVE OR VOLCANIC ROCK MASSES

These are most commonly found in the form of lava flows, which are generally sheetlike in nature. Certain lava flows, such as those of the Columbia Lava Plateau in the northwestern United States between the northern Rocky Mountains and the Cascade Range, cover hundreds of square miles to depths of almost a mile. Lava flows are also common in many parts of Arizona,

California, New Mexico, Colorado, and other western and southwestern states.

Some lava flows are associated with volcanoes and others are the result of fissure flows. Many of these lava flows exhibit a typical columnar jointing (Fig. 25). Others consist largely of rough blocky masses of scoria.

Extrusive igneous products may also be in the form of volcanic ash, dust, and bombs (see page 46). In certain areas of extensive volcanic activity large cinder cones have been formed. Sunset Crater National Monument near Flagstaff, Arizona, is one of the better-known craters of this type. Other popular localities which show the results of volcanic activity and have excellent exposures of extrusive rocks are Lassen Volcanic National Park and Lava Beds National Monument in northern California, Crater Lake National Park in southern Oregon, Capulin Mountain National Monument (a cinder cone) in northern New Mexico and Craters of the Moon National Monument in southern Idaho.

PLUTONS OR INTRUSIVE IGNEOUS ROCK MASSES

Intrusive, or plutonic igneous rocks have been intruded or injected into the surrounding rocks. Intrusions of this type normally occur at great depth, consequently igneous intrusive bodies may be seen only after the overlying rocks have been removed by erosion. Some of the more common **plutons** or intrusive bodies are discussed below.

Dikes. A dike is a tabular or wall-like mass of igneous rock that cuts across bedding planes when introduced into sedimentary rocks (Fig. 29). Dikes commonly result from magma being injected into cracks and joints in the rocks, and range in size from a few feet to many miles in length. They are quite common in volcanic areas, and are commonly associated with volcanic necks (see below).

Sills. These are tabular bodies of igneous rocks that spread out as essentially horizontal sheets between beds or layers of rocks. They differ from dikes in that the igneous rocks lie parallel to the bedding plane. The Palisades of the Hudson

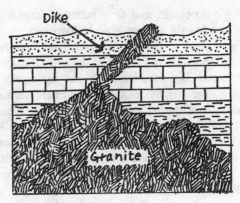

Fig. 29. Igneous dike.

River in New York and New Jersey represent the face of a great sill that is hundreds of feet thick.

Laccoliths. Laccoliths are lenslike or mushroom-shaped intrusive bodies that have relatively flat under surfaces and arched or domed upper surfaces. They are intruded between the bedding planes and differ from sills in that they are thicker in the center and become thinner near their margins. Many of the domed mountains in the Judith Mountains of Montana and the Henry Mountains of Utah have been formed by laccoliths.

Batholiths. These, the largest of igneous intrusions, are irregularly shaped and may cover thousands of square miles. Batholiths extend great distances within the earth and become larger with depth. The Idaho batholith covers 16,000 square miles; other great batholiths have been exposed in the cores of the Rocky Mountains and Sierra Nevada.

Stocks. These are similar to batholiths but cover an area of less than 40 square miles. Stone Mountain near Atlanta, Georgia, is a good example of a stock.

VOLCANOES

Volcanoes are vents in the earth's crust through which molten rock and other volcanic products are extruded. Volcanoes and their related phenomena, such as fumaroles and hot springs, are among the most interesting of all geologic processes, and their activities have been mentioned in the earliest historical writings.

The typical volcano is a cone-shaped mountain with a funnel-shaped crater at the top (Fig. 30). This crater is connected with the underground magma chamber by means of a central vent or conduit, and during periods of eruption steam, dust, ashes, stones, and molten rock (called lava) emanate from the vent. The **magma chamber** is located far beneath the surface of the earth and is a reservoir containing hot molten rock material, which may be either intruded into the earth's crust or extruded upon the surface.

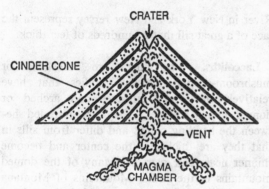

Fig. 30. Volcanic cone with crater.

DISTRIBUTION OF VOLCANOES

The volcanoes of the earth appear to be concentrated within certain well-defined geographic belts or zones (Fig. 31). Volcanic zones occur most frequently in areas of crustal instability within or near regions of recent mountain-building activities, and the two major zones are associated with large fault, or fracture, zones in the earth's crust. These fault zones, as noted in Chapter 2, are associated with plate boundaries. However, certain volcanoes—for example, those of the Hawaiian Islands—are believed to be caused by plumes, or "hot spots," located beneath certain plates.

The circum-Pacific belt, or zone, is the most important and contains most of the world's active volcanoes. It borders the Pacific Ocean along the continental margins of Asia and the Americas. This zone, commonly called the "Pacific ring of fire," includes the volcanoes of South and Central America, Alaska, the Aleutian Islands, Japan, the Philippines, and the East Indies.

The Mediterranean Zone extends in an east-west direction and includes the volcanoes of the Mediterranean basin, the West Indies, Hawaii, and the Azores. In addition to the above zones, volcanoes are also located in the Atlantic, Pacific, and Indian Oceans, in Iceland, and in the Antarctic.

The United States has several active volcanoes worthy of mention, among them, Lassen Peak in Lassen Volcanic National Park, California, Mount Katmai and Mount Aniakchak in Alaska, the several active volcanoes of Hawaii, and Mount St. Helens of the Cascade Range in Washington. There are also many cones of extinct or dormant volcanoes in the United States. Some, like Mount St. Helens, may unexpectedly resume activity after hundreds—or thousands—of years of quiescence. Such familiar mountains as Mount Rainier in Washington, Mount Hood in Oregon, Mount Shasta in California, and Mount St. Elias in Alaska are cones of this type. Some well-known Mexican volcanoes are Parícutin, Popocatepetl, and Orizaba.

THE ACTIVITY OF VOLCANOES

As noted above, some volcanoes are active, while others have not erupted within historic times. In order to indicate the relative activity of volcanoes, they have been classified as **active, dormant,** and **extinct.** Those volcanoes that are continually or periodically in a state of eruption are classified as active volcanoes. A volcano that is now inactive, but has been known to erupt within modern times is classed as dormant. There are many examples of so-called "dormant" volcanoes, such as Mount Vesuvius in Italy, or Mount St. Helens in the United States, experiencing violent eruptions after many centuries of inactivity. If a volcano is not known to have erupted within historic times, it is said to be extinct. Here again, Nature has shown the tendency to disregard classification, for Lassen Peak, an "extinct" volcano in California, and Mount St. Helens suddenly became active after a long period of quiescence. Volcanologists tell us that probably the only volcanoes that are truly extinct are those that have been eroded almost to the level of their magma chamber.

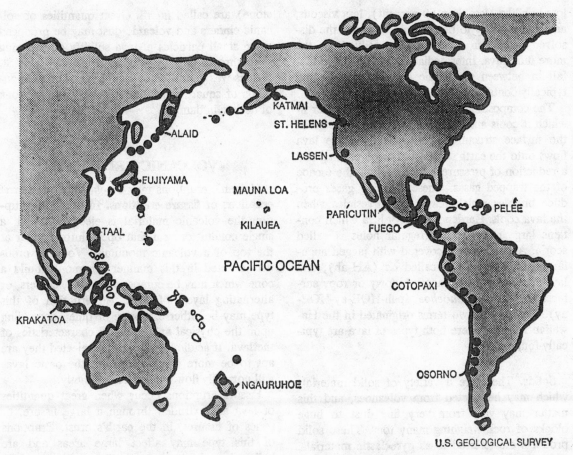

Fig. 31. Map showing distribution of major areas of volcanic activity.

VOLCANIC PRODUCTS

When volcanoes erupt they may eject a large variety of material which may vary from gases to large fragments of rocks.

Gases. The gases that are emitted from volcanoes are composed largely of water vapor, with varying amounts of carbon dioxide, hydrogen sulfide, and chlorine. During an eruption these escaping gases may become mixed with vast quantities of volcanic dust and often rise from the crater in great dark clouds which may be seen for many miles. As in the case of the 1980 eruption of Mount St. Helens, dust from such eruptions may be carried by winds for great distances. Although these dusty clouds of steam are frequently referred to as "smoke," it should be noted that they are not caused by fire.

Liquids. The liquids produced by volcanoes are the lavas—great quantities of white-hot molten rock. Lava is more typically extruded from the crater in the top of the volcano, but it is not uncommon for the lava to break through the sides of the cone and escape by means of fissures developed along zones of weakness.

Not all lavas are alike in their chemical and physical properties, and these properties may be reflected by the manner in which the volcano erupts. The chemical composition of the lava will affect its viscosity, which will in turn affect its rate and distance of flow. Chemical composition will also affect the shape of the cone, and will have some bearing on the surface structure of the rock formed when the molten rock solidifies.

Because of the different characteristics of lavas, geologists have classified them as **acidic, basic,** and **intermediate.** The acidic lavas are high in silica content (65 to 75 percent), usually very viscous, and frequently explosive. Basic lavas are low in silica (less than 50 percent), less viscous, and not as likely to be explosive because the dissolved gases can escape more easily from the more fluid lava. Intermediate lavas are those that fall in between the acidic and basic types and typically contain 50 to 60 percent silica.

The composition of the lava and the manner in which it cools and solidifies are often reflected in the surface structure of the rock. As the lava flows onto the earth's surface there is cooling and a reduction of pressure, which permits the escape of the trapped gases. These escaping gases produce bubbles which leave empty vesicles when the lava cools. Hardened cindery lava which contains large numbers of irregular holes is called scoria. A lava surface covered with jagged angular blocks of scoria is called *aa* (AH-ah), and lavas with relatively smooth billowy or ropy surfaces are called *pahoehoe* (pah-HOE-ay-HOE-ay). These latter two terms originated in the Hawaiian Islands, where both types of lava are typically found.

Solids. There are a variety of solid materials which may be ejected from volcanoes, and this matter may vary from very fine dust to huge blocks of rock weighing many tons. These solid products are referred to as **pyroclastic** materials, or **tephra.** One of the more interesting and unusual types of pyroclastics is the **volcanic bomb.** These spherical or pear-shaped objects (Fig. 32) are formed from large masses of lava that harden as they swirl through the air. In addition to large masses of lava, large, broken, angular fragments of rock may also be ejected from the volcano. The larger pieces are known as volcanic blocks and the smaller pieces (about the size of a small

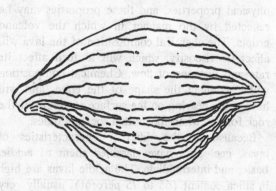

Fig. 32. Volcanic bomb.

stone) are called **lapilli.** Great quantities of volcanic **cinders** and **volcanic** dust may be produced when small particles of lava solidify after having been thrown into the air. Dust from Mount St. Helens was deposited over an area of many thousands of square miles and caused many millions of dollars in damage.

VOLCANIC ERUPTIONS

Volcanic eruptions may be classified as **central eruptions** or **fissure eruptions.** In a central eruption the volcanic material is ejected through a single conduit or vent that opens into a crater at the top of a volcanic mountain. Volcanic products erupted in this manner commonly build a cone which may be composed of lava, cinders, or alternating layers of both. An eruption of this type may be either explosive or quiet, depending upon the physical and chemical characteristics of the lava. If acidic lavas are being ejected they are apt to be more explosive, while the basic lavas will normally flow out relatively quietly.

Fissure eruptions occur when great quantities of lava are extruded through a large fissure, or series of fissures, in the earth's crust. Eruptions of this type may affect large areas and are believed to be responsible for our great lava plains and basalt plateaus. Most of these lava plains were formed in prehistoric times and volcanic action is no longer present in the immediate vicinity of the flows. The only fissure eruption within modern times occurred in Iceland in 1783. During this eruption a great flood of lava began pouring out along a large fissure near Mount Skapta and eventually covered an area of 218 square miles. As noted above, however, there is much evidence to indicate that large fissure eruptions have occurred at many times during the geologic past.

TYPES OF VOLCANOES

One of the more commonly used classifications of volcanoes recognizes four principal types of volcanoes: the Peléan, Vulcanian, Strombolian, and Hawaiian types.

Peléan. The Peléan or **explosive** type of volcano erupts with violent explosions which eject great quantities of gas, volcanic ash, dust, and large rock fragments. Eruptions of this type are believed to occur in volcanoes whose vents have been plugged by solidified magma. The gases accumulating in the magma chamber eventually develop pressures great enough to blow out this plug and the resulting explosion is often violent enough to completely blast away a large part of the mountain. Eruptions of this type are often accompanied by destructive clouds of volcanic gases and dust, and are among the most disastrous types of explosions known to man. An example of this type of explosion occurred in 1902 at Mount Pelée on the Island of Martinique in the West Indies. After eruptions in 1762 and 1851, the volcano gave no sign of life and was thought to be extinct, but in 1902 it erupted with such violence that the top of the mountain was blown off. This eruption was accompanied by a huge black cloud of hot gas and dust which descended upon the city of St. Pierre and took an estimated thirty thousand lives. The recent eruptions of Mount St. Helens were of the Peléan type. However, there is much evidence to suggest that many of its earlier eruptions were accompanied by large quantities of lava.

Vulcanian. The Vulcanian type of volcano is characterized by very viscous lavas, which solidify soon after they come in contact with the air. The lava in the crater crusts over between eruptions, and each later eruption takes place through breaks in this crust. This type of eruption typically produces large quantities of ash, lava, and great clouds of dust and gas. Mount Vesuvius in Italy is noted for its great numbers of eruptions followed by periods of quiet and is a typical example of the Vulcanian type of volcano.

Strombolian. This type of volcano is in constant action and is in contrast to the more typical volcano which has alternating periods of activity and quiescence. Stromboli, an island of the Lipari group in the Mediterranean Sea off the northern coast of Sicily, is the classic example of this type of volcano. The volcano is constantly active, and explosive eruptions come at well-spaced intervals. These explosions are accompanied by the emission of viscous lavas and large amounts of pyroclastics. Both the Strombolian

and Vulcanian types of volcanoes have also been referred to as **intermediate** volcanoes.

Hawaiian. The Hawaiian, or **quiet,** volcano is characterized by less viscous lavas which permit the escape of gas with a minimum of explosive violence. The lava is typically extruded from the crater, although flank eruptions may occur through fissures in the side of the mountain. Eruptions are commonly accompanied by small explosions of escaping gas, which may whip the lava into a froth that may later solidify into scoria. Probably the best-known volcano of this type is Mauna Loa in the Hawaiian Islands. This volcanic mountain rises 13,680 feet above sea level, and its oval-shaped crater is about five miles in circumference. The walls of this great crater are almost vertical and it is believed to be about 1000 feet deep. Kilauea is another very active Hawaiian volcano.

LANDFORMS PRODUCED BY VOLCANIC ACTIVITY

Volcanic activity and the extrusion of lava result in four principal types of **volcanic edifices** or landforms: plateau basalts or lava plains, volcanic mountains, craters, and calderas.

Plateau or Flood Basalts and Lava Plains. These are formed when great floods of lava are released by fissure eruptions and spread in sheet-like layers over the earth's surface. Some of these lava flows are quite extensive, and the Columbia River Plateau of Oregon, Washington, Nevada, and Idaho is covered by 200,000 square miles of basaltic lava which originated from such an eruption. This great basalt plateau represents the accumulation of many individual lava flows, which attain a thickness of 4000 feet in some places.

The Craters of the Moon National Monument in Idaho is part of the Columbia Plateau and includes what is probably the most recent evidence of fissure eruption in this part of the United States. Other large basalt plateaus occur in other parts of the world, and among these are the Deccan Plateau of India and the Paraná Plateau of South America.

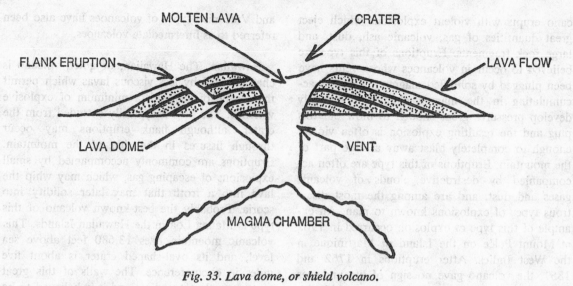

Fig. 33. Lava dome, or shield volcano.

Volcanic Mountains. These are mountains that are composed of the volcanic products of central eruptions, and are classified as **explosion cones** or **cinder cones**, **composite cones** (also called stratovolcanoes and stratocones), and **lava domes** or shield volcanoes.

Explosion cones are formed solely by explosive eruptions and consist of successive, steeply inclined layers of pyroclastics disposed around a central crater. Cones of this type seldom exceed 1000 feet in height and are often the result of one volcanic explosion. Typical examples of this kind of mountain are Capulin Mountain in northern New Mexico, Cinder Cone in Lassen Volcanic National Park, and Sunset Crater in northern Arizona.

Composite or stratovolcanoes are steeply sloping volcanoes composed of alternating sheets of lava and pyroclastic material. They are cone-shaped mountains with concave sides and may be as much as 12,000 feet high. The alternating layers of lava and pyroclastics are evidence of intermittent periods of quiescence and explosive eruption. Some famous composite volcanoes are Mount Vesuvius in Italy, Mount Fuji in Japan, and Mount Rainier in Washington. Prior to the May 18 eruption of Mount St. Helens, it was one of the more symmetrical of the world's stratovolcanoes.

Lava domes or shield volcanoes are broad, gently sloping volcanic domes, characteristically exhibiting a gently rounded convex upper surface (Fig. 33). This type of volcanic mountain is composed of large numbers of overlapping basaltic lava flows which originated from the central vent or from flank eruptions through fissures. The great volcanoes of Hawaii are typical of this type of mountain.

Volcanic Craters. These are funnel-shaped depressions in the tops of volcanic mountains through which central eruptions take place. Most craters have been produced as a result of explosive volcanic activity and are seldom more than a mile in diameter or more than a few hundred feet deep.

Calderas. Calderas are nearly circular, basin-shaped depressions in the tops of volcanoes, and are much larger than craters. There are two types of calderas: one is brought about as the result of **explosive activity** and the other as a result of **collapse** or **subsidence.** Explosion calderas are created as the result of violent volcanic explosions which have displaced large amounts of rock. Collapse or subsidence calderas are produced when the upper part of the volcano collapses because of the sudden withdrawal of the supporting magma. Some calderas are believed to have been formed by the combined effects of explosion and collapse. Crater Lake in Crater Lake National Park, Oregon, occupies a great caldera which may have been formed by collapse of a now-extinct volcano. The caldera is filled with a lake which covers an area of approximately twenty square miles and is as much as 2000 feet deep. Wizard Island, a small cinder cone, is located within the caldera and rises about 800 feet above the lake. This cone was formed by eruptions that occurred after the top of the volcano, Mount Mazama, was destroyed.

THERMAL AREAS

In many areas of volcanic or other igneous activity there is evidence of volcanic gases, steam, or hot water escaping from the earth. These places are called **thermal areas** and are closely associated with volcanism or igneous activity.

Fumaroles. These are vents or cracks in the earth's surface through which steam and gas issue. Steam emanates from certain fumaroles in Italy in sufficient quantities to generate power. Some fumaroles are characterized by the emission of large quantities of sulfurous vapors and these have been called **solfataras.**

Hot Springs. Hot springs are formed when ground water is heated by large masses of magma that are located relatively near the surface. Many of these springs, such as the famous hot springs of Arkansas, are the sites of health and bathing resorts.

Geysers. A geyser is a special type of hot spring that intermittently erupts a column of steam and hot water. Geysers originate in areas where ground temperatures are unusually high, and where long narrow fissures are likely to be present in the rocks. The ground water at the bottom of these fissures is heated to a temperature far above the boiling point of water (212° F). This superheating of the bottom water is made possible because of the pressure exerted by the water that lies above it. As the water in the bottom of the fissure expands, it causes some of the overlying water to overflow onto the surface. This overflow relieves part of the pressure and allows the superheated water to explode into steam, ejecting a great column of water into the air. Some geysers, such as Old Faithful in Yel-

lowstone National Park, erupt with amazing regularity, but most geysers are quite erratic in their performance. There are, at present, some one hundred geysers and three thousand noneruptive hot springs known in Yellowstone National Park. Other areas where geysers occur are Iceland, New Zealand, and Japan.

Some thermal and volcanic areas (such as those in Iceland) are associated with plate boundaries. Others—for example, the Hawaiian Islands (Fig. 14) and Yellowstone National Park —appear to be situated above local "hot spots" or **plumes** in the earth. These hot, pipelike features (page 18) are believed to carry heat and mantle material from the lower part of the mantle up to the crust, thereby producing hot spots at the surface.

Certain thermal areas have great amounts of natural steam. In northern California, Iceland, New Zealand, and Italy this steam has been harnessed as a source of geothermal energy. Although sometimes rather highly touted as an energy source, its occurrence is far too localized to be of much value in solving the world's future energy progems.

WHAT CAUSES VOLCANISM?

As noted earlier, lava comes from localized pockets of magma contained within the crust or upper mantle. The exact way in which magma originates is not known at present. However, it is known that there cannot be a great reservoir of molten rock within the earth because of the way that the earth transmits certain seismic (earthquake) waves. Evidence from these seismic waves proves that the material forming the crust is largely solid. It is further believed that magma cannot come from very deep in the earth (not below about 240 miles) because the composition and behavior of the earth's material appear to undergo radical changes at about these depths. The evidence for this is again derived from earthquake waves and other experimental studies.

One explanation that has been advanced for the origin of magma is that it is due to the local reduction of pressure within the crust. This may occur as the result of bending or breaking of the rocks that overlie the magma reservoir.

It has also been suggested that the melting of rock may be caused by increased temperatures produced by the breakdown of radioactive minerals in the rocks. It is known (from temperature measurements in wells and mines) that the crustal rocks get progressively hotter with increasing depth. If the temperature rise was uniform, rocks should be hot enough to melt at depths of about 20 miles. But they do not melt because pressures are too high. Rocks must expand when they melt. Therefore, high-confining pressure can prevent melting until the temperature rises far above the normal melting point. If pressure is reduced locally, the material at high temperature can then melt and may form a body of magma.

The exact source of volcanic heat is not known. It may be a part of the earth's original heat that has not yet escaped. It may also result from the accumulation of heat from the small amounts of radioactive elements in the earth's crust, or of heat generated by pressure ionization within the earth.

Measurements show that the temperature increases at an average rate of about one degree centigrade per 100 feet. Because pressure also increases with depth, the temperature at which rocks melt becomes higher. Local release of pressure can thus lower the melting point of rock to cause melting. Also, rocks are very poor conductors of heat; this fact may help explain the localized development of magma in the crust or mantle.

Within recent years the theory of plate tectonics has provided still more clues to the causes of volcanism. We have seen that most volcanoes are products of lithosphere-plate motions, and the "Pacific ring of fire" (Fig. 31) is evidence of one type of this volcanic activity. The chains of volcanoes in the island arcs (such as the Aleutian Islands) and continental margins (such as the Andes) around much of the ocean form above subducting oceanic plates. The main volcanic axis is typically about 80 miles above the inclined zone of earthquakes that marks the descent of the lithosphere plate into the deep mantle. Thus, processes related to the descent and to that depth must control the melting of the magmas. As an example we can again mention Mount St. Helens. Many geologists believe that the magma that feeds St. Helens is generated as the relatively small Juan de Fuca plate descends beneath the North American plate (Fig. 34).

The theory of plate tectonics also helps us to understand certain volcanic areas that are not associated with rifting or subduction along plate boundaries. The Hawaiian Islands consist of a series of volcanic cones rising thousands of meters from the floor of the Pacific Ocean. This string of volcanoes has largely been built in succession—each one to the northwest being older than that to the southeast. The island of Hawaii—the largest of the chain—rises more than 30,000 feet above the ocean floor; and its active volcanoes typically erupt every few years.

This great chain of volcanoes continues northwestward as the foundation for coral atolls as far as Midway, and then as seamounts (eroded, submerged volcanic cones) all the way to Kamchatka in northeast Russia. It is interesting to note that the general age progression of

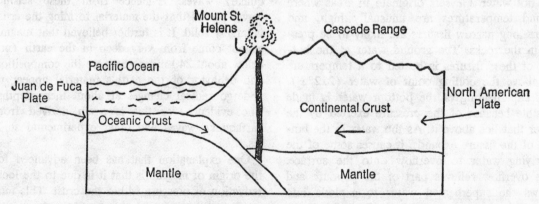

Fig. 34. Subduction of Juan de Fuca plate beneath North American plate and possible relation to Mount St. Helens.

the volcanoes and seamounts continues throughout: the older cones lie to the northwest and the younger volcanoes are to their southeast.

The occurrence of this intraplate volcanism and the age progression may be due to the fact that the Pacific plate is drifting slowly over a "hot spot" in the deeper mantle. Molten rock associated with this plume keeps rising through the plate above. Thus, as the plate continues its northward journey, it is leaving behind a string of volcanoes and their eroded remnants (Fig. 14).

In summary, the ultimate causes of igneous activity appear to be related to the same internal processes that cause earthquakes, raise mountains, and produce metamorphism. These forces are the result of the complex interaction of many factors which are still not thoroughly understood. Thanks, however, to the explosion of geologic knowledge generated by research resulting from interest in the theory of plate tectonics, we now know much more than we did just a decade ago.

EFFECTS OF VOLCANOES ON HUMANS

Volcanic activity is sometimes tremendously destructive, but in general volcanoes cause much less damage than earthquakes, hurricanes, and tornadoes. Explosive eruptions may occur without warning, sometimes causing much property damage and loss of life. The damage is done by heavy falls of dust, ash, and bombs, and by suffocating gases. Damage is especially severe when explosions are directed sideward instead of upward, and when clouds of hot gas and dust move rapidly down the mountain slopes. Milder explosive eruptions can ruin agricultural land for several years by depositing thick layers of dust and ash, sometimes over an area many miles from the volcano. Although lava flows generally move too slowly to cause loss of life, they may cause extensive property damage when they invade densely populated areas.

Volcanic activity does have beneficial effects in that the weathering of many volcanic rocks yields a very fertile soil material. Such weathering produces readily available mineral matter for plant growth and forms a youthful soil with good texture for cultivation.

Throughout the ages, water vapor given off by volcanoes has helped to fill the oceans, and the carbon dioxide given off has made possible the survival and evolution of plants. Without plants there would be virtually no animal life on earth. Hence, in an indirect way it may be that humans might not be here today if it were not for the gases given off by volcanoes.

Certain volcanic rocks are used extensively as building stone and road material. When crushed, the rocks make excellent foundation material for roads and airfields. Some solidified volcanic ash is widely used in warm climates because of its excellent insulating properties. Pumice and volcanic ash are used as abrasives because they consist of fairly hard material with sharp points and edges. Agate and opal are sometimes found in cavities in lava, where they were deposited by hot water.

Volcanoes are also responsible for some of the world's most beautiful scenery. In general, the movement of molten rock builds up the land surfaces locally by forming volcanic mountains, by flooding large areas with lava, and by elevating the surface when molten rock is intruded underneath. Thus, the landscape is changed and in many places the scenery is enhanced.

SOME FAMOUS VOLCANIC ERUPTIONS

The volcano **Krakatoa,** located in Sunda Strait between Java and Sumatra, exploded in 1883 with what was probably the greatest explosion in the history of all mankind. This great blast threw fragmental material many miles into the air, and falling ashes were distributed over 300,000 square miles; in fifteen days volcanic dust from the explosion had encircled the earth. The violent activity of Krakatoa was responsible for the generation of great sea waves, some as much as 100 feet in height, which destroyed hundreds of villages and drowned an estimated 36,000 persons.

Mount Vesuvius is famous for its large number of explosive eruptions and has been studied in great detail. This volcano, located on the Bay of Naples in southern Italy, erupted in 79 A.D. with such violence that the Roman cities of Pompeii and Herculaneum were completely buried. There was another great eruption of Vesuvius in 1906, at which time explosions reduced the height of the mountain by several hundred feet, and lava broke through the northwest flank of the cone and flowed for many months.

Lassen Peak in northern California erupted in 1914 after a two-hundred-year period of inactivity. During this eruption clouds of steam and ash issued from the crater, and one column of steam rose to a height of 10,000 feet above the crest of the mountain. Its unexpected activity is believed to have been the result of great earthquakes in Alaska and California which preceded the 1914 eruption. The peak, known also as Mount Lassen, is surrounded by lava flows, and excellent examples of volcanic rocks, hot springs, mud pots, and other activities related to volcanism may be seen in this area. (A mud pot is a type of hot spring consisting of a shallow pit filled with hot, normally boiling mud and very little water.)

Parícutin, one of the most recent and most publicized of volcanoes, has provided us with much information about the birth, development, and death of a volcano. This volcano, located about 200 miles west of Mexico City, showed its first signs of activity in February 1943, and was marked by extensive lava flows and explosions of pyroclastic material. A 350-foot cinder cone had been formed at the end of the first week's activity, and this cone attained a height of about 1400 feet by the end of the first year. Eruptions ceased in February, 1952, after nine years of activity, and Parícutin now appears to be dead.

Mount St. Helens—a perfectly formed stratovolcano in Washington's Cascade Range—suddenly erupted on May 18, 1980, after 123 years of inactivity. Following two months of earthquake activity, St. Helens exploded with a force estimated to be the equivalent of 50 million tons of TNT! A billowing cloud of steam, ash, and dust reached heights of 10 to 12 miles, and 1300 feet of the mountain's top were blown away. Most of the damage was done by a great blast of volcanic gases and pyroclastics, which was followed by huge mudflows and attendant floods which destroyed wildlife and tens of thousands of acres of timber. People miles away from the explosion were killed and large areas of Washington, Oregon, Montana, and Idaho were blanketed with suffocating layers of volcanic dust. At least 35 persons died in the blast and scores were listed as missing. Estimates of damage were in excess of $2 billion.

CHAPTER 5

SEDIMENTARY ROCKS

Those rocks which are exposed on the earth's surface are especially vulnerable to the agents of erosion. They may be attacked chemically, or be worn and broken by mechanical means such as rolling along the bottom of a stream. These rock fragments are commonly picked up and transported by wind, water, and ice, and when the transporting agent has dropped them they are generally referred to as **sediments.** Sediments are

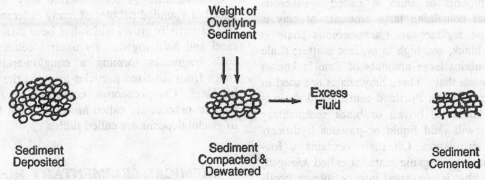

Fig. 35. How sediments become lithified by compaction and cementation to form sedimentary rock.

typically deposited in layers or beds called **strata.** When sediments become compacted and cemented together (a process known as **lithification**), they form sedimentary rocks (Fig. 35). These rocks, represented by such common types as sandstone, shale, and limestone, make up about 75 percent of the rocks exposed on the earth's surface.

KINDS OF SEDIMENTARY ROCKS

Sedimentary rocks are generally classified as either **clastic** or **chemical,** according to the source of the rock materials which form them.

CLASTIC OR DETRITAL SEDIMENTARY ROCKS

Clastic sediments are composed of rock fragments which have been derived from the decomposition or disintegration of igneous, sedimentary, or metamorphic rocks. Rocks formed from these worn-down rock particles are also called **detrital** or **fragmental** sedimentary rocks. Because the sediments which form these rocks are normally transported by mechanical means (wind, water, or ice), they have also been referred to as **mechanical sediments.**

Clastic rocks are composed of rock particles of varying size and this size differentiation has been used as a basis of classification for these rocks. Table 2 shows the most generally accepted size ranges of the materials composing clastic sedimentary rocks.

ROUNDED, SUBROUNDED, AND SUBANGULAR ROCKS

SIZE	FRAGMENT	AGGREGATE
Over 256 mm.	Boulder	Boulder gravel, boulder conglomerate
64–256 mm.	Cobble	Cobble gravel, cobble conglomerate
4–64 mm.	Pebble	Pebble gravel, pebble conglomerate
2–4 mm.	Granule	Granule sand
1/16–2 mm.	Sand	Sand, sandstone
1/256–1/16 mm.	Silt	Silt, siltstone
Under 1/256 mm.	Clay	Clay, shale

TABLE 2. This classification has been made by the Committee on Sedimentation, Division of Geology and Geography, National Research Council.

Some of the more common types of clastic sedimentary rocks are described below.

Shale. The most abundant of all sedimentary rocks, shale is formed from silt and clays which have hardened into rock. Shale (Fig. 36) is characteristically fine-grained, thinly bedded, and split easily along bedding planes (the dividing planes which separate individual layers or beds of sedimentary rocks). Shale containing appreciable amounts of sand is called **arenaceous** shale; that containing large amounts of clay is said to be **argillaceous. Carbonaceous** shale is typically black, and high in organic matter; shale which contains large amounts of lime is known as **calcareous** shale. These limy shales are used in the manufacture of Portland cement. **Oil shale** is a finely laminated brown or black sedimentary rock that will yield liquid or gaseous hydrocarbons or distillation. Oil shale contains a fossilized insoluble organic material called **kerogen,** which is what is converted into petroleum products.

Sandstone. Composed essentially of cemented grains of sand, sandstone has a granular texture and is the second most abundant of all sedimentary rock. In addition to quartz, sandstone may consist of sand-sized particles of calcite, gypsum, or various iron compounds. **Arkose** is a special type of sandstone which contains fragments of feldspar as well as quartz. Sandstone is used as an abrasive (for sandpaper) and as a building stone.

Conglomerate. A conglomerate may be composed of rounded pebbles of many different sizes. It is essentially gravel which has been mixed with sand and held together by natural cement. The rock fragments forming a conglomerate may range from silt-sized particles to rocks the size of boulders. Conglomerates composed largely of angular pebbles are called **breccias;** those formed in glacial deposits are called **tillites.**

CHEMICAL SEDIMENTARY ROCKS

Sediments which have been precipitated from material dissolved in water are called chemical sediments and form **chemical sedimentary rocks.** Some chemical sediments are deposited directly from the water in which the material is dissolved; for example, rock salt may be precipitated from solution upon evaporation of seawater. Such deposits are generally referred to as **inorganic chemical sediments.** Chemical sediments which have been deposited by or with the assistance of plants or animals are said to be **organic** or **biochemical sediments.** Oysters, for example, extract calcium carbonate from seawater and use it to build a calcareous or limy shell. When the oyster dies, its shell commonly remains on the sea floor where it is eventually incorporated into the bottom sediments.

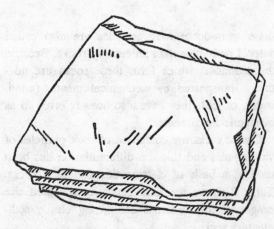

Fig. 36. Shale showing bedding planes.

Inorganic Chemical Sedimentary Rocks. Sedimentary rocks formed from sediments created by inorganic processes are discussed below.

Limestone—Limestone is composed primarily of one mineral: calcite ($CaCO_3$). There are many varieties of limestone, and some are formed by inorganic means, such as direct precipitation, while others are organic in origin. **Travertine,** which forms stalactites and stalagmites in caves, is a crystalline, usually banded variety of limestone. **Tufa,** a spongy, porous, inorganic limestone, is formed when calcite is deposited around springs and streams.

Dolomite—Known also as magnesium limestone, dolomite [$CaMg(CO_3)_2$] is formed when some of the calcium in limestone is replaced by magnesium. Exactly how this replacement occurs is not completely understood.

Evaporites—Sedimentary rocks that are derived from minerals precipitated from seawater are termed evaporites. These include gypsum ($CaSO_4 \cdot 2H_2O$), anhydrite ($CaSO_4$, calcium sulfate without water), and halite or rock salt ($NaCl$). Extensive evaporite deposits occur in western Texas and southeastern New Mexico, and in Michigan, Ohio, and New York; some of these are of considerable economic value.

Biochemical or Organic Sedimentary Rocks. These rocks consist of sediments formed from the remains and/or secretions of organisms.

Organic Limestone—Most limestones are organic in origin and these rocks frequently contain the remains of the organisms responsible for their formation. **Coquina** is a type of limestone composed of shells and coarse shell fragments, **reef limestones** are composed of corals and other lime-secreting organisms, and **chalk** is a porous, fine-textured variety of limestone composed of the calcareous shells of micro-organisms such as foraminifers (Chapter 20).

Coal—Coal is composed largely of carbonized plant remains. An important fuel of industry, coal is usually found in layers, associated with other sedimentary rocks. In its formation coal passes through several stages. Peat, composed of partially carbonized plant material, marks the first stage; **lignite** or brown coal is the second stage. Further changes may convert the lignite to bituminous or soft coal, and bituminous coal which has been metamorphosed will turn into anthracite or hard coal.

Other organic sedimentary rocks are **radiolarite,** composed largely of the siliceous exoskeletons of tiny one-celled organisms called radiolarians, and **diatomaceous earth,** formed primarily from siliceous remains of microscopic plants called diatoms.

PHYSICAL CHARACTERISTICS OF SEDIMENTARY ROCKS

Sedimentary rocks possess definite physical characteristics and display certain features which make them readily distinguishable from igneous or metamorphic rocks. Some of these more important characteristics should be considered here.

Stratification or Bedding. Probably the most characteristic feature of sedimentary rocks is their tendency to occur in strata or beds (Fig. 37). Each stratum or bed is separated by a **bedding plane** which marks the top of one bed and the bottom of the bed next above it. These strata are formed as geologic agents such as wind, water, or ice gradually deposit their load of sediment. Changes in the carrying agent (such as reduced stream or wind velocities) will affect the texture of the sediments and the thickness of the beds.

Texture. The size, shape, and arrangements of the materials which form a sedimentary rock will determine its texture. Conglomerates exhibit a coarse texture, whereas a fine-grained limestone has a fine texture. Sands are classified as fine-grained, coarse-grained, etc. In general, textures are usually said to be **clastic** if formed from broken rock and mineral fragments, and **nonclastic** if they are more or less crystalline or granular.

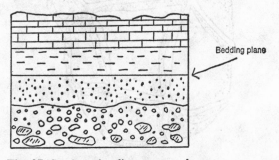

Fig. 37. Section of sedimentary rock strata.

Ripple Marks. Little waves or ripples of sand are commonly developed on the surface of a beach, sand dune, or the bottom of a stream. Ripples of this type have also been preserved in certain sedimentary rocks (Fig. 38) and may provide the geologist with information about the conditions of deposition when the sediment was originally deposited.

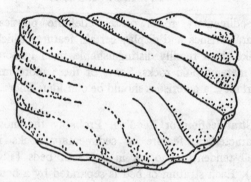

Fig. 38. Ripple marks in limestone.

Mud Cracks. It is not uncommon to find mud cracks that have formed on the bottom of dried-up lakes, ponds, or stream beds. These polygonal (many-sided) shapes give a honeycomb appearance to the surface (Fig. 39). Such cracks preserved in sedimentary rocks suggest that the rock was subjected to alternate periods of flooding and drying.

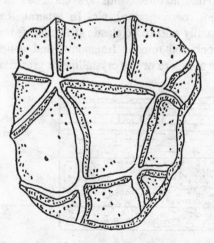

Fig. 39. Mud cracks preserved in stone.

Concretions. Some shales, limestones, and sandstones contain spherical or flattened masses of rock that are generally harder than the rock enclosing them. These objects, called concretions (Fig. 40) are commonly formed around a fossil or some other nucleus. Concretions range from as little as one inch to several feet in length or diameter. Because concretions are usually harder than the enclosing rock, they are often left behind after the surrounding rock has been eroded away.

Fig. 40. Concretion.

Geodes. Geodes are rounded concretionary rocks that are hollow and frequently lined with crystals (Fig. 41). Geodes are most likely to occur in limestone but they may also be found in certain shale formations. The formation of geodes is discussed in Chapter 10.

Fig. 41. Geode with crystals lining interior cavity.

Color. Such areas as the Painted Desert and Grand Canyon of Arizona are noted for their brilliantly colored formations of sedimentary rocks. The color of these, and other rocks, is largely dependent upon the chemical composition of the rock. Hematite (Fe_2O_3), one of the most common coloring agents in sedimentary rocks, produces a pink or red color. Limonite may produce yellow-colored rocks, manganese various shades of purple, and rocks of high organic content (such as carbonaceous shale) are likely to be gray to black in color. In addition, weathering may affect the color of a rock. Thus, a rock that contains iron may be dark on a fresh surface, yet oxidation, brought about by chemical weathering, may result in a yellowish brown color on the weathered surface.

Fossils. Fossils are the remains or evidence of ancient plants and animals that have been preserved in the earth's crust. Fossils normally represent the preservable hard parts of some prehistoric organism that once lived in the area in which the remains were collected (Fig. 42).

Most fossils are found in sedimentary rocks; only rarely do they occur in igneous or metamorphic rocks. The original hot molten rocks would have had no life in them, and the metamorphic rocks have been so greatly altered or distorted that any fossils which might have been present in the original rock have been destroyed. Even in sedimentary rocks, however, only a small fraction of the plants and animals of the geologic past have left any record of their existence.

Fig. 42. Trilobite, a typical paleozoic fossil.

Sedimentary Facies. When applied to sedimentary rocks, the term **facies** describes an accumulation of deposits that have distinctive characteristics and grade laterally into other sedimentary deposits which, although formed at the same time, exhibit quite different characteristics (Fig. 43). A **facies change** is said to occur when there is a lateral or vertical change in the type of rock or fossils present in sedimentary deposits of the same age. Such variations are caused by, and are an indication of, a change in the environment of deposition (Fig. 44).

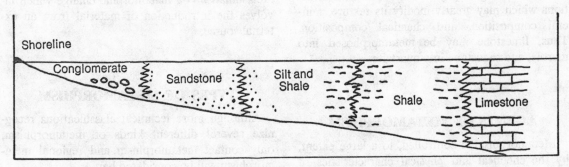

Fig. 43. Cross section of the sedimentary rocks resulting from consolidation of sediments.

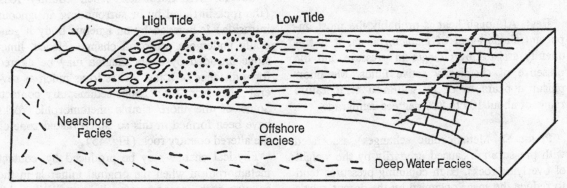

Fig. 44. Generalized cross section of the continental shelf and continental slope showing types of sedimentary facies.

CHAPTER 6

METAMORPHISM AND METAMORPHIC ROCKS

Metamorphic rocks are rocks (originally either igneous or sedimentary) that have been buried deep within the earth and subjected to high temperatures and pressures. These new physical conditions usually produce great changes in the solid rock (this includes rock in a plastic state) and these changes are included under the term **metamorphism** (Greek *meta,* "change," and *morphe,* "form" or "shape").

During the process of metamorphism the original rock undergoes physical and chemical alterations which may greatly modify its texture, mineral composition, and chemical composition. Thus, limestone may be metamorphosed into marble, and sandstone into quartzite.

AGENTS OF METAMORPHISM

Metamorphism is controlled, to a large extent, by the chemical and physical characteristics of the original rock and by the agent and degree of metamorphism involved.

Heat. Although heat is probably the most important single agent of metamorphism, it is frequently assisted by changes in pressure and the presence of chemically active fluids. Metamorphism appears to occur within a temperature range of about 100 to 800 degrees centigrade.

Pressure. Metamorphic changes associated with pressure are caused primarily by the weight of overlying rocks. High confining pressures tend to reduce the space occupied by the parent rock's

mineral constituents, produce recrystallization, and/or result in the formation of new minerals. Differential pressures can result in rock flowage which causes changes in texture and may result in foliation (see page 59).

Chemically Active Fluids. Hydrothermal ("heated water") solutions associated with magma may react with surrounding rocks to bring about chemical change. This may produce **metasomatism**—a metamorphic change which involves the introduction of material from an external source.

TYPES OF METAMORPHISM

Although more technical classifications recognize several different kinds of metamorphism, only contact metamorphism and regional metamorphism will be considered here.

Contact Metamorphism. When country rock (the rock intruded by or surrounding an igneous intrusion) is invaded by an igneous body it generally undergoes profound change. Hence, limestone intruded by a hot magma may be altered for a distance of a few inches to as much as several miles from the igneous sedimentary contact. Some of the more simple metamorphic rocks have been formed in this so-called **baked zone** of the altered country rock (Fig. 45).

Physical change may be produced by contact metamorphism when the original minerals in the country rock are permeated by magmatic fluids which often bring about recrystallization. This process, which typically produces either new or larger mineral crystals, may greatly alter the texture of the rock. In addition, the magmatic fluids commonly introduce new elements and compounds which will modify the chemical composition of the original rock and result in the formation of new minerals.

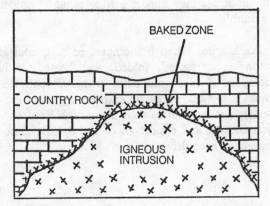

Fig. 45. Baked zone in country rock surrounding an igneous intrusion.

Regional Metamorphism. This type of metamorphism develops over extensive areas and takes place when rock layers undergo strong structural deformation during the formation of mountain ranges. The great pressures exerted as the rock layers are folded, fractured, and crumpled generally produce widespread and complex metamorphic change. Such pressures may result in tearing or crushing of the minerals, obliteration of any indication of fossils or stratification, realignment of mineral grains, and increased hardness.

TEXTURE OF METAMORPHIC ROCKS

The rearrangement of mineral crystals during metamorphism results in two basic types of rock texture: foliated and nonfoliated.

Foliated Metamorphic Rocks. Foliated rocks are metamorphic rocks in which the minerals have been flattened, drawn out, and arranged in parallel layers or bands (Fig. 46). There are four basic types of foliation: slaty, phyllitic,

schistose, and gneissic. Each of these, and some common rocks which exhibit them, is discussed below.

Slate. A metamorphosed shale, slate is characterized by a very fine texture in which mineral crystals cannot be detected with the naked eye. It does not show banding and splits readily into thin even slabs. Slate occurs in a variety of colors, but is usually gray, black, green, and red. Its characteristic slaty cleavage (not to be confused with mineral cleavage) makes it especially useful for roofing, blackboards, and sidewalks.

Phyllite. Derived from the Greek word *phyllon* (a leaf), phyllites are more fine-grained than schists but coarser than slate. On freshly broken surfaces they have a characteristic silky luster or sheen due to the presence of fine grains of mica. Most have been formed from shales which have been subjected to pressures greater than those required to produce slate, but not of sufficient intensity to produce schists.

Schist. Schist is a medium- to coarse-grained foliated metamorphic rock formed under greater pressures than those which form slate. It consists principally of micaceous minerals in a nearly parallel arrangement called **schistosity** (Fig. 46). Schists usually split readily along these schistose laminations or folia, which are usually bent and crumpled. Commonly derived from slate, schists may also be formed from fine-grained igneous rocks. They are named according to the predominant mineral, such as mica schists, chlorite schists, etc.

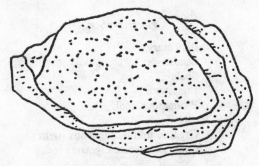

Fig. 46. Schist, a foliated metamorphic rock.

Gneiss. Gneiss (pronounced "nice") is a very highly metamorphosed coarse-grained banded rock. This rock is characterized by alternating bands of darker minerals such as chlorite, biotite mica, or graphite (Fig. 47). The bands are typically folded and contorted, and although some gneisses resemble schists, they do not split nearly as easily. Banding may be an indication of stratification in the original bedded sedimentary rock, or caused by the alteration of coarse-grained igneous rocks containing light- and dark-colored minerals.

In general, gneisses have undergone a greater degree of metamorphism than have schistose rocks and are commonly formed as a result of intense regional metamorphism.

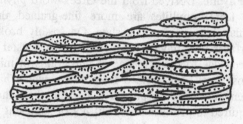

Fig. 47. Gneiss, a banded metamorphic rock.

Nonfoliated Metamorphic Rocks. These are metamorphic rocks which are typically massive or granular in texture and do not exhibit foliation. Although some nonfoliated rocks resemble certain igneous rocks, they can be differentiated from them on the basis of mineral composition.

Quartzite. Quartzite is formed from metamorphosed quartz sandstone. One of the most resistant of all rocks, quartzite is composed of a crystalline mass of tightly cemented sand grains. When formed from pure quartz sand, quartzite is white; however, the presence of impurities may stain the rock red, yellow, or brown.

Marble. A relatively coarse-grained, crystalline calcareous rock, marble is a metamorphosed limestone or dolomite. It is formed by recrystallization, and any evidence of fossils or stratification is usually destroyed during the process of alteration. White when pure, the presence of impurities may impart a wide range of colors to marble.

Anthracite. When bituminous, or soft, coal is strongly compacted, folded, and heated, it is transformed into anthracite, or hard, coal. Because it has undergone an extreme degree of carbonization, anthracite coal has a high fixed carbon content and almost all of the volatile materials have been driven off.

GRANITIZATION

Although the magmatic origin of granite has been generally accepted since the late eighteenth century, some geologists do not believe that granite is an igneous rock. They suggest that granite is a metamorphic rock created from parent rocks through the process of **granitization.** The exact operation and extent of this process is not clearly understood, but some investigators believe that there is a rearrangement of crystal structures in a solid or partially solid state. Others apply the term to the formation of granitic rock from sedimentary rock regardless of whether melting has occurred.

PARENT ROCK	METAMORPHIC ROCK
Sedimentary	
Sandstone	Quartzite
Shale	Slate, phyllite, schist
Limestone	Marble
Bituminous coal	Anthracite coal, graphite
Igneous	
Granitic textured igneous rocks	Gneiss
Compact textured igneous rocks	Schist

TABLE 3. Some common igneous and sedimentary rocks and their metamorphic equivalents.

CHAPTER 7

DEFORMATION OF CRUSTAL ROCKS

The earth's crustal rocks have undergone great structural change in the geologic past. These rocks continue to be altered today by three major geologic processes: erosion, volcanism, and tectonism. Of these, **tectonism** (Greek *tekton,* "builder") is by far the most important cause of rock deformation.

TECTONISM

Tectonic movements normally occur slowly and imperceptibly over long periods of time. But some—for example, an earthquake—may take place suddenly and violently. In some instances the rocks will move vertically, resulting in uplift or subsidence of the land. They may also move horizontally, or laterally (sidewise), as a result of compression or tension. The two major types of tectonic movements, **epeirogeny** (vertical movements) and **orogeny** (essentially lateral movements) are discussed below.

Epeirogenic Movements. Relatively slow movements accompanied by broad uplift or submergence of the continents are termed epeirogenic movements. Such movements affect relatively large areas, and typically result in tilting or warping of the land. An uplift of this type may raise wave-cut benches and sea cliffs well above sea level; features of this sort are common along certain parts of the Pacific Coast. In a like manner, parts of the Scandinavian coast are rising as much as three feet per century. Subsidence of the continents may also take place. Thus, continental

areas sink slowly beneath the ocean and become submerged by shallow seas. Similar movements have caused the British Isles to become isolated from continental Europe and bays to be formed in drowned valleys along the New England coast. (Submergence may, of course, also be caused by a rise in sea level.)

Rock strata involved in epeirogenic movements are not usually greatly **folded** or **faulted** (fractured). As noted above, however, such strata may undergo large-scale tilting or warping.

Orogenic Movements. These are more intense than epeirogenic movements, and the rocks involved are subjected to great stress. These movements, known also as **orogenies** or mountain-making movements, normally affect long narrow areas, are accompanied by much folding and faulting, and are generally thought to have been caused by horizontal compression. Igneous activity and earthquakes also commonly occur with this type of crustal disturbance. Although orogenic movements are slow, they do occur somewhat more rapidly than epeirogenic movements.

HOW ARE ROCKS DEFORMED?

How can rocks which seem so strong and rigid be crumpled and broken? The force or pressure that causes rock movement is called **stress.** Stress can be in the form of **tension,** a stretching stress that increases volume; **compression,** a squeezing stress that reduces volume; or **shear,** which produces change of shape without change of volume.

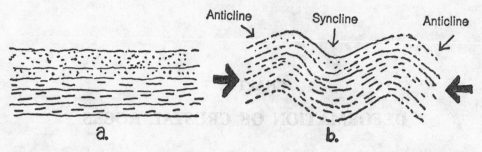

Fig. 48. Deformation of sedimentary rock layers. (a) Original sedimentary layers in undisturbed position. (b) Compression (horizontal squeezing indicated by arrows) produces folding to form anticlines and a syncline.

As earth materials are subjected to stress, they are deformed as they undergo change in shape or volume or both. This response to stress is called **strain.**

Elastic Deformation. An elastic solid substance will, after undergoing a change in shape or volume under stress, return to its original condition when stress is removed. This can be compared to the elasticity of a rubber band that is stretched and then released to assume its original shape.

Plastic Deformation. In plastic deformation a solid substance undergoes a continuous change in shape. This change is permanent, for the material does not assume its original shape. This is analogous to molding a piece of clay (Fig. 48).

Rupture. In this type of deformation rocks literally reach their "breaking point" as the stress applied exceeds the rocks' strength. Displacement of rock due to rupture is believed to cause most earthquakes.

ISOSTASY

In Chapter 2 we learned that the earth's crust and upper mantle are broken into rigid lithospheric plates consisting of both continental and oceanic crustal rocks. The stronger, more rigid slabs of the lithosphere float on the weaker underlying asthenosphere (Fig. 7), which flows plastically in both vertical and horizontal directions. As the plates drift in the asthenosphere, the lateral flow of the asthenosphere maintains a balance between the weight of the slabs of lithosphere. This **isostatic balance** has been explained by the **theory of isostasy.**

The theory states that at considerable depth within the earth different segments of the crust will be in balance with other segments of unequal thickness. The differences in height of these crustal segments is explained as the result of variations in density. Consequently, the continents and mountainous areas are high because they are composed of lighter rocks; the ocean basins are lower because they are composed of denser (heavier) rocks (Fig. 49). As the continents are eroded and sediments deposited in the ocean, the ocean basin is depressed because of the added weight of the accumulating sediments. This causes displacement of the plastic subcrustal rocks which push the continents up. The upward displacement of the continent is aided by erosion, which removes rock materials, thus making the continents lighter and more susceptible to uplift.

How can crustal segments float? Quite different explanations were proposed by two English scientists in the mid-1800s. According to G. B. Airy (an astronomer), the crustal segments might be compared to two icebergs floating in the sea. Both are of the same density but they float in seawater of greater density than the ice. If one iceberg rises three times as far above the water as the other, this larger iceberg will be found to lie three times as far *beneath* the surface of the ocean. The iceberg's "roots" enable it to maintain **isostatic balance** (or equilibrium). By the same token, mountain ranges—which contain rocks of relatively low density—float much higher above the asthenosphere than do slabs of more dense oceanic crust. Moreover, continental crust composing the mountains extends into the asthenosphere, forming roots like those of icebergs (Fig. 49).

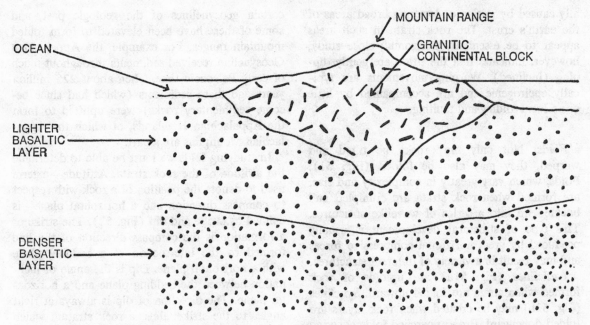

Fig. 49. *Relatively light granitic rocks of continent resting on denser basaltic substratum.*

Another explanation was proposed by J. H. Pratt, a geographer. He postulated that the substratum upon which the crust floats is of equal density, but that various segments of the earth's crust *differ* in density. He assumed that mountainous segments are of a lesser density than, say, crustal segments forming the ocean floor. Thus, the crust everywhere would extend equally into the denser substratum without the mountain roots proposed by Airy (Fig. 50).

Utilizing information derived from more recent research on isostatic balance, it now appears that either the Pratt or Airy hypothesis can be applied to various parts of the crust.

STRUCTURAL FEATURES PRODUCED BY TECTONISM

Tectonic movements, whether epeirogenic or orogenic, will result in rock deformation. Under surface conditions, ordinary rocks are relatively brittle and will fracture or break when placed under great stress. Deeply buried rocks, however, are subject to such high temperatures and pressures that they become somewhat plastic. When subjected to prolonged stress these rocks are likely to warp or fold.

Broad Warps. As noted above, warping is usu-

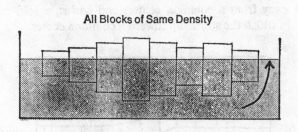

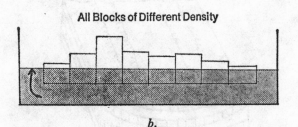

Fig. 50. *Two explanations of isostasy. (a) Airy interpretation assumes all blocks have the same density and are floating in a denser material. (b) Pratt hypothesis postulates a crust composed of different materials of different densities floating in a denser material.*

ally caused by raising or lowering broad areas of the earth's crust. The rock strata in such areas appear to be essentially horizontal; close study, however, indicates that the strata are gently **dipping** (inclined). Warping movements are typically epeirogenic and are accompanied by little or no local folding and faulting.

Folds. Not only may rocks be tilted and warped, they may also be folded (Fig. 51). Folds, which vary greatly in complexity and size, are formed when rock strata are crumpled and buckled up into a series of wavelike structures. This type of structural development is usually produced by great horizontal compressive forces and may result in a variety of different structures.

Anticlines (Fig. 51a) are upfolds of rock formed when strata are folded upward. **Synclines** (Fig. 51b) may be created when rock layers are folded downward. Broad uparched folds covering large areas are called **geanticlines;** large downwarped troughs are known as **geosynclines.** Great thicknesses of sediments have accumulated in certain geosynclines of the geologic past, and some of these have been elevated to form folded mountain ranges. For example, the Appalachian Geosyncline received sediments throughout much of early Paleozoic time. Then about 225 million years ago these sediments (which had since become sedimentary rocks) were uplifted to form the Appalachian Highlands, of which the Appalachian Mountains are a part.

In studying folds we must be able to determine the **attitude** of the rock strata. Attitude—a term used to denote the position of a rock with respect to compass direction and a horizontal plane—is defined by **strike** and **dip** (Fig. 52). The strike of a formation is the compass direction of the line formed by the intersection of a bedding plane with a horizontal plane. Dip is the angle of inclination between the bedding plane and a horizontal plane. The direction of dip is always at right angles to the strike; thus, a rock stratum which dips due north would strike east-west.

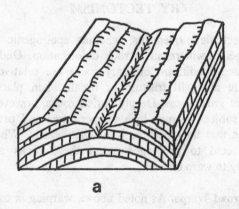

a

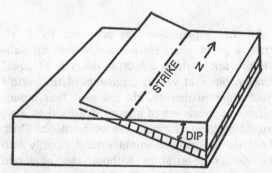

Fig. 52. Strike and Dip. The beds strike north-south and dip to the east.

Other types of folds include **monoclines,** simple steplike folds which dip in only one direction (Fig. 53); **domes,** a fold in which strata dip away from a common center; and **basins,** a fold in which the strata dip toward a common center.

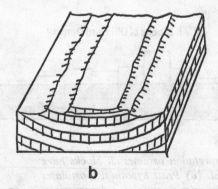

b

Fig. 51. Types of folds
  (a) Anticline   (b) Syncline

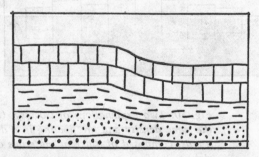

Fig. 53. Monocline.

Fractures. Rocks subjected to great stress near the surface are apt to fracture, thus producing joints and faults. A fracture along which there has been little or no movement is called a **joint** (Fig. 54). Joints occur in sets and are usually parallel to one another. Fractures of this sort have formed in igneous rocks as a result of contraction due to cooling and are common in certain dikes and sills. Joints are also created by tension and compression when rocks undergo stress due to warping, folding, and faulting.

Joint systems are developed when two or more sets of joints intersect. These intersecting joint patterns may be helpful in certain quarrying operations and in developing porosity in otherwise impervious rocks. Jointing will also hasten weathering and erosion, for they render the rocks more susceptible to attack from rain, frost, and streams.

Faults are fractures in the earth's crust along which movements have taken place (Fig. 55). The rocks affected by faulting are displaced along the **fault plane.** If the crust is displaced vertically, the rocks on one side of the fault may stand higher than those on the other. This may result in a cliff called a **fault scarp.** Large-scale faulting of this type may produce **fault-block mountains,** such as the Sierra Nevada in California and the Lewis Range in Montana.

Some knowledge of fault terminology is prerequisite to an understanding of the different types of faults. (The parts of faults are illustrated in Fig. 55.) The rock surface bounding the lower side of an inclined fault plane is known as the **footwall** and that above as the **hanging wall.** The **strike** of a fault is the horizontal direction of the fault plane; **dip** is determined by measuring the inclination of the fault plane at right angles to the strike. **Displacement** refers to the amount of movement that has taken place along the fault plane.

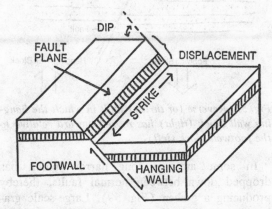

Fig. 55. *Normal fault showing principal parts and terms used in describing faults.*

The various types of faults are classified largely by the direction and relative movement of the rocks along the fault plane. A **normal or gravity fault** is one in which the hanging wall has moved downward with respect to the footwall (Fig. 56). If the hanging wall has moved upward with respect to the footwall, a **reverse fault** or **thrust fault** is produced (Fig. 57). A **strike-slip fault** will be produced if the movement is predominantly horizontal parallel to the fault plane (Fig. 58).

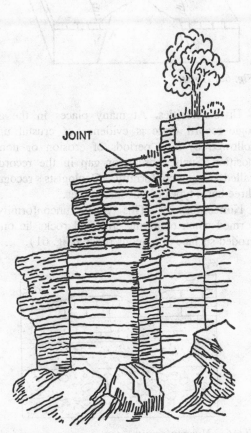

Fig. 54. *Vertical joints in limestone cliff.*

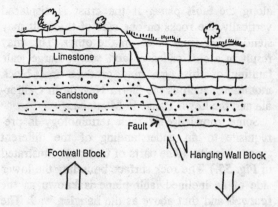

Fig. 56. Normal fault in which the hanging wall block (right) has moved downward relative to the footwall block (left).

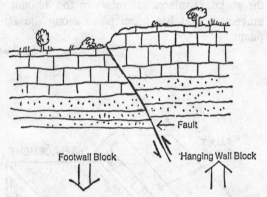

Fig. 57. Reverse (or thrust) fault in which the hanging wall block (right) has moved upward relative to the footwall block (left).

In some areas a long narrow block has dropped down between normal faults, thereby producing a **graben** (Fig. 59). Large-scale grabens are called **rift valleys.** Two examples of grabens are the upper Rhine Valley and the depression containing the Dead Sea. Sometimes blocks will be raised between normal faults; these elevated blocks are called **horsts** (Fig. 60).

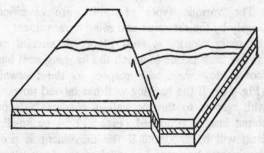

Fig. 58. Strike-slip fault. (Note the road offset in center of block.)

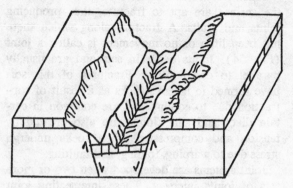

Fig. 59. Graben.

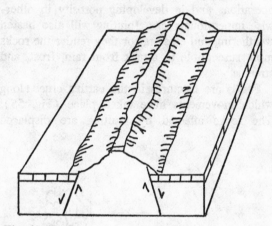

Fig. 60. Horst.

Unconformities. At many places in the geologic record there is evidence of crustal uplift followed by long periods of erosion or nondeposition. Such a break or gap in the record is called an unconformity. Geologists recognize three basic types of unconformities.

Nonconformity—This type of unconformity is formed when overlying stratified rocks lie on an eroded surface of igneous rocks (Fig. 61).

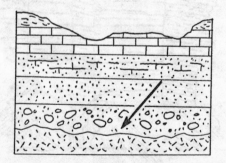

Fig. 61. Nonconformity. Arrow points to eroded igneous surface overlain by sedimentary strata.

Disconformity—In unconformities of this type, the rock layers above and below the unconformity are parallel (Fig. 62).

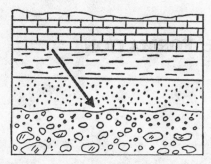

Fig. 62. Disconformity. Note parallel beds above and below unconformity.

Angular Unconformity—In this, a relatively obvious type of unconformity, the beds above the unconformity are not parallel to the beds below it (Fig. 63). This type of unconformity indicates that the lower series of rocks were tilted or folded prior to their erosion and the subsequent deposition of the overlying beds.

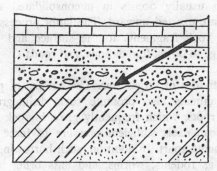

Fig. 63. Angular unconformity. Note tilted beds underlying parallel beds.

EVIDENCE OF CRUSTAL MOVEMENTS

In addition to warping, folding, fracturing, and unconformities, the earth's crust contains much conclusive evidence that myriad tectonic movements have taken place in the geologic past. We have already learned, for example, that the fossilized remains of sea plants and animals may be found thousands of feet above sea level. Common also are elevated beaches, coastal plains, and wave-cut cliffs and sea caves. Such features strongly suggest a drop in sea level or an uplift of the continent (possibly both). Similarly, drowned river valleys indicate a rising sea and/or a subsiding landmass.

The occurrence of earthquakes is evidence that similar movements are taking place today. A good example of this can be seen in the Yakutat Bay area of Alaska. Here, in 1899, faulting caused some parts of the coast to be raised as much as 47 feet. Likewise, during the San Francisco earthquake of 1906 the horizontal movement along the fault plane caused certain fences and roads to be offset as much as 20 feet.

Meanwhile, studies related to plate tectonics and associated geologic phenomena clearly indicate that large segments of the crust have not only moved in the past but continue to move—at a measurable rate—to this day.

CHAPTER 8

WEATHERING AND SOIL FORMATION

Weathering, the process whereby rocks undergo natural chemical and physical change at or near the surface of the earth, is one of the most important of all geologic processes. It provides much of the material from which sedimentary rocks are formed, is important in the shaping of surface landforms, and is responsible for the formation of soil.

Rock fragments produced by weathering are removed by **erosion**—the loosening and carrying away of rock debris by natural agents. Weathering and erosion are constantly at work wearing away the rocks of the earth's surface.

MECHANICAL WEATHERING

Mechanical weathering takes place when a rock is reduced to smaller fragments without undergoing a change in chemical composition. This type of weathering, known also as **disintegration,** may be the result of a variety of physical forces.

Expansion and Contraction Resulting from Temperature Changes. In some places, particularly in certain mountainous regions, the rocks are subjected to drastic temperature changes almost daily. Rocks on a high mountain peak expand as they are heated in the daytime, and contract when subjected to freezing temperatures at night. This process, repeated over long periods of time, will cause small cracks and crevices which permit other agents of weathering, such as frost wedging or solution to attack the rock. Heat from forest and prairie fires may also hasten the physical breakdown of rocks. In spite of the

effects outlined above, geologists are still undecided as to the precise role of temperature variations in rock disintegration.

Frost Action. When water freezes in the cracks or pores of rocks it expands. This process of expansion may be of two kinds: **frost wedging** or **frost heaving.** Both kinds exert sufficient pressure to break down the rock. In frost wedging these pressures are directed laterally; in frost heaving, which usually occurs in unconsolidated rocks, they are exerted upward. The latter process may force rock fragments to the surface and cause damage to posts, foundations, and roads.

Activities of Organisms. The actions of plants and animals also promote rock disintegration. Tree roots, which frequently grow in rock crevices, can exert sufficient pressure to force rock fragments apart. In addition, such burrowing animals as rodents, worms, and ants bring to the surface rock particles to be exposed to the action of weathering. Also included here are many of the activities of man. Large-scale rock disintegration commonly accompanies such operations as road construction, mining, quarrying, and cultivation.

CHEMICAL WEATHERING

Chemical weathering, or **decomposition,** produces a chemical breakdown of the rock, which may destroy the original minerals and produce new ones. Physical weathering simply produces smaller fragments of the parent rock; chemical weathering produces rock materials that are basically different from the original rock. Although chemical changes occur in a variety of ways, the more common processes of decomposition are oxidation, hydration, carbonation, and solution.

Oxidation. Oxidation occurs as oxygen, assisted by moist air, combines with minerals to form oxides. Rocks and minerals containing iron compounds are especially susceptible to this type of decomposition. The oxidation of iron compounds, which produces rust, is also responsible for the color of many red, yellow, and brown rocks and soils. In addition, certain iron compounds (for example, pyrite) form acids when oxidized. These acids attack the rocks and thereby hasten the process of decomposition.

Hydration. The chemical union of water with another substance is called hydration. Rocks and minerals subjected to this process frequently produce new compounds, especially hydrous silicates and hydrous oxides. Some examples of this are the conversion of anhydrite to gypsum and the reaction between hematite and water to produce limonite. Hydration is also the process by which feldspars are converted into clay minerals.

In addition to the chemical effect of hydration, there is a physical expansion of the minerals during this process. This creates zones of weakness within the rock which accelerate its physical breakdown.

Carbonation. Carbon dioxide (CO_2), which is generally present in air, water, and soils, commonly unites chemically with certain rock minerals, greatly altering their composition. Substances produced in this manner (carbonates and bicarbonates) are relatively soluble and therefore easily removed and carried away. In addition, the union of carbon dioxide and water produces carbonic acid (H_2CO_3), an effective agent in attacking such minerals as calcite and dolomite.

Solution. Solution, the process whereby minerals and rocks are dissolved in water, plays an important part in chemical weathering. Although water has a solvent effect on all minerals, solution is greatly accelerated with the addition of carbonic acid or acids derived from the decom-

position or body wastes of organisms. Most of this work is carried on by percolating ground waters which remove minerals from the rock and soil as they seep downward. Solution weathering, known also as **leaching,** may also dissolve the cementing agents in sedimentary rocks and bring about their physical breakdown.

RATES OF WEATHERING

The forces of erosion are continually at work, removing the relatively thin veneer of loose weathered rock materials which overlie the bedrock. **Bedrock,** solid rock which lies in a relatively undisturbed position beneath the weathered rock debris, deteriorates as it becomes exposed to the various agents of weathering.

The rate at which the bedrock will be weathered depends largely upon such factors as the composition of the rock, its physical condition, climatic conditions, and the type of topography (the physical features or configuration of the land surface).

Composition of the Rock. The mineral and chemical composition of a rock is an important factor in determining the extent to which it will weather. In general, igneous rocks are relatively resistant to mechanical weathering, but more susceptible to chemical weathering. Many sedimentary rocks, especially limestones and dolomites, are highly vulnerable to decomposition by carbonation and solution. The nature of the cementing material (the substance holding the rock particles together) is also a determining factor. A **siliceous** sandstone (with silica as the cementing agent) is more enduring than a **calcareous** sandstone in which calcite is the cementing agent. Certain metamorphic rocks, especially quartzite, are among the most durable of all rocks.

Physical Condition of the Rock. Rocks that contain holes, cracks, and crevices allow weathering agents to penetrate deeply within them, thus hastening their destruction. Solid, unbroken rock surfaces are considerably more weather-resistant.

Climatic Conditions. The type of climate present has a decided effect upon the nature and rate of weathering. Weathering, especially the chemical type, takes place more rapidly in warm, moist climates which have an abundance of rainfall. In warm, dry climates, weathering is apt to be primarily mechanical and proceeds relatively slowly; the same is true of very cold regions.

Topography. Weathering proceeds most rapidly in areas where land slopes are steep. Rock debris is removed rapidly in such areas, and new surfaces are continually exposed to weathering processes. With an increase in altitude there is an increase in rainfall and a decrease in temperature which will also influence the rate of weathering.

EFFECTS OF WEATHERING

As bedrock is attacked by the various processes of physical and chemical weathering, some of the following special effects may be produced.

Differential Weathering. In differential weathering, different portions of an exposed rock mass weather at different rates. This type of weathering permits the more resistant parts of the rock to stand in relief after the removal of the softer or more soluble rock material. Differential weathering may come about as the result of structural or mineral differences, variations in cement, or the presence of concretions (Chapter 7). It is responsible for such spectacular scenic areas as Bryce Canyon National Park in Utah and Petrified Forest National Park in Arizona.

Exfoliation. Exfoliation occurs when thin flakes, or more or less curved slabs, peel (or **spall**) off exposed rock surfaces (Fig. 64). There is some disagreement as to the exact cause of exfoliation, but it would appear to be the result of the combined effects of alternating temperature changes and relief of pressure. As these slabs of rock slide away they leave rounded rock masses called **exfoliation domes.** Such famous landmarks as Stone Mountain in Georgia and Half Dome in Yosemite National Park, California, have been formed by exfoliation.

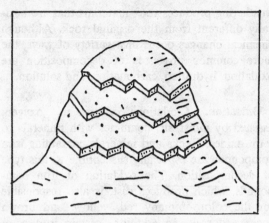
Fig. 64. Granite dome caused by exfoliation.

Spheroidal Weathering. Under certain conditions, exfoliation may continue until boulders are reduced to rounded, more or less spherical bodies (Fig. 65). This type of weathering phenomenon is more common in fine-grained igneous rocks, but may also occur in massive shale formations.

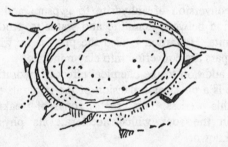
Fig. 65. Boulder showing spheroidal weathering.

Talus. Weathered rock debris at the bottom of a steep mountain, cliff, or slope is called talus (Fig. 68). Some accumulations of talus, known as talus deposits, or **sliderock,** are hundreds of feet thick. Talus deposits are generally formed as a result of frost action or some other form of physical weathering, and are deposited as a result of gravitation.

SOILS

The most important products of the forces of weathering are soils. **Soil** consists of decomposed and disintegrated mantle rock which has been altered to the extent that it can support plant life.

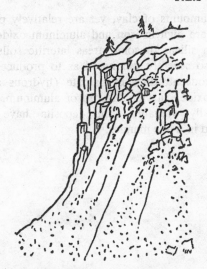

Fig. 66. Talus slope formed of weathered rock debris at foot of cliff.

Most soils contain a certain amount of **humus,** dark organic material produced by the decomposition of plant and animal materials.

Although a number of factors ultimately determine the type of soil to be developed in a given area, the more important of these are (1) composition of the parent (original) rock, (2) climate, (3) topography, (4) time, and (5) plant and animal activity. These factors must also be considered in soil classification, a subject which will be discussed below.

TYPES OF SOILS

The upper six or eight inches of the soil is called **topsoil,** and below this is a lighter, more compact, less fertile layer, the **subsoil.** Soils which have been derived from the bedrock upon which they rest are called **residual soil. Transported** soils have been carried to their present location by wind, water, gravity, or glaciers; they typically contain rock types different from the bedrock below them.

Soil Profiles. Different kinds of soils exhibit their own characteristic soil profile—a succession of soil **horizons** (or layers) each of which differs from those above or below it. The nature of these three horizons in a mature, or well-developed, soil is important in soil classification and is discussed below.

The A-horizon, the uppermost layer in the soil profile, is the topsoil. It typically contains varying amounts of humus and has usually undergone a certain amount of leaching. Beneath this is the B-horizon, or subsoil, which in moist climates contains considerable amounts of clay and iron oxides but little organic material. The lowermost C-horizon is comprised largely of slightly altered parent rock which grades downward into the bedrock (Fig. 67).

Classification of Soils. Soil scientists classify soils according to the prevailing climate in which they are developed and the vegetation which is associated with them. There are a number of different soil groupings, but only three, pedalfers, pedocals, and laterites, will be discussed here.

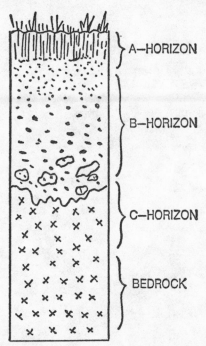

Fig. 67. Typical soil profile showing A-, B-, and C-horizons.

Pedalfers are characteristic of areas with temperate humid climates and generally develop under heavy vegetation. High in iron and alumina, the B-horizon is usually rich in clays and iron oxides and has a brown or red color. The light gray, sandy A-horizon is typically high in organic content.

Pedocals contain relatively large amounts of

calcium carbonate. They normally develop in areas of low rainfall and relatively high temperatures, and support grasses and brush. The lower part of the pedocal soil profile contains appreciable accumulations of calcium carbonate, which has been leached out of the horizons above it.

Lateritic soils, or **laterites,** are typical of moist, tropical regions which support jungle vegetation. Usually red or yellow in color, laterites contain large amounts of clay, yet are relatively porous. They are high in iron and aluminum oxides and low in silica. In some areas lateritic soils have been so severely weathered as to produce valuable concentrations of bauxite (hydrous aluminum oxide), a valuable ore of aluminum. Commercially valuable iron deposits have been formed in a like manner.

CHAPTER 9

RUNNING WATER

THE WORK OF RUNNING WATER

Running water is undoubtedly the most important agent of erosion. It probably does more to wear away the land than all the other agents of erosion combined. Streams (water flowing over the land in more or less distinct channels) are continually altering the surface features of the earth and carving out the major landforms so familiar to us all.

Each year precipitation equal to approximately four billion tons of water falls on all the land surface of the earth. Although the annual rate of precipitation varies greatly from one area to another, the average annual precipitation on land is estimated to be forty inches of water. Of this, about 22 to 30 percent becomes runoff—water that flows from the land. Most of our surface streams are formed as a result of this runoff.

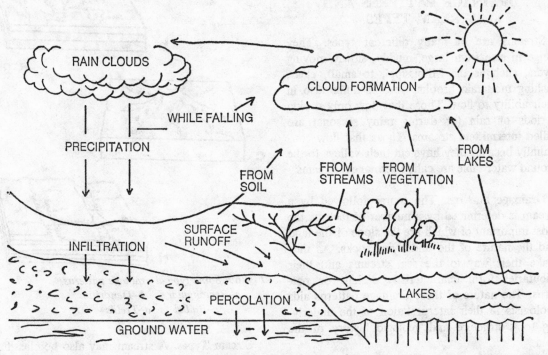

Fig. 68. The hydrologic cycle.

THE HYDROLOGIC CYCLE

In order that we may more fully understand the origin and ultimate disposal of stream waters, it will help to have some knowledge of the hydrologic cycle. This cycle is a continuous process whereby water is evaporated from the seas, carried inland and precipitated as rain or snow, and eventually returned to the sea (see Fig. 68).

Most of the water on the earth is meteoric in origin, that is, it has been derived from the atmosphere as rain or snow. As mentioned earlier, an estimated 22 to 30 percent of this water is carried back to the sea as runoff, but much of it sinks into the ground by infiltration to become **ground water.** Most of this water is returned to the atmosphere by evaporation or transpiration. The latter is a process whereby plants breathe back water vapor into the atmosphere. In addition to water that is disposed of by runoff, infiltration, or evaporation, some water is retained on the surface for long periods as glacier ice. (Glaciers are discussed in Chapter 11.)

DRAINAGE PATTERNS AND STREAM TYPES

Streams are of many different types. They range in size from large, muddy, slowly moving rivers, such as the Mississippi, to small, clear, rushing mountain brooks. Streams differ also in their ability to flow. Those that flow only during periods of rain (or during rainy seasons) are called **intermittent** streams. Those that flow continually because they have cut their valleys to the ground water table are called **permanent** streams.

Drainage Patterns. The course followed by a stream is determined by a number of factors, the most important of which are the slope of the land and the nature of the underlying rocks. As they make their way to the sea, streams and their tributaries form characteristic designs or patterns. The nature of these drainage patterns aids geologists in their interpretation of the underlying rock structure and geologic history of the area.

Most drainage patterns, because of the way tributaries enter the main stream channel, resemble the branching of a tree and are said to be **dendritic** (Fig. 69b). This treelike pattern is typical of areas underlain by flat-lying sedimentary rocks or massive igneous or metamorphic rocks. A **radial** pattern is developed when drainage flows out in all directions from a central area such as the top of a mountain (Fig. 69c). When tributaries join larger streams at right angles, a **trellis** pattern is developed (Fig. 69d). This type of pattern is typical of regions where tilted rock layers of unequal resistance crop out. In such areas, valleys develop along outcrops of weak rock and the more resistant layers stand out as divides. A **rectangular** pattern (Fig. 69a) may occur in areas where the underlying bedrock is highly fractured; this pattern is similar to the trellis pattern (compare Figs. 69a and 69d).

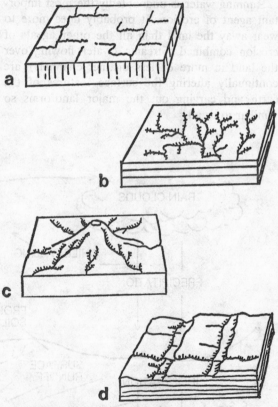

Fig. 69. *Some typical drainage patterns*
a–Rectangular   b–Dendritic
c–Radial   d–Trellis

Stream Types. A stream may also be classified according to the relationship between its course and the underlying rocks. A **consequent** stream is one whose direction of flow follows the original slope of the land. This type of stream typically develops in areas of low relief, such as a coastal plain. A **subsequent** stream is one whose direction of flow has been altered by fractures of folds, or by differences in the hardness of the underlying rocks. The channels of this type of stream usually follow beds of soft rocks, such as shale. On the other hand, an **antecedent** stream will adhere to its original course in spite of any uplift that might have taken place along its course. (Subsequent streams commonly show up as tributaries to the antecedent stream in a trellis type of drainage pattern—see Fig. 69d.) **Superimposed** (or superposed) streams are those that have cut through the softer overlying strata in which they originated and imposed themselves on the older underlying rocks. The rocks which underlie superimposed streams have different composition and structure than those in which the original channel was developed.

THE WORK OF STREAMS

In general, the work of running water starts with rain, much of which is disposed of by runoff. The water may start its work as a sheet of water (**sheetwash**), but ordinarily will soon be diverted into a stream. The amount of runoff in an area may be increased by (1) steep slope, (2) low permeability of surface materials, (3) lack of vegetation, and (4) short, heavy, or prolonged gentle rains.

TYPES OF STREAM EROSION

Stream erosion occurs by means of several processes, most of which act in co-operation with each other. A variety of factors ultimately determine the degree and type of erosion that will take place in a given area.

Abrasion. The abrasive ability of a stream depends upon its **load**—the amount of material carried by a stream at a given time. Each sand grain, pebble, or boulder carried becomes a cutting tool capable of deepening and widening the stream bed. Known also as mechanical stream erosion, abrasion occurs as rock particles rub against each other or against bedrock as they are transported by the stream. In addition, much damage is done by **impaction** as rock fragments knock against bedrock or each other.

Abrasion is most effective where stream flow (velocity) is rapid, stream load is heavy, and much debris is being rolled along the bottom. The effects of this type of stream erosion may be seen in smooth well-rounded pebbles and boulders, and in undercut banks along the sides of many streams.

Solution. Running water also has a dissolving or corroding effect on the rocks over which it flows. This type of stream erosion occurs as water containing carbonic acid (derived from the air and vegetation) dissolves minerals in the bedrock. Such relatively soluble rocks as limestone, gypsum, and dolomite are most likely to be affected by the solvent action of stream water.

Direct Lift or Hydraulic Action. The ability of a stream to lift and transport materials is most effective in places where the bedrock is highly fractured and/or poorly cemented. Strong currents may force water into cracks along the stream channel thus removing rock material from the banks or bed of the stream.

RATE OF STREAM EROSION

The rate at which running water will erode depends on several factors, the most important of which are discussed below.

Stream Size. The volume of water carried by a stream will have a marked effect on its ability to erode. Larger volumes of water are capable of carrying larger loads, which in turn increases the ability of the stream to abrade. Thus erosion will be most active when rivers are at flood stage and transporting large amounts of material.

Stream Gradient and Velocity. Gradient refers to the slope down which the stream flows. Stream gradients vary from place to place; they are usually higher at the source or head of the stream and become relatively low at its mouth. The velocity of a stream increases when gradients are steep, there are large volumes of water, and the stream channel is straight, narrow, and relatively free of obstacles.

Laminar and Turbulent Flow. If a stream channel is relatively smooth, free of obstructions, and velocity is rather low, the water flows in rather smooth sheets parallel to the walls of the stream channel. This is called laminar flow. Turbulent flow is caused when the stream is slowed down by friction between the water and banks and when there are obstructions and irregularities in the channel. These break up the smooth, laminar flow and the water tumbles along in eddies or swirls (Fig. 70). Turbulent flow is highly effective in eroding stream channels and in transporting sediment.

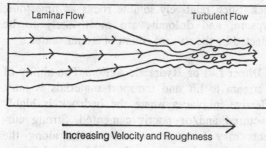

Fig. 70. Aerial view of a wide, smooth stream channel (left) grading into a narrow, rough channel (right) as related to laminar and turbulent flow. Individual lines show paths followed by separate water particles.

THE EFFECTS OF STREAM EROSION

The erosional work of streams is responsible for a variety of interesting geologic phenomena. Among these are stream-cut valleys and gullies, waterfalls and rapids, potholes, stream piracy, meanders, cutoffs, and oxbow lakes.

Stream-cut Valleys and Gullies. Running water moving over the earth's surface cuts a depression or channel which may ultimately become a valley. Most valleys start as gullies, which become wider, deeper, and longer with each rain. The gully is lengthened by **headward** erosion—erosion **uphill** and at the point where water pours into its upper end. Continued erosion produces V-shaped valleys which are deepened by eroding

of the stream bed and widened by erosion of its banks (Fig. 71). Such erosion may continue until the stream reaches **base level**—the lowest gradient at which the water will flow or erode its valley.

Fig. 71. Typical V-shaped valley produced by stream erosion.

The degree to which valley development will proceed depends largely upon (1) the volume of the stream, (2) its velocity, (3) the nature of its load, and (4) the resistance of the bedrock. Some valleys are deepened more rapidly than they are widened. Such valleys may be referred to as ravines, gorges, or canyons. The development of stream-cut valleys is discussed later.

Rapids and Waterfalls. Where there is a sudden drop in the stream slope the movement of the water is accelerated and rapids may be formed. When the stream bed makes a sudden vertical or nearly vertical drop, a waterfall occurs (Fig. 72). Many waterfalls, for example, Niagara Falls, are formed as the stream bed passes from resistant rock to rock that is relatively soft. As the Niagara River plunges over a cliff capped by resistant limestone, it falls on rock material which is much less resistant. The force of the cascading water scours into the shale at the base of the cliff, undercutting the limestone and allowing it to break off. This process of undermining brings about the retreat of the falls upstream. As a result of undermining, Niagara Falls appears to be retreating at the rate of four to five feet per year. Some falls, such as Yellowstone Falls in Yellowstone National Park, are formed when streams pass over igneous intrusions and erode volcanic ash deposits downstream. Others, like those of Yosemite National Park, are formed when hanging valleys (see Chapter 11) enter the main valley.

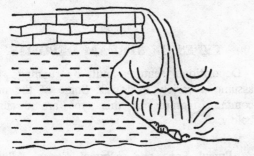

Fig. 72. Cross section of a waterfall. (Note the resistant limestone which caps the fall.)

Potholes. When rapidly moving streams produce whirlpools, the swirling current drives water (and its load of sand, gravel, etc.) in a rotary motion. The rock fragments caught up in this whirl will eventually grind out a shallow, circular depression in the bed of the stream. Holes formed in this manner are called potholes and range from a few inches to as much as twenty feet in diameter.

Stream Piracy. Sometimes a stream will be so lengthened by headward erosion that it will intercept the banks of another stream and divert it into its own channel. This phenomenon, known as stream piracy or stream capture, comes about as a result of differences in the rate of stream erosion.

Meanders, Cutoffs, and Oxbow Lakes. When the gradient of a stream is such that there is approximate balance between the amount of material that it erodes and the amount it deposits, it is called a **graded stream.** Such a stream no longer cuts downward but uses most of its energy to carry its load. However, lateral erosion or **sidecutting** does occur, and the valley bottom continues to grow wider. As the valley grows, the stream channel normally occupies only a relatively small part of the valley floor. This permits the stream to take a wandering, winding course characterized by many wide S-shaped bends called **meanders** (Fig. 73a).

Some meanders become so curved that only a narrow neck of land separates the ends of the meander. During times of flood a stream may shorten its course by making a cutoff across the neck, and thus isolate the meander from the rest of the stream. If water remains in the abandoned

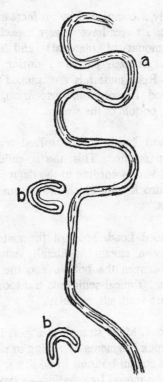

Fig. 73. Stream meanders (a) and oxbow lakes (b).

arcuate section of the channel, it is called an **oxbow lake** (Fig. 73b).

Braided Streams. A braided stream is one that is characterized by a series of complex channels which unite and diverge again and again. It is also filled by numerous sand bars—accumulations of sand deposited by an overloaded stream.

HOW STREAMS CARRY THEIR LOADS

A stream, like all agents of erosion, picks up most of its load as it wears away the earth materials with which it comes in contact. Each year as much as a billion tons of sediments are worn from the earth's surface, transported by streams, and deposited in the sea. These rock fragments will be the sedimentary rocks of future geologic time.

As noted earlier, the carrying ability of a stream depends largely upon the velocity and volume of the water. An increase in volume is commonly accompanied by an increase in velocity. Hence streams have greater **capacity** (carry a larger amount of material) and **competency** (carry larger-sized particles) during periods of flooding. Rock materials thus picked up may be transported in solution, suspension, or rolled along the bottom of the stream.

Dissolved Load. The dissolved materials are carried in solution. This, the so-called invisible load, will vary according to the degree of solubility of bedrock with which the stream may come in contact.

Suspended Load. Most of the material transported by a stream is literally suspended or "hung" between the bottom and the surface of the stream. Typical sediments transported in this manner are sand, silt, and clay.

Bed Load. Many streams transport large quantities of rock fragments by rolling or sliding them along the stream bottom. In addition, rock particles may be moved by **saltation**—a type of movement whereby rocks move forward by means of a series of short jumps. Rock fragments transported by any of the movements described above are said to be moved by **traction** and make up the **bed load** of the stream.

STREAM DEPOSITION

A stream deposits its load when the competency and capacity of the stream are decreased. Some of the causes of such decreases are (1) reduction in stream gradient, (2) decrease in volume, (3) loss of velocity, (4) obstacles in the stream channel, (5) widening of the stream bed, (6) overloading, (7) freezing, and (8) emptying into quiet or slower moving bodies of water. Material thus deposited is called **alluvium.**

Alluvial deposits contain materials which have been sorted according to size and as a consequence are stratified (deposited in layers) with the coarser materials on the bottom. In addition, alluvial materials are usually composed of rock fragments which have been smoothed or rounded by stream abrasion.

TYPES OF STREAM DEPOSITS

Depositional features built by running water assume a variety of forms. Some of the more common features of this type are discussed below.

Alluvial Fans and Alluvial Cones. Alluvial fans are moderately sloping fan-shaped deposits found at the foot of mountains. Characteristic of semiarid zones, these accumulations of silt, sand, gravel, and boulders are deposited when fastflowing mountain streams lose their gradient and flow out on level ground at the foot of the mountain. Deposits of this type which have very steep slopes are called alluvial cones. In certain areas of the western United States a number of alluvial fans join each other at the foot of a mountain range to form **piedmont alluvial plains** or **bajadas** (ba-ha′-das).

Deltas. When a stream flows into a larger body of water such as a sea or lake, its velocity is suddenly decreased and much of its load is dropped. Deposits formed under these conditions are called deltas. Some deltas, such as those of the Mississippi River, covering approximately 12,000 square miles, and the Nile (10,000 square miles), are quite extensive and have been studied in considerable detail. Deltaic deposits are responsible for the formation of some of our most fertile farm land. As the delta becomes larger, the main stream may overflow and form new channels called **distributaries.**

Flood Plains. Known also as **river plains** or **valley flats,** flood plains are formed when a river in flood overflows its banks. The velocity is reduced when the stream leaves its channel and much of the load is deposited on the valley floor. The Mississippi River has developed a large flood plain, especially along its lower reaches.

Stream Terraces. If a flood plain should undergo erosion the remnants of the flood plain are known as stream terraces. Such terraces are topographically higher than the surrounding flood plain.

Natural Levees. When a stream flows over its banks onto the flood plain, the greatest loss of load takes place along the banks of the channel. The coarsest materials of the load are deposited here, and this tends to build up a ridge or an embankment called a natural levee. Some of these may rise fifteen to twenty feet above the surrounding flood plain and afford protection to the adjacent lowlands during time of flood.

CYCLES OF EROSION

According to some geologists, erosion follows a rather well-defined cycle, although we seldom find a perfect example of a completed cycle. Sometimes a cycle will be interrupted by **rejuvenation.** This occurs when an area that has been eroded almost to base level will again be elevated, bringing about increased stream gradients and renewed erosion. In general, however, the erosion cycle begins with the erosion of an area down to base level, followed by a fresh uplift, when erosion begins anew.

Although geologists disagree as to the validity of this concept, there is no doubt that it does provide us with much information about the development of streams and landscapes. How this concept has been applied to the development of stream valleys is discussed below.

DEVELOPMENT OF A STREAM VALLEY

When tectonic movements lift a region well above base level, the streams proceed to erode the surface back down to base level. The end result of this continued erosion is a **peneplain** (peneplane), an extensive area of low relief and low elevation. This erosional process, known as the stream valley erosion cycle, occurs in three rather well-defined stages—youth, maturity, and old age. (The same stages are experienced by the rivers which occupy these valleys.) The character and features of the various stages of the cycle of stream valley erosion are shown in Table 4.

VALLEY CYCLE

	YOUTH	MATURITY	OLD AGE
Transverse Profile			
Gradient	steep	moderate	low, gentle
Erosion	deepening valley	widening and deepening	widening valley
Channel Trend	straight	begins to meander	broad meanders
Valley Bottom	little or no flood plain	distinct flood plain	broad flood plain
Tributaries	few and small	maximum number	few and large
Special Features	rapids, waterfalls	some oxbow lakes	many oxbow lakes, natural levees, marshy flood plain

TABLE 4. By permission from *Physical Geology Laboratory Manual* by H. E. Eveland, William C. Brown Book Company, Dubuque, Iowa, 1966.

Youthful Stage. Youthful valleys are deep, steep-sided, and V-shaped; no flood plains have been developed. Streams occupying youthful valleys are still well above base level and are actively engaged in cutting downward into their beds. These are said to be youthful streams and are characterized by fairly straight courses, rapids, waterfalls, and relatively few tributaries. Such features are most likely to be present near a stream's headwaters.

Mature Stage. As rivers deepen their valleys they decrease their gradients. At this stage, there will no longer be rapids or waterfalls, and the channel will normally develop meanders. Valley maturity is further indicated by flat-floored valleys with distinct flood plains, wide meander belts, and occasional oxbow lakes.

Old Age Stage. Continued erosion will result in valleys that are extremely broad and shallow and marked by extensive flood plain deposits and numerous oxbow lakes. Such valleys, and the streams responsible for them, are said to be in old age. Old streams are normally rather sluggish, have a low gradient, and their channels are marked by many meanders, oxbows, and natural levees.

Rejuvenation. We learned earlier that the cycle of valley development may be interrupted by rejuvenation. When this occurs, the streams, as a result of increased gradients, will cut deeper into the valley floor where they may form a series of steplike terraces. Rejuvenation may also permit the stream to produce entrenched, or incised, meanders. These develop when an uplifted meandering stream continues to follow its original winding pattern but cuts deeply into the underlying rock.

CHAPTER 10

GROUND WATER

We have learned that water which falls as rain may be disposed of by runoff, evaporation, or infiltration. The water that seeps into (or infiltrates) the ground becomes ground water. Known also as **subsurface** or **underground** water, this water is found in the pores and crevices in the rocks and soils of the upper part of the earth's crust.

Most of the water which is found in the ground is **meteoric** water—it is derived from rain or snow which soaked into empty spaces in the rocks. This is the most important source of ground water.

A relatively small percentage of ground water has originated as **magmatic** water. Such water originates beneath the earth's surface and is formed chemically from igneous masses which are buried there. Because this water is making its

initial appearance in the hydrologic cycle, it is known also as **juvenile water**.

Connate water is water that was trapped in a sedimentary deposit at the time the sediments were accumulating. It is this type of water which is commonly found associated with deposits of petroleum. Connate water is typically salty and may be ancient sea water which was trapped in the sediments at the time of deposition. Like magmatic water, connate water forms only a small portion of the ground water.

MOVEMENT OF GROUND WATER

Gravity causes ground water to circulate downward and to fill all available empty spaces from the bottom upward. This is possible be-

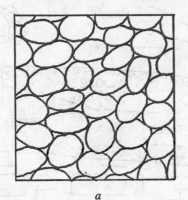 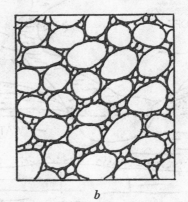

Fig. 74. Porosity in sedimentary deposits. The porosity of a is greater than b because the grains of a are all about the same size. Smaller grains fill spaces between larger grains in b, thereby reducing pore space.

cause rocks that are porous will absorb much of the infiltrating surface water. If the rocks are permeable, they will permit the ground water to move freely through them and underground circulation is further facilitated. Rocks that are porous and permeable and permit the free flow of ground water are called **aquifers.**

Rocks differ greatly in their degree of **porosity** and **permeability** (Fig. 74). Porosity may vary from less than 1 percent in certain massive, unweathered igneous rocks to as much as 30 percent in the case of certain sandstones. Some rocks, though not originally porous, may become permeable as a result of solution cavities, fractures, etc. Rocks which will not permit water to go through them are said to be **impermeable** or **impervious.**

THE WATER TABLE

That portion of the earth's crust in which all available pore space has become filled with water is called the **zone of saturation** or **phreatic zone** (Fig. 75). The upper limit of this zone is known as the **water table.**

The rocks and soil through which ground water passes on its way to the zone of saturation is called the **vadose zone** or the **zone of aeration.** The rocks in the vadose zone never become completely saturated. Instead, there is always some air present and this may combine with the water to hasten the decomposition of the surrounding rocks.

The depth at which the water table will be encountered beneath the surface varies greatly in different regions. Two of the more important factors that affect the level of the water table are the amount of rainfall in the region and the topography of the land.

For example, the water table may be lowered considerably during dry seasons, causing wells to go dry. On the other hand, excess precipitation may result in the water table being brought nearer the surface. Topography is also a factor in controlling the depth of the water table. In general, it conforms roughly to the surface configuration of the land. Therefore, the water table is nearer the surface in valleys and occurs at greater depths in the hills and mountains.

Wherever the water table intersects the surface

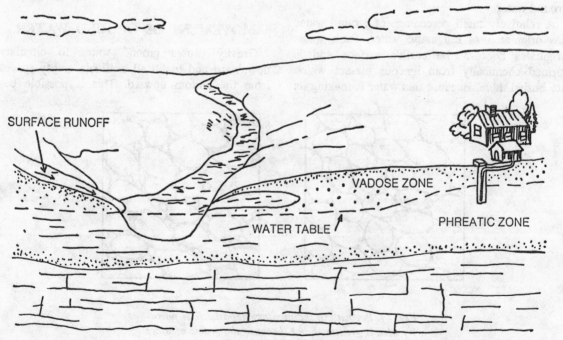

Fig. 75. Cross section illustrating relation of water table to vadose zone and phreatic zone.

of the ground, a body of water will collect to form pools, lakes, or swamps.

In some areas, ground water may collect in an aquifer which overlies an impermeable layer and becomes separated from the normal water table (Fig. 76). This is called a **perched water table** because it is found higher than the normal water table.

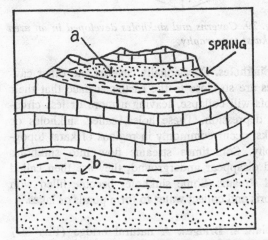

Fig. 76. A perched water table (a). The normal water table is indicated at (b).

HOW GROUND WATER REACHES THE SURFACE

Although much underground water is brought to the surface by means of wells, most ground water reaches the surface as a result of natural seepage, such as in springs.

Wells. A hole dug into the ground to a depth which reaches the water table is called a well. If it is to be considered permanent, a well must be deep enough so that the water table will never be below its bottom, even during very dry periods. Wells should penetrate the zone of saturation as deeply as possible and great care must be exercised to see that they do not become polluted.

Artesian wells are wells in which the hydrostatic (water) pressure is sufficient to cause the water to rise above the level at which it was first encountered (it may or may not flow out upon the surface of the earth). Artesian wells may produce great quantities of water, and since they are not dependent on seasonal rainfall they tend to be more reliable than ordinary wells.

Certain conditions must prevail before an artesian well can be developed. The aquifer, usually sandstone or gravel, should dip away from the surface and have impermeable rocks above and below it (Fig. 77). In addition, the aquifer should be exposed in an area of adequate rainfall to replenish the artesian system, and at an altitude higher than the site of the well. These conditions will produce hydrostatic pressures sufficient to develop artesian wells.

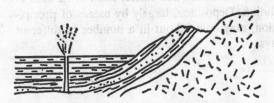

Fig. 77. An artesian well.

Springs. A spring is developed when ground water comes to the surface and flows out more or less continuously. **Hillside** springs occur in hilly regions where the water table intersects the land surface (Fig. 78). **Fissure** springs are naturally formed artesian wells. The water reaches the surface through fissures (cracks) in the rocks and flows out with considerable force. **Hot** springs (or thermal springs) contain water that has been heated by contact with heated rocks in the subsurface. Such areas as Hot Springs, Arkansas, Yellowstone National Park, Wyoming, and Lassen Volcanic National Park, California, are famous for their hot springs.

The water in a mineral spring contains an unusually large amount of dissolved mineral matter. Some of the minerals found in such springs are sodium chloride, sulfur, and magnesium sulfate. Others contain gases such as carbon dioxide or the ill-smelling hydrogen sulfide.

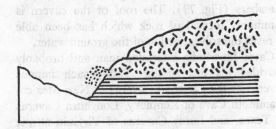

Fig. 78. Hillside spring along bedding plane.

Geysers are rather specialized hot springs which erupt intermittently. (Geysers were discussed in some detail in Chapter 4.)

Fig. 79. Caverns and sinkholes developed in an area of karst topography.

GEOLOGIC WORK OF GROUND WATER

Ground water is an effective agent of erosion, transportation, and deposition, and does its work on a relatively large scale. It erodes principally by chemical action and carries most of its load in solution. Deposition, largely by means of precipitation, may come about in a number of different ways.

EROSION BY GROUND WATER

Frequently carbon dioxide from the air and decaying organic matter in the soil combine with ground water to form carbonic acid. This acid-charged ground water makes a very effective agent of erosion, especially in areas of soluble sedimentary rocks.

As ground water circulates through rocks such as limestone or dolomite, the rock is dissolved and carried away in solution. Consequently, the underlying bedrock may become honeycombed with caverns, and sinkholes and natural bridges may develop on the surface. Land surfaces characterized by such features are said to have **karst topography** (named for the Karst region of Yugoslavia and Italy). In the United States karst topography is developed in parts of Kentucky, Tennessee, and Florida.

Caverns. Caverns (or caves) are formed when ground water, by means of solution, enlarges cracks into a series of underground tunnels and chambers (Fig. 79). The roof of the cavern is commonly formed of rock which has been able to resist the solvent action of the ground water.

Caves have long interested man and probably provided his first shelter. Today such famous caverns as the Carlsbad Caverns of New Mexico, Mammoth Cave of Kentucky, Longhorn Caverns of Texas, and Luray Caverns of Virginia attract hundreds of thousands of tourists each year.

Sinkholes. Occasionally caverns and other cavities are so close to the earth's surface that their roofs will collapse, leaving a more or less circular depression. These holes, called sinkholes or sinks, occur commonly in regions of karst topography. Sometimes streams flow into sinkholes and disappear underground; they are then called **lost streams.** Some sinkholes become filled with debris and collect water to form ponds or lakes.

Natural Bridges. A natural bridge (Fig. 80) may develop when a stream flows into an opening in the rock, dissolves a tunnel, and emerges on a cliff or slope on the other side. Portions of the tunnel may collapse and be carried away; the natural bridge is all that remains of the tunnel.

Fig. 80. Natural bridge.

DEPOSITION BY GROUND WATER

When ground water becomes oversaturated with mineral material, it is forced to deposit some of it. This deposition may be caused by (1) an increase in temperature, (2) a decrease in pressure, or (3) the loss of water by evaporation. Some of the depositional features formed by ground water are discussed below.

Spring Deposits. Certain ground waters contain such large quantities of dissolved materials that they deposit their load shortly after reaching the surface. Such deposits often form terraces and cones around hot springs and geysers. Calcareous material formed in this manner is called **travertine;** exceptionally porous travertine is referred to as a **calcareous tufa.** When siliceous material is deposited around hot springs, it is known as **siliceous sinter,** or **geyserite** when deposited around the vent of a geyser.

Cavern Deposits. As might be suspected, much ground water deposition takes place in the subsurface. Calcium carbonate in the form of travertine is most commonly deposited, but concentrations of gypsum and rock salt may also occur.

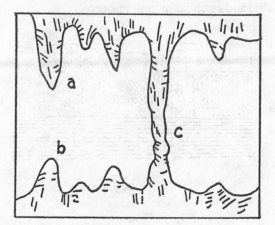

Fig. 81. Cave formations.
a–Stalactite b–Stalagmite c–Column

Calcite-laden ground water dripping continuously from the same spot will eventually produce calcareous icicle-like deposits called **stalactites** (Fig. 81a). These hang from the cavern roof. **Stalagmites** are mound-shaped masses of calcium carbonate which are built up on the floor of the cavern at the point where water drips from a stalactite (Fig. 81b). Stalactites and stalagmites may eventually unite to form a **column** (Fig. 81c).

Cementation. Ground water plays an important part in the cementation of rock particles.

This occurs when minerals carried by ground water are precipitated between loose grains, thus bonding them together. In this way a loose sand may be converted into a hard sandstone when silica is deposited between the constituent sand grains.

Concretions. Concretions are formed when ground water precipitates minerals around a nucleus such as a leaf (Fig. 82), shell, pebble, or some other object. Concretions may assume a variety of shapes and exhibit a wide range in size.

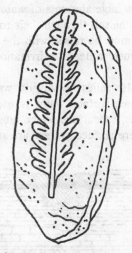

Fig. 82. Fern leaf in limestone concretion.

Geodes. More or less spherical cavities which have been wholly or partially filled with inward-pointing crystals are called **geodes.** Although formed underground, geodes that are found at the earth's surface typically result from the following sequence of events: (a) the formation of a marine shale or limestone; (b) the development of a spherical cavity in the rock; (c) the precipitation in the cavity of mineral matter from underground solutions; and (d) erosion that exposes the geode on the earth's surface.

Fissure Deposits or Veins. When supersaturated ground water is deposited in cracks or crevices, mineral veins are formed. Calcite and quartz veins are common, and such veins sometimes carry concentrations of metallic minerals such as gold, silver, and copper.

Replacement or Petrifaction. The process whereby ground water dissolves one type of material and substitutes another in its place is known as replacement. When organic material has been replaced we say that petrifaction has occurred. Thus, when the woody cells of a tree are replaced by silica, petrified wood is formed (see Chapter 19).

GROUND WATER AND HUMAN NEEDS

Ground water serves humankind in a host of ways. It is vital to agriculture because some plants require large amounts of water, which they absorb from the soil through their roots. Crops in arid regions must be raised with the aid of irrigation, and much water for irrigation is derived from wells.

Industry also relies heavily on water supplies. Although much surface water is used for industrial purposes, subsurface water must be utilized in areas where surface waters are not available.

Heavy industrial demands can rapidly deplete precious ground water supplies. In some areas ground water has become polluted by industry. In others rapid withdrawal of excessive amounts of ground water has caused the earth's surface to subside. This can result in damage to surface structures and can leave certain places subject to disastrous flooding.

Other human activities, particularly the disposal of wastes and/or chemically toxic materials, can also pollute ground water. By carefully evaluating ground water conditions and their relation to the surrounding rocks (Fig. 83), safe waste disposal sites can usually be selected.

The search for ground water has become a rather specialized science, and both state and federal agencies have **hydrologists** (scientists who specialize in the study of water) who are continually seeking new methods of finding and conserving ground water—one of our most valuable and essential natural resources.

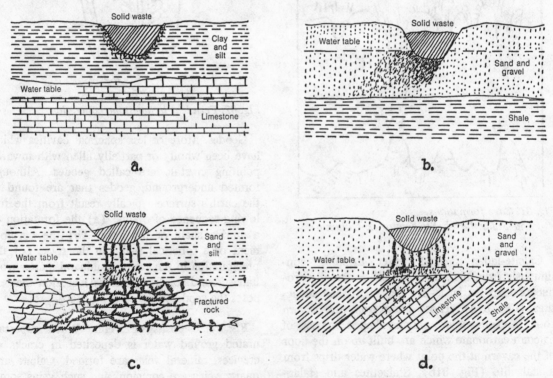

Fig. 83. Relation of waste-disposal site selection to subsurface geologic conditions. Note that with the exception of a (where the site is underlain by impermeable rocks) ground water has been contaminated by pollutants reaching the water table through permeable rocks.

CHAPTER 11

GLACIERS AND THE GEOLOGIC WORK OF ICE

Glaciers are large, slow-moving masses of land ice formed by the recrystallization of snow. These great bodies of flowing ice once occupied as much as 30 percent of the world's land area, but today cover little more than 10 percent of the earth's surface.

Periods of glaciation have occurred several times during the history of the earth, but the great Ice Age of Pleistocene time (Chapter 22) has provided us with the clearest and most recent record of glacial activity. During this time a great ice sheet covered much of Canada, northern Europe, and the northern part of the United States (Fig. 84). The last great ice sheet retreated from the United States about ten to fifteen thousand years ago. But before it disappeared it had reached as far south as St. Louis, and covered approximately five million square miles.

Glacial periods normally produce great physical and biological changes in the region of glaciation. During Pleistocene time the sea level was lowered as the water was frozen into glacial ice. When the glaciers began to melt, much of the water was returned to the sea, causing the sea level to rise. In addition to bringing about changes in sea level, there is much evidence to indicate that the earth's crust sagged or became warped under the great weight of ice sheets. Other changes include formation of new lakes and swamps (including the Great Lakes), the changed course of rivers, and the migration of plants and animals as climates became colder.

Let us now examine the effects of glaciation, both past and present, and learn more about the

Fig. 84. *Distribution of ice sheets during Pleistocene time.*

role of these great ice masses in shaping the earth's surface and its history.

HOW GLACIERS FORM

In areas where snowfall is sufficiently heavy and the average annual temperature sufficiently low, the snow remains throughout the year. In regions with temperate or tropical climates, the snow will remain year round on only the highest mountains. However, in the frigid zones even land which lies only slightly above sea level may be perpetually covered by snow and ice. The lower limit of perpetual snow is known as the **snow line.** Determined largely by latitude, the snow line is found at lower altitudes as the latitude increases. For example, at 90° N latitude (the north pole) the snow line is at sea level. At the equator (0° latitude) the snow line may be as much as 18,000 feet above sea level.

It is above the snow line, in massive accumulations of snow called **snow fields,** that glaciers are born. As the snow freezes and compacts, it turns into granular, pellet-sized ice particles called **firn** or **névé.** This material, covered by subsequent snows, is gradually compressed until finally the lower level of the snow field is compacted into a great mass of ice. Eventually, the firn undergoes changes which transform the entire mass into glacier ice. When sufficient glacier ice has accumulated, the force of gravity tends to move it slowly downslope.

KINDS OF GLACIERS

Geologists usually divide glaciers into three groups: (1) valley or alpine glaciers, (2) piedmont glaciers, and (3) ice sheets or continental glaciers.

Valley Glaciers. Known also as alpine or mountain glaciers, **valley glaciers** originate in snow fields at the heads of mountain valleys. Their downward movement follows old stream-cut valleys, which are sometimes filled from wall to wall with rivers of glacier ice. Valley glaciers range in area from several hundred square yards to many square miles, and in length from a few hundred yards to more than seventy-five miles. Such glaciers occur in the Alps and in the Himalaya, Rocky, Sierra Nevada, and Cascade mountains. Mount Rainier in Washington is well known for the many glaciers which course down its slopes.

Piedmont Glaciers. Sometimes two or more valley glaciers emerge from adjacent mountain valleys onto the plains below. Here the lower ends of the glaciers unite to form a broad rounded mass of ice called a **piedmont** glacier. One of the better-known glaciers of this type is the Malaspina Glacier on the western side of Yakutat Bay in Alaska. Covering an area of about 1500 square miles, Malaspina Glacier is formed by the union of several valley glaciers that moved down the slopes of nearby Mount St. Elias.

Ice Sheets or Continental Glaciers. The broad sheetlike ice masses that cover large land areas are known as **ice sheets** or **continental** glaciers (smaller, relatively localized ice sheets are called **ice caps**). Usually very thick, these glaciers spread outward from the center of a landmass until they may cover much of a continent—highlands and lowlands alike. Occasionally an isolated mountain peak known as a **nunatak** will be found projecting above the surface of the ice.

The world's largest ice sheet, that of the Antarctic, covers most of the continent of Antarctica—an area almost twice the size of the United States. In places this great ice mass is as much as 10,000 feet thick. The Greenland ice sheet is also quite large; it has a surface area of approximately 670,000 square miles and a maximum thickness of possibly 11,000 feet.

MOVEMENT OF GLACIERS

To the casual observer a glacier appears to be a stationary mass of ice. But glaciers, like rivers, move—although much more slowly. The rate of forward progress ranges from less than an inch to as much as one hundred feet per day (the latter occurring under rather extreme conditions). Factors which affect the rate of movement include (1) size of the glacier (the thicker it is the faster it will move), (2) slope and topography of the land, (3) temperature of the area (the glacier moves faster as temperatures become higher), and (4) the amount of unfrozen water in the glacier.

The nature of glacial movement is not completely understood, for it appears to be a rather complex process. In general, however, glaciers appear to move as the force of gravity and pressure from the weight of accumulating ice causes the ice in the lower levels of the glacier to become plastic and subject to slow flowage. Ice in this lowermost portion of the glacier is said to be in the **zone of flow;** the less plastic ice in the upper part of the glacier occupies the **zone of fracture** (see Fig. 85). In addition, alternate periods of melting and refreezing produce contraction and expansion of the ice which may further glacial motion.

Fig. 85. Cross section through a typical valley glacier.

Glacial movement is somewhat like stream movement in that glaciers move more rapidly in the middle than along their sides, and faster on top than along the bottom. Friction along the sides and bottom of the glacier will retard movement there. As a glacier follows the twisting path of its valley and passes over irregularities in the valley floor, tension may cause fractures to develop in the rigid, more brittle ice in the zone of fracture. These fractures produce fissures, called **crevasses** (Fig. 85) some of which may be hundreds of feet long. Crevasses may be concealed by a thin crust of snow which breaks at the slightest weight. Because of this they are a constant source of danger to persons traveling over the glacier's surface.

Glaciers continue to move until they reach an area where warm air causes the ice to melt as fast as the glacier advances. The ice front then becomes stationary. The glacier will eventually retreat if the ice wastes more rapidly than it advances.

Many glaciers continue to move until they reach the sea, where large pieces of the glacier may break off to form icebergs. These float away and eventually melt as they reach warmer waters.

GEOLOGIC WORK OF GLACIERS

Like all other geologic agents, the work of glaciers consists essentially of erosion, transportation, and deposition. Taken together, these processes are called **glaciation.**

GLACIAL EROSION

So great is the erosive power of glaciers that few objects will deter them as they plow down their valleys or override prominent land features to blanket an entire continent. Glacial erosion is accomplished by (1) **plucking** or **quarrying**—the glacier dislodges and picks up protruding fragments of bedrock; (2) **abrasion**—the ice-plucked blocks and other rock debris scratch and polish the bedrock over which the glacier passes; and (3) **plowing** or **sledding**—loose material is pushed ahead of the glacier, or rock material may fall from valley walls and come to rest on top of the ice.

Erosion by Valley Glaciers. A valley glacier is a very effective agent of erosion and will greatly modify the area it occupies. Valley glaciers originate in **cirques**—great semicircular depressions which have been developed by deepening and enlarging the head of a mountain valley. When several cirques develop close together, the ridges separating them may become very sharp and jagged, producing knife-edged ridges called **arêtes.** When two cirques erode into a ridge from opposite sides, they may meet to form a **col** or **pass.** A **matterhorn peak,** or **horn,** is produced in late stages of glaciation after the summits of preglacial mountains have been reduced to isolated peaks. When glacier ice disappears, a cirque may become filled with water to form a glacial lake called a **tarn.** Some of these features are illustrated in Fig. 86.

Valley glaciers have their greatest effect on the valleys which they occupy. Such valleys will be modified in a number of ways as the glacier grinds away the valley walls and smooths the valley floor. Young valleys traversed by glaciers will be widened and deepened and the form changed from a V to a U shape (Fig. 87). In addition, the valley walls and floor are scratched, grooved, and polished by the rock debris being carried in the glacial ice. Marks thus produced are called **glacial striae** if they are scratches, **glacial grooves** if they are very deep. Projections in the valley floor are smoothed and rounded to form **roches moutonnées** (Fig. 88a) a French term meaning

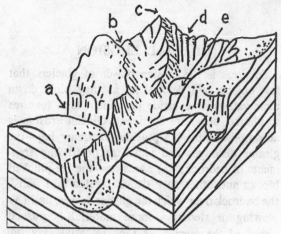

Fig. 86. Features developed by valley glaciers.
a–Hanging valley   b–Col
c–Horn   d–Cirque
e–Tarn

"sheep rocks." Moreover, much of the valley floor over which the glacier moves may be ground to powder or **rock flour.**

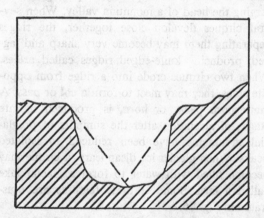

Fig. 87. Typical U-shaped glacial trough, or valley. (Broken line shows valley profile before glaciation.)

The main glacial valley (known also as a **glacial trough**) is usually more deeply eroded than are the tributary or side valleys leading into it. Thus, when the glaciers melt, these tributaries are left hanging high above the main valley floor. Valleys of this type are called **hanging valleys,** and streams flowing through them commonly form steep waterfalls where they plunge into the deeper main valleys. Yosemite Falls in Yosemite National Park is a typical example of this kind of waterfall. Indeed, Yosemite Valley in California

is one of the classic glaciated areas of the world, and here may be seen outstanding examples of most of the products of valley glaciation.

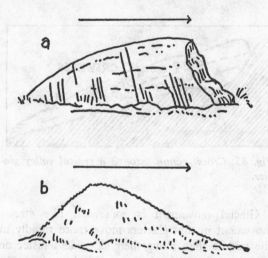

Fig. 88. a–Roche Moutonnée, or "Sheep Rock" b–Drumlin. Arrows signify direction in which ice moved.

As a glacier flows from the mountains into the sea, the ice may excavate its valley below sea level. When the glacier melts, the sea will invade the valley, thereby producing a **fiord.** These deep, steep-walled, narrow arms of the sea are especially characteristic of the coast of Norway.

Erosion by Ice Sheets. Ice sheets, because of their great thickness and extent, may completely override major surface features. Thus mountains and hills as well as valleys may be subjected to glacial erosion. Beneath the ice the rocks will be quarried, scratched, and grooved, as evidenced by glacial striations and roches moutonnées. Ice sheets may also produce **drumlins,** streamlined, elliptical hills formed parallel to the direction in which the ice moved (Fig. 88b).

In general, continental ice sheets tend to smooth out surface irregularities which inhibit movement of the ice sheet, and soil and mantle rock may be removed from large areas.

GLACIAL TRANSPORTATION

Glaciers are capable of carrying great quantities of earth materials, and some of these rock fragments may be quite large. Consequently, a glacier's load will normally include finely pulverized rock flour and huge boulders, with all sizes of rocks in between.

Much of this material is transported on top of the glacier and constitutes the **superglacial load.** The material frozen in the interior of the glacier is termed the **englacial load,** while the **subglacial load** consists of the rocks and soil carried on the bottom of the ice mass. It is the subglacial load that is responsible for much of the abrasive action of a glacier.

Valley glaciers carry more materials on their surface than do ice sheets or continental glaciers. This is because much debris falls from the valley walls and accumulates on top of the glacier. In addition, part of the load may be pushed along in front of the advancing ice.

Ice sheets are normally so thick that they gather very little debris to be carried as superglacial load. They normally are not capable of transporting as much material as a valley glacier, and most of the load is frozen into the bottom of the ice or shoved along ahead of it.

GLACIAL DEPOSITION

As noted above, a glacier's load consists of rocks and soil randomly intermingled without regard to size, weight, or composition. When the ice melts it will drop the debris, forming a variety of deposits which are designated as **glacial drift.** There are two types of drift: **till,** glacial drift which has not been stratified or sorted by water action but has been deposited directly by the ice, and **outwash,** or stratified drift, composed of materials that have been sorted and deposited in definite layers by the action of glacial meltwater.

Unstratified Deposits or Till. Laid down directly by the ice, deposits of till are composed of rock fragments of varying size, many of which are polished or bear glacial striae. Deposits of till form topographic features known as **moraines—** ridges or mounds of boulders, gravel, sand, and clay deposited by a glacier. There are several types of moraines, each being named with respect to its relation to the glacier. A **terminal moraine,** or **end** moraine, is a mound of till formed at the terminus, or end, of a glacier. Terminal moraines

mark the former position of the ice front. **Recessional** moraines are deposits of till left at various points as a glacier recedes or is temporarily stable. Irregular deposits of till deposited by retreating melting glaciers are called **ground** moraines. Drumlins are commonly developed on ground moraine surfaces.

Each of the moraines described above is characteristic of both ice sheets and valley glaciers. The latter, however, produce two types of moraines that are not developed by ice sheets. Valley glaciers will commonly display **lateral** moraines, which are ridges formed on each side of a glacial valley. They consist of material that has been eroded from the sides of the valley or has fallen from the valley sides onto the glacier's surface to be carried along by the ice (Fig. 89a). When two valley glaciers join to form a single stream of ice, the lateral moraines unite to form a single **medial** moraine (Fig. 89b).

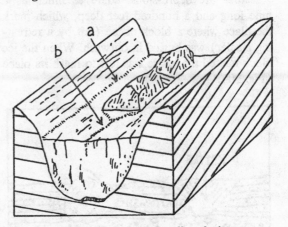

Fig. 89. Cross section through valley glacier.
a–Lateral moraine   b–Medial moraine

Erratics are large stones or boulders which have been transported by glaciers and which are different from the underlying bedrock. Erratics, some of which may weigh many tons, have been found hundreds of miles from their place of origin. An elongated line of erratics derived from a common source is called a **boulder train.**

Stratified Deposits or Outwash. Rock materials deposited by streams of glacial meltwater are called outwash. Known also as **glaciofluvial** deposits, this stream-sorted material may produce a variety of landforms. Some of the more common outwash deposits are discussed below.

Outwash plains are broad, fan-shaped deposits of fine drift deposited in front of the glacier; they are characteristic of ice sheets. In a valley glacier most of the outwash deposits are left along the valley floor, forming features known as **valley trains.**

Eskers are long, winding ridges of stratified drift which resemble railroad embankments. This material was apparently deposited in ice tunnels by streams which ran along the bottom of the glacier. Although eskers may be many miles in length and from ten to as much as one hundred feet high, they are only a few feet wide.

Kames, small, rather steep-sided flat-topped hills of stratified drift, are formed by material that collected in circular depressions in the glacier. Layered deposits of sand and gravel formed between the side of a wasting glacier and the adjoining valley wall are called **kame terraces.**

Kettles are depressions, some as much as a mile long and a hundred feet deep, which mark the place where a block of ice (left by a retreating glacier) was buried in outwash. When the ice block melted the kettle was left to mark its place (Fig. 90).

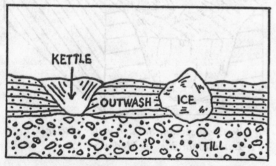

Fig. 90. Formation of a kettle in outwash. Block of ice at right is buried in outwash; when ice melts, a depression (the kettle) remains.

CAUSES OF GLACIAL PERIODS

What causes periods of glaciation? Unfortunately, geologists have not yet found the complete answer to this rather complex problem.

However, a study of the record of glacial activities of the past and observations on many of our present-day glaciers have given rise to a number of theories as to the ultimate cause of glacial activity. A few of the factors believed to have some bearing on this problem are briefly mentioned below:

1. Elevation of the lands. Periods of glaciation seem to coincide with times when the continents are known to have been high. Lower temperatures prevail at higher altitudes and a drop in mean annual temperature at a time when lands are high may produce a period of glaciation.

2. Variation in the amount of heat received from the sun. The sun is the source of the earth's heat energy, and the amount of energy thus generated is known to have fluctuated as much as 3 percent in the past forty years. Although this is not enough to cause glaciation, larger fluctuations may have occurred in the geologic past. Variations in the amount of solar energy received by the earth's surface might also have been produced by occasional clouds of volcanic dust. Or perhaps the earth's orbit around the sun was different than it is today, thus producing a longer, colder winter season.

3. Variations in carbon dioxide and water vapor in the atmosphere. There is considerable evidence to suggest that both carbon dioxide and water vapor help the earth to retain heat derived from the sun. A decrease in these substances would permit more heat to escape by radiation, thus bringing about a colder climate. Enlarged and elevated land areas may have decreased the amount of water vapor in the atmosphere and thus decreased its ability to retain solar heat.

4. Continental drift. Evidence from plate tectonics (Chapter 2) suggests that continental drift has placed the continents in positions that favor glaciation.

In addition to the above, such factors as periods of greatly increased volcanic activity, an increase in the amount of cosmic dust in space, melting of the arctic ice cap, and changes in the circulation of the oceans have been suggested as possible causes of glaciation.

CHAPTER 12

MASS WASTING AND WIND EROSION

MASS MOVEMENT OF ROCK AND SOIL

Mass movement, or **mass wasting**, takes place as earth materials move downslope in response to the forces of gravity. This type of erosion is apt to occur in any area with slopes steep enough to allow downward movement of rock debris.

CAUSES OF MASS MOVEMENT OF EARTH MATERIAL

All land surfaces slope to a certain degree, and the ability of a slope to resist gravity depends largely upon the cohesive ability or strength of the earth materials forming it. Some of the factors which help gravity overcome this resistance are discussed below.

Water. Although mass wasting may occur in either wet or dry materials, water greatly facilitates downslope movements. It may soften clays, making them slippery, add weight to the rock mass, and, in large amounts, may actually force rock particles apart, thus reducing soil cohesion.

Freezing and Thawing. Water contained in rock and soil expands when frozen. Alternate periods of freezing and thawing will loosen rock materials, and in some instances ice expansion may be great enough to force rocks downhill. This action is most effective at high altitudes where freezing and thawing occur almost every day.

Undercutting. Undercutting by streams or by man-made excavations may remove support and allow overlying material to fall.

Organic Activities. Animals such as deer or cattle walking on the surface knock materials downhill. Burrowing animals cast rocks and soils out of their holes as they dig; these are commonly piled up downslope.

Shock Waves. Strong vibrations caused by faulting, blasting, and heavy traffic can also exert sufficient stress on rock materials to start their movement downhill. An example of this is the landslide which occurred in Yellowstone National Park in August 1959. This mass movement of rock material, which buried twenty-eight campers, was triggered by an earthquake.

KINDS OF MASS MOVEMENTS

Mass movements may occur suddenly and violently as in a landslide, or almost imperceptibly as in the case of soil creep. Let us now consider the various forms of rapid and slow mass movements.

RAPID MOVEMENTS

Most of the more rapid movements of earth materials are the results of forces which have been gradually weakening the mantle rock over long periods of time. Some of the more common types of rapid mass wasting are described below.

Talus. Talus consists of weathered rock fragments piled up at the foot of a cliff or mountain. Talus builds up gradually as weathered rock particles are dislodged from the cliff face and roll downslope.

Landslides. The most spectacular and violent of all mass movements, landslides, are characterized by the sudden movement of great quantities of rock and soil downslope. Such movements typically occur on steep slopes that have large accumulations of weathered material. Water from rain or snow may seep into the mass of steeply sloping rock debris, adding sufficient weight to start the entire mass sliding. **Avalanches** are rapid movements of snow with some soil and rocks, and **rock slides** are especially destructive landslides which involve movement of the bedrock as well as the mantle rock.

There are numerous accounts of destructive landslides which have taken place within recent times. One of the better-known catastrophes of this type occurred in Canada at Frank, Alberta. Here, in 1903, forty million cubic yards of rock suddenly broke loose from the face of three-thousand-foot Turtle Mountain, and descended upon the little coal-mining town of Frank. This huge rock mass rushed two miles across the valley and four hundred feet up the opposite side. The total period of movement for this great rock slide was less than two minutes, but approximately seventy residents of Frank lost their lives in this brief span of time.

Slump, a special type of landslide, occurs as large masses of the slope move downward and outward due to gravitational pull. Such movements are most likely to occur in unconsolidated materials, and are usually caused by undercutting or steepening of the slope to the extent that it can no longer support its own weight. Slump is a common occurrence along the banks of streams or the walls of steep valleys (Fig. 91).

Fig. 91. A slump block. (Note curved plane of slippage beneath arrows).

Mudflows. Large flowing masses of rocks, soil, and water mixed to mudlike consistency are termed mudflows. Mass wasting of this type typically occurs as certain arid or semi-arid mountainous regions are subjected to unusually heavy rains. Usually originating in steep-walled gulches or canyons, mudflows course down the valley and may cause widespread destruction of objects in their path.

Earthflows. Differing from mudflows in the amount of water that they contain, earthflows usually move more slowly than the more fluid masses of mud.

SLOW MOVEMENTS

Although the slower types of mass movement normally lack the sudden and spectacular action that marks rapid mass wasting, their total geologic effect is probably considerably greater than those which occur more quickly.

Soil Creep. Gravity also moves rock material downslope by means of soil creep. This movement, usually so slow as to be imperceptible, normally occurs on moist slopes not steep enough for landslides. As the mantle rock slowly moves downhill it may tilt trees, displace fences, and deform rock strata (Fig. 92). Soil creep may be accelerated by frost wedging (see page 68), alternate freezing and thawing, and by certain plant and animal activities.

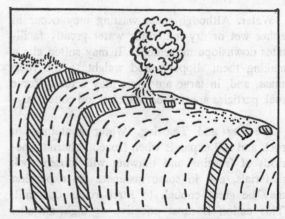

Fig. 92. Soil creep. Note downslope migration of strata, tilting the tree.

Solifluction. Solifluction is a downslope movement typical of areas where the ground is normally frozen to considerable depth. The actual soil flowage occurs when the upper portion of the mantle rock thaws and becomes water-saturated. The underlying, still frozen subsoil acts as a "slide" for the sodden mantle rock which will move down even the most gentle slope. Solifluction is characteristic of arctic, subarctic, and high mountain regions.

WIND EROSION

Wind (air in motion) is a very effective geologic agent. Although not normally as spectacular as the work of certain other gradational agents, wind erosion is, nonetheless, an important landforming process. As might be expected, wind works most effectively in arid and semiarid regions. However, even moist regions will experience periods of drought, and during such times the soil becomes loose and subject to removal by wind. In addition, wind-blown dust may be transported for great distances and deposited in areas in which climates are prevailingly humid.

HOW THE WIND ERODES

Wind by itself has little if any effect on solid rock. But winds of high velocity will pick up a load of rock fragments which may become effective tools of erosion. These winds may erode by deflation or abrasion.

Deflation. In regions of arid and semiarid climates and where the vegetative cover is sparse, loose rock and soil particles are apt to be blown away by the wind. This process of blowing away, known as deflation, may create several types of distinctive features. For example, broad shallow depressions termed **blowouts** may be developed where wind has scooped out soft unconsolidated rocks and soil. **Lag gravels** are formed when the wind blows away finer rock particles, leaving behind a residue of coarse gravel and stones. **Desert pavement** may be produced when large pebbles, boulders, and patches of bedrock are exposed in such a manner that they fit tightly together to form a relatively smooth surface. Some

of these stones may exhibit a dark, enamel-like coat of iron or manganese called **desert varnish.**

Abrasion. The wind abrades by means of loose sand and dust particles which are transported as part of its load. Wind abrasion acts as a natural sandblasting process to wear away solid objects. The destructive action of these windblown abrasives may wear away wooden telegraph poles and fence posts, and scour or groove solid rock surfaces. Windows which are constantly exposed to the impact of wind-blown sand may eventually become pitted, chipped, or frosted. The sand grains which are used in the abrasive process are also subjected to wear; they, too, will become pitted, worn, and reduced in size.

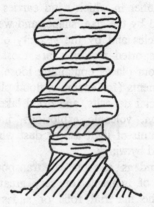

Fig. 93. Rock pedestal formed by wind erosion.

Wind abrasion also plays a part in the development of such landforms as **table rocks** and **pedestals**—isolated rocks which have had their bases undercut by wind-blown sand (Fig. 93). Moreover, certain shallow hillside caves appear to have been developed with the help of wind erosion. **Ventifacts** are another interesting and relatively common product of wind erosion. These are pebbles, cobbles, and in some instances boulders which have been polished, faceted, or grooved by wind-blown sand. Ventifacts are formed when the wind blows sand against the side of the stone, shaping it into a flat surface (Fig. 94). If the prevailing winds change directon, faces may be developed on other sides of the stone. Stones formed with one flat face commonly have a single sharp edge and these are called **einkanters** (German, "one-edge"); triangular-shaped, three-faced ventifacts are called **dreikanters** (German, "three-edge").

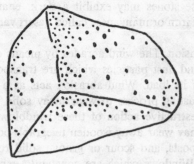

Fig. 94. Ventifact, an angular stone shaped by the wind.

TRANSPORTATION BY THE WIND

The manner in which wind carries its load is determined by the size, shape, and weight of the rock particles and by the velocity of the wind. Wind-transported materials are most commonly derived from places containing loose, weathered rock fragments (for example, flood plains, beach sands, glacial deposits, and dried lake bottoms). In addition, volcanic explosions may produce large amounts of light ash or dust which will be transported by winds.

The wind is capable of transporting large quantities of material for very great distances. Part of the material rolls or slides along the ground. This, the **bed load,** is said to move by **traction.** Some sand particles move by **saltation** —a series of leaping or bounding movements. If the velocity of the wind is great enough, particles may be transported in **suspension.** Most of the suspended load is carried within a few feet of the ground, but lighter dust particles may be lifted upward into higher, faster-moving wind currents. Material caught up in these upper-level wind currents may be transported for many thousands of miles.

WIND DEPOSITION

The wind will begin to deposit its load when its velocity is decreased, or when the air is washed clean by falling rain or snow. A decrease in wind velocity may be brought about when the wind "dies down" or strikes some obstacle (trees, fences) in its path.

The major types of wind-blown deposits (known also as **eolian** deposits) are **dunes** and **loess.**

DUNES

Sand dunes are mounds or hills of sand which have been deposited by the wind. Dunes vary in shape and size according to the nature of the wind, available quantity of sand, and the amount and distribution of the vegetative cover.

How Dunes Are Formed. Dunes are formed in areas where there is a sufficient amount of loose, unprotected sand and winds strong enough to move it. Areas of this type include sandy deserts, sandy flood plains, and sandy beaches along lake shores or sea coasts. The dune is started by an obstacle that causes a drop in the speed of the wind, perhaps a tree or a fence. When the velocity drops, a small deposit of wind-blown material will accumulate on the sheltered (lee) side of the obstruction. As the mound of sand grows it becomes a more efficient windbreak and thus increases the amount of deposition. This process continues until the dune is at least several feet high, and might possibly continue until it is several hundreds of feet high.

Dunes formed in areas where the wind blows steadily from a single direction develop a characteristic profile (Fig. 95). Such dunes have a relatively long gentle slope on the windward side and a short steep slope on the lee side. Small furrows, known as **ripple marks,** are commonly found on the windward slope of the dune.

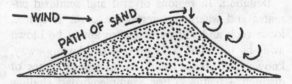

Fig. 95. Profile of typical sand dune. Arrows denote paths of wind currents.

Migration of Dunes. Most sand dunes are not stationary. Instead, they slowly migrate as the wind blows sand up the gentle windward slope and over the crest, thus allowing it to fall down the steep leeward side. The repeated occurrence of this process will result in the dune moving in a leeward direction, a movement called **dune mi-**

gration. Although normally a rather slow movement (seldom as much as twenty-five feet per year), some dunes are known to have moved as much as one hundred feet in one year. Migration will continue until the dunes become covered with vegetation, which will protect the sand from the wind. Dunes of this type are said to be **fixed** or **stabilized.** Migrating dunes have been known to advance over forests, farm lands, railroads, highways, and villages. In some instances man has arrested the movement of sand by planting grass, shrubs, or trees or by erecting protective fences.

TYPES OF SAND DUNES

Dunes vary greatly in size and shape, depending on the velocity and direction of the wind and on the amount of sand available in the area.

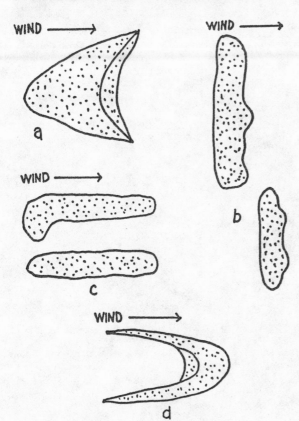

Fig. 96. Types of sand dunes. Arrows denote direction of prevailing winds.

a—Barchan   b—Transverse

c—Longitudinal   d—Parabolic

Barchans. Crescent-shaped dunes characterized by two long, curved extensions pointing in the direction of the wind are called barchans (Fig. 96a). Such dunes are formed in areas where winds blow steadily and from a single direction.

Transverse Dunes. Formed especially along sea coasts and lake shores, transverse dunes develop with their long axis at right angles to the wind (Fig. 96b). Sand ridges of this type may be ten or fifteen feet high and as much as a half mile in length.

Longitudinal Dunes. A long ridgelike dune developed parallel to the wind is called a longitudinal dune (Fig. 96c). **Seif dunes** are a special type of longitudinal dune which resemble the shape of an Arabian sword. Seif dunes may be as much as seven hundred feet high and six hundred feet long. They are commonly grouped together to form ridges which may extend for many miles across the country.

Parabolic Dunes. These U-shaped dunes resemble barchans. However, the tips of parabolic dunes point toward the wind, whereas the tips of the barchan point downwind (Fig. 96d).

LOESS

The finer particles carried by the wind may accumulate to form deposits of dust known as loess. A yellowish, fine-grained, nonstratified material, loess is composed of small angular fragments of a variety of minerals. The materials forming loess are derived from surface dust originating primarily in deserts, river flood plains, glacial outwash deposits, and deltas. Loess is quite cohesive and possesses the property of forming steep bluffs with vertical faces.

Loess is well known for its ability to form fine-textured, fertile, yellowish soils, and in areas of sufficient rainfall such soils are of considerable agricultural importance. Some of the more extensive loess deposits occur in the lower Mississippi River Valley, the pampas of Argentina, and in northern China.

DESERTS

Deserts—areas where the amount of precipitation received is less than the potential evaporation—cover roughly 30 percent of the earth's land surface. One of the more hostile environments to life, deserts may be either extremely hot or very cold. Precipitation is less than ten inches per year, droughts are common, and vegetation is sparse.

Many **hot deserts** such as the Sahara of North Africa are found primarily in the tropics or sub-tropics. Others—for example, the Mohave Desert of the southwestern United States and the deserts of Central Asia—occur in the middle latitudes. Desertification in hot areas typically occurs in regions that are far from sources of moisture, isolated from moisture by high mountains, in coastal areas along which there are onshore winds and cold-water currents, and/or high pressure areas where descending air masses produce warm, dry air.

Cold deserts are characterized by temperatures that are so low that the atmosphere cannot hold much moisture. Deserts of this type are found in Greenland, Antarctica, and elsewhere.

CHAPTER 13

OCEANS AND SHORELINES

We have already learned that the oceans of the world cover approximately 71 percent of the earth's surface and that most of the soil which has been eroded from the land is eventually deposited in the sea. In addition to their geologic importance, oceans are of value as routes of commerce, regulators of climates, and the primary source of all water.

ORIGIN OF THE OCEANS

Despite the fact that they are so widespread, the oceans are but a thin film of water that fills the ocean basins and laps onto the margins of the continents (Fig. 97). The origin of the hydrosphere—of which the oceans comprise more than 97 percent—can be traced back more than 4 billion 500 million years ago.

Where did all of this water come from? It is believed to have been originally locked up in the primordial earth. At some early stage in the earth's formation, our planet began to release water and various gases from its interior, primarily by means of volcanic activity. This process is called **outgassing** or **degassing**. According to one theory, outgassing primarily occurred as the earth gradually cooled during the first 500 million years of its history. However, it has also been suggested that there has been a gradual release of these materials by volcanic action throughout much of geologic time. Indeed, there is evidence to suggest that this process is still occurring today.

The water and gases that produced the hydrosphere also formed the atmosphere. Rock debris added to the oceans by the weathering of crustal rocks and smaller amounts of matter from space also contributed to the basic composition of the oceans.

COMPOSITION OF OCEAN WATER

The composition of ocean water has remained constant in composition throughout most of geologic time. This has been possible because of a balance of inflow of dissolved materials supplied by rivers plus the precipitation of sediments. Of what is seawater composed? One scientist has defined it as a weak solution of almost everything. More specifically, some seventy elements have been identified in ocean water, but others are most certainly present. About 3.5 percent of average seawater, by weight, consists of dissolved salts (see Table 5). These dissolved salts give

ION	PERCENTAGE OF ALL DISSOLVED MATTER
Chloride (Cl^{-1})	55.07
Sodium (Na^{+1})	30.62
Sulfate (SO_4^{-2})	7.72
Magnesium (Mg^{+2})	3.68
Calcium (Ca^{+2})	1.17
Potassium (K^{+1})	1.10
Bicarbonate (HCO_3^{-1})	0.40
Bromine (Br^{-1})	0.19
Strontium (Sr^{+2})	0.02
Total	99.97

TABLE 5. The major constituents dissolved in ocean water.

the oceans their "saltiness" or salinity. Sodium chloride (common salt) comprises more than three-fourths of the total dissolved solids. Where do these salts come from? The greater part of them have been leached from the soil and transported to sea by streams.

The salt content of an ocean may vary from place to place. For example, waters may be saltier in regions where excessive evaporation occurs, and less saline in areas of cold climate, heavy rainfall, or where large rivers enter the ocean.

DISTRIBUTION OF THE OCEANS

The oceanic waters of the earth have a combined area of about 140 million square miles. In the Southern Hemisphere the oceans cover about 81 percent of the surface, while in the Northern Hemisphere they cover approximately 61 percent of the surface (Fig. 97). The oceans are intercommunicating bodies of water; therefore a ship can sail from one ocean to all of the others. Oceans include also their adjoining gulfs and bays; thus, the Mediterranean and Baltic seas are considered to be parts of the Atlantic Ocean.

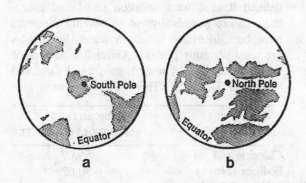

a   b

Fig. 97. The Southern Hemisphere (a) has been called the water hemisphere because most of the earth's landmasses are located north of the equator (b).

DIVISION OF THE WORLD OCEAN

The **world ocean** consists of the three major oceans—the Atlantic, Pacific, and Indian—which are all interconnected. The Pacific, the largest and deepest ocean, makes up approximately three-eighths of the total water area. At the equator, its widest part, the Pacific is about 10,000 miles wide.

The second largest ocean, the Atlantic, comprises roughly one-fourth of the total area of the oceans and ranges from 2000 to 4200 miles in width. The Indian Ocean is third in size, being about 6000 miles in diameter and composing about one-eighth of the area of the sea.

Although not considered to be oceans, other large and well-defined bodies include the so-called Arctic Ocean, the Mediterranean Sea, and the Baltic Sea, all of which are generally included as part of the Atlantic Ocean. The Antarctic Sea is not considered an ocean because it surrounds a continent and lacks clearly defined physical boundaries.

DEPTH OF THE OCEANS

As noted above, the Pacific is the deepest of all oceans, having an average depth of about 14,000 feet. At its deepest part, the Marianas Trench in the western Pacific is more than 36,000 feet deep. The Indian Ocean is second deepest, with a mean depth of approximately 13,000 feet, while the Atlantic Ocean has a mean depth of about 12,800 feet. Those parts of the ocean floor which are more than 18,000 feet below sea level (the surface of the ocean) are called **deeps.** There are about fifty-seven known deeps; Pacific deeps include the Marianas Trench off the island of Guam, and the Swire Deep, or Philippine Trough (35,430 feet), located northeast of the island of Mindanao. The deepest part of the Atlantic Ocean, more than 29,000 feet, is in the Milwaukee Deep, or Puerto Rico Trough, located just north of Puerto Rico.

The oceans are much deeper than the lands are high. The average depth of the sea is 13,000 feet (about two and one-half miles), while the average elevation of the land is about 2600 feet (about one-half mile). Thus, if the continents were eroded and the material composing them placed in the oceans, the earth would be covered by a universal sea approximately two miles deep.

THE OCEAN FLOOR

The bottoms of the ocean basins (depressed portions of the earth's surface lying between continental land masses) were once thought to be flat, featureless plains. We now know that parts of the ocean floor are marked by mountain ranges, plateaus, and other relief features similar to those of the land. In general, however, the submarine topography is not as rugged as that of the earth's surface.

The floor of the ocean has been divided into four divisions: the continental shelf, continental slope, continental rise, and deep-sea floor or abyssal plain (Fig. 98).

appears to be an extension of the Hudson River; other canyons, however, are not associated with extended river valleys and their origin is not completely understood. Certain of these have been explained as the result of submarine earth movements, tidal scour (erosion produced by tidal action), changes in sea level during periods of glaciation, and turbidity currents (currents of turbid or muddy water moving relative to the surrounding water because of higher density).

Continental Rise. The continental rise is a broad wedge of sediment that has accumulated along parts of the base of the continental slope. It is formed as sediment is swept down the slope

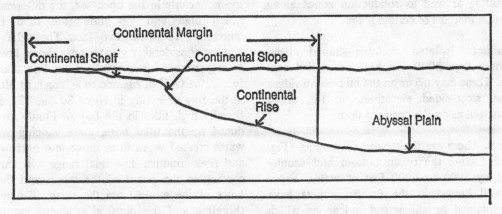

Fig. 98. Cross section of ocean floor showing major elements of topography.

Continental Shelf. The flooded, nearly flat margins of the continents are called the continental shelves (Fig. 98). Sloping gently outward from the shores of the continents, these shelves have an average width of about forty miles and an average depth of about four hundred feet.

Continental Slope. The slope of the sea floor increases rather sharply at the outer edges of the continental shelves (Fig. 98). These slopes descend rather abruptly (some dropping as much as 30,000 feet in a relatively short distance) to the deeper parts of the ocean. In some places the surfaces of the continental slope and continental shelf are marked by deep **submarine canyons.** One of these, the Hudson Submarine Canyon, is about 2400 feet deep, 3 miles wide, and about 125 miles long. The Hudson Submarine Canyon

and is dispersed at its base. Because of the subtle gradients between the continental slope, rise, and abyssal plain, the rise may be difficult to recognize topographically.

Abyssal Plain. That part of the ocean floor extending seaward from the base of the continental slope is called the abyssal plain (Fig. 98). The flattest surfaces on the earth, the abyssal plains are found at depths ranging from 10,000 to 20,000 feet beneath the surface of the sea. They are largely composed of fine sediment and make up about 42 percent of the ocean floor.

The deep ocean floor does not consist exclusively of the flat abyssal plains. In places there are areas of considerable relief, just as there are on the landmasses. Among the more important such features are:

Mid-oceanic Ridges. The ocean basins are dominated by a nearly continuous system of mountain ranges extending for a distance of more than 31,000 miles. This mid-ocean ridge is present in all oceans and nearly bisects the Atlantic and Indian oceans (Fig. 4). The mid-oceanic ridges and their relation to earthquakes, volcanic activity, and plate tectonics were discussed in Chapter 2.

Deep-sea Trenches. Also called ocean deeps, these are long, narrow, deep basins in the deep-sea floor. Many occur at the foot of the continental slope, and although their origin is not fully known, they may be associated with submarine faulting as well as subduction zones along continental margins of certain plates.

Seamounts. Isolated mountain-shaped elevations more than 3000 feet high are called seamounts. These may occur on the mid-ocean ridges (narrow, steep-sided elevations on the ocean floor) as well as on the deep-sea floor.

Guyots. These are flat-topped seamounts (Fig. 99) rising from the ocean bottom and usually covered by 3000 to 6000 feet of water. Especially well known in the Pacific, guyots have been explained as submerged volcanoes which have been truncated by wave action.

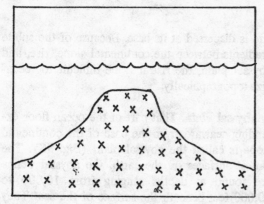

Fig. 99. A guyot. Such structures are typically covered by 3000 to 6000 feet of water.

MOVEMENTS OF THE SEA

Anyone who has witnessed the ceaseless, restless motion of the sea can easily understand its effectiveness as a geologic agent. Tides, currents, and waves, the principal types of movements of ocean water, are continually at work producing changes in the rocks along the shore.

The causes of the unceasing motion of the sea are varied and complex. Basically, however, they may be attributed to tides, wind, changing density of sea water, and rotation of the earth.

Tides. The periodic rise and fall of the sea (once every twelve hours and twenty-six minutes) produces the tides. Tides cause the ocean waters to rise gradually for about six hours and thirteen minutes and to recede slowly for an equal period of time. The effect of the tides is not too noticeable in the open sea, the difference between high and low tide (the **tidal range**) amounting to about two feet. The tidal range may be considerably greater near shore, however. It may range, for example, from less than two feet in the Gulf of Mexico to as much as fifty feet in the Bay of Fundy in Nova Scotia. The exceptionally high tides in the Bay of Fundy are produced by the **tidal bore,** an advancing wall of water created when tides move into narrow bays and river mouths. The tidal range will vary according to the phase of the moon and the distance of the moon from the earth. The type of shoreline and the physical configuration of the ocean floor will also affect the tidal range.

Most tides are caused by the gravitational pull of the moon on the waters of the earth; the gravitational force exerted by the sun may also raise tides. In addition, the tidal effects of both the sun and the moon may be aided by centrifugal force developed by the rotation of the earth.

Currents. The oceans have localized movements of masses of seawater called ocean currents. These may be caused by prevailing winds, tides, variations in salinity of the water, rotation of the earth, and concentrations of turbid or muddy water. Changes in water density due to temperature changes will also cause currents. The Gulf Stream, which runs along the Atlantic Coast, is a current of this type.

In addition to the ocean currents, there are several types of shore currents which are restricted to coastal regions. These include: **under-tow,** a stream of water which returns seaward along the bottom underneath the incoming waves; **rip currents** (also caused by water returning to the ocean), swift currents running close to and parallel to the shoreline; and **longshore currents,** caused by waves which strike the shore at an oblique angle, creating currents that move parallel to the shoreline. Longshore currents, as will be noted later, are of considerable importance in shaping shorelines.

Waves. Waves are produced by the friction of wind on open water. Essentially an up-and-down movement of the water, wave motion also moves the surface water in the direction that the wind is blowing. Breakers are formed when the wave comes into shallow water near the shore. The lower part of the wave is retarded by the ocean bottom, and the top, having greater momentum, is hurled forward causing the wave to break.

Varying greatly in size, waves may be slight ripples or giant storm waves twenty-five to fifty feet in height. The latter may do great damage to coastal property as they race across coastal lowlands driven by winds of gale or hurricane velocity. Giant waves may also be produced as a result of earthquakes on the ocean floor. These waves, called **tsunamis,** are the largest and most destructive of all ocean waves. They are discussed in some detail in Chapter 15.

GEOLOGIC WORK OF THE SEA

The geologic work of the sea, like that of previously discussed geologic agents, consists of erosion, transportation, and deposition. The sea accomplishes its work largely by means of waves and wave-produced currents; their effect on the seacoast may be quite pronounced.

MARINE EROSION

As waves attack the shore they erode by a combination of several processes. How rapidly the shore will be worn away will depend, of course, upon the resistance of the rocks composing it and the intensity of wave action to which it is subjected.

Processes of Marine Erosion. Wave erosion may be accomplished in a variety of ways. Destruction by hydraulic action occurs as waves beat upon poorly consolidated sediments or loosely jointed rock. The coast also undergoes abrasion as wave- and current-carried rock fragments scour and grind against it. Seacoasts having outcrops of soluble rocks such as limestone may also be affected by solution.

Features Formed by Marine Erosion. The erosional landforms caused by wave erosion are common features of many shorelines. Some of the more typical features of this type are discussed below.

Sea Cliffs. Known also as **wave-cut cliffs,** sea cliffs (Fig. 100) are formed by wave erosion of the underlying rock followed by the caving-in of the overhanging rocks. Such cliffs are essentially vertical and are common at certain localities along the New England and Pacific coasts of North America.

Wave-cut Bench. Extending seaward from the base of most sea cliffs are relatively flat platforms called wave-cut benches or **wave-cut terraces** (Fig. 100).

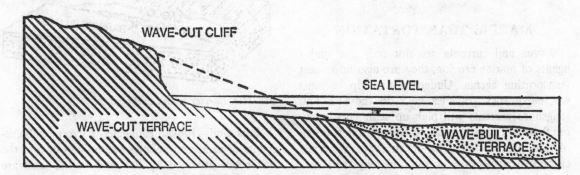

Fig. 100. Features formed by marine erosion and deposition.

Headlands or Promontories. Finger-like projections of resistant rock extending out into the water are known as headlands or promontories (Fig. 101). Indentations between headlands are termed **coves.**

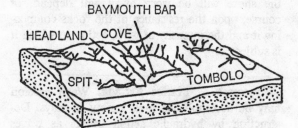

Fig. 101. Shoreline features caused by marine erosion and deposition.

Sea Caves, Sea Arches, and Stacks. Continued wave action on a sea cliff may hollow out cavities which will form sea caves (Fig. 102). Waves may cut completely through a headland to form a sea arch; should the roof of the arch collapse the rock left separated from the headland is called a stack (Fig. 102).

Fig. 102. Coastal figures developed by marine erosion.

> *a—Sea cave developed in wave-cut cliff*
> *b—Stack*

MARINE TRANSPORTATION

Waves and currents are not only the major agents of marine erosion, they are also important transporting agents. Undertow and rip currents will carry rock particles back to the sea, and longshore currents will pick up sediments, moving them out from shore into deeper water. Some of this material is carried in solution. Materials carried in suspension or solution may drift seaward for great distances and eventually be depos-

ited far from shore. While being carried by waves and currents, sediments undergo additional erosion, becoming rounded and reduced in size.

MARINE DEPOSITION

When waves or currents suffer reduced velocity they will deposit their load. In addition, some rock particles will be thrown up on the shore by the breaking waves. Most of the sediments thus deposited consist of rock fragments derived from the mechanical weathering of the continents, and they differ considerably from terrestrial or continental deposits.

Features Formed by Marine Deposition. Although erosion may be taking place along one part of the seacoast, marine sediments are being deposited elsewhere. These depositional features, like those formed by marine erosion, are characteristic of most shorelines.

Beaches. Beaches are coastal deposits of debris which lie above the low-tide limit in the shore zone. They are transitory features, and although most beaches are sandy, they may also consist of pebbles, cobbles, shells, mud, or a combination of these materials.

Barrier Islands. Long narrow accumulations of sand lying parallel to the shore and separated from the shore by a shallow lagoon are called barrier islands. Known also as **barrier beaches,** these depositional features are common along much of the Atlantic Coast from New Jersey to Miami (Fig. 103).

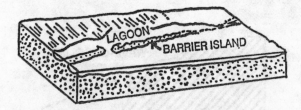

Fig. 103. Barrier island and lagoon.

Spits and Hooks. Elongate, narrow embankments of sand and pebbles extending out into the water but attached by one end to the land are called spits (Fig. 103). When the free end of a spit curves landward a hook or recurved spit is formed.

Tombolos. A tombolo is a bar of sand or gravel connecting an island with the mainland or another island. Islands associated with tombolos are known as **tied islands.** The Rock of Gibraltar is a tied island, connected to the Spanish coast by means of a tombolo. (Some geologists consider a tombolo to consist of both the island and the connecting bar rather than just the bar as defined above.)

Wave-built Terraces. Sediments deposited in deep water beyond a wave-cut terrace may form deposits referred to as wave-built terraces (Fig. 100).

LIFE IN THE OCEAN

The sea abounds with countless plants and animals of many types. These organisms float, swim, or crawl about, or burrow in the floor of the ocean. Others, such as certain calcium-secreting plants and corals, build great calcareous masses called **reefs.**

Most marine life exists in the shallow marginal or **epicontinental** seas that border the continents; many of our fossiliferous rock formations were deposited in similar seas of prehistoric time.

CORAL REEFS

Coral reefs, previously mentioned as products of ocean organisms, are ridges of calcareous rock at or near the surface of the sea. They consist, in part, of great accumulations of the lime skeletons of reef-building corals. These small animals, found only in the sea, generally live in colonies in warm (no colder than 68° F.), clear water at depths of less than 150 feet. Corals of this type extract dissolved calcium carbonate from the seawater and use this material to build their shells. Other calcium-secreting plants and animals also live in the reefs. When these organisms die, their remains are added to the calcareous mass and new corals grow on top of them. Thus, the reef continues to grow for long periods of time.

The largest known coral reef, the Great Bar-

rier Reef off the east coast of Queensland, Australia, extends for a distance of more than 1200 miles and varies from ten to ninety miles in width. It is separated from the mainland by a wide lagoon, the Inland Water Way, which is an important route of commerce. Fossil coral reefs have been found in many parts of the world in rocks of various ages.

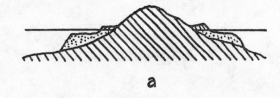

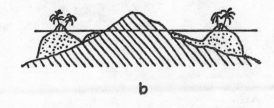

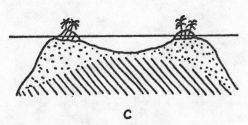

Fig. 104. Sequence of coral reef formation according to Subsidence Hypothesis of Darwin.
a–Fringing reef   b–Barrier reef   c–Atoll

Geologists and oceanographers have long speculated as to how the various types of coral reefs and coral islands have been formed. One of the more commonly accepted theories was proposed by Charles Darwin in 1842. According to his **Subsidence Hypothesis,** there are three stages of coral reef formation (see Fig. 104). At first, a fringing reef is formed as corals grow in shallow water near the shore of an island. With the passage of time the island gradually subsides while the corals continue to grow on top of the reef. Gradually the reef enlarges; it becomes separated from the shrinking island by a lagoon, and a barrier reef is created. The final stage, in Darwin's hypothesis, results in an **atoll,** a roughly circular reef surrounding a lagoon which covers the now-submerged island.

A later idea, the **Glacial-Control Hypothesis,** proposed in 1910 by Professor R. A. Daly of Harvard, suggests that barrier reefs and atolls were formed on truncated volcanic islands as a result of changes in sea level during the Ice Age. Unfortunately, neither of these hypotheses satisfactorily explains all coral reef structures. It has been suggested, therefore, that coral reefs may be formed as a result of both subsidence and glacial-control.

CHAPTER 14

LAKES AND SWAMPS

Lakes and swamps are found in many parts of the world and many of them are of great importance to human welfare.

LAKES

A lake may be defined as a body of standing water occupying a depression in the land. Varying greatly in size, lakes may range from less than an acre to many thousands of square miles in area. They also vary greatly in depth; some lakes are only a few feet deep and may dry up during periods of drought, while others are many thousands of feet deep. The largest known lake is the Caspian Sea with an area of about 169,000 square miles. (The term "sea" is misused in this sense, for such bodies of water as the Dead Sea and Salton Sea are actually saline lakes.) The world's deepest lake, Lake Baikal in eastern Siberia, has a depth of more than 5400 feet.

Lakes are to be found at all altitudes. Lake Titicaca, located between Chile and Peru, is 12,500 feet above sea level. At the other extreme, the Dead Sea in Israel and Jordan is almost 1300 feet below sea level.

Some lakes, especially the larger ones, have considerable effect on the people who live near them. They may, for example, supply water for drinking and industrial purposes, regulate the temperature of the adjoining lands, provide recreational areas, and be used as transportation routes. Because of this it is not uncommon to find large cities and industrial areas built up around many of our larger lakes.

ORIGIN OF LAKE BASINS

Lake basins may be formed in a variety of ways and by a number of different geologic processes. The more important of these are discussed below.

Crustal Movements. Some basins have been formed as a result of warping, folding, or faulting of the strata. For example, Lake Superior occupies a basin that was originally formed by structural deformation and later enlarged by glacial action. **Rift valley lakes** are created when great fault blocks (see Chapter 7) sink down between high steep walls. Usually quite deep, lakes of this type often form a chain along the floor of the valley. Such a chain exists in the Great Rift Valley that extends from the Dead Sea to Lakes Nyassa and Tanganyika in eastern Africa.

Lakes are sometimes formed as a result of rock displacement which accompanies earthquakes; a local sinking of the ground may produce depressions suitable for lake formation. Reelfoot Lake in northwestern Tennessee was formed in this way after the New Madrid earthquake of 1811–12.

Volcanic Activity. The effects of volcanism may form lakes of two different types. Lava flows may dam up part of a stream valley, causing the stream to back up and form a lake. Snag Lake in Lassen Volcanic National Park has been formed in this manner. In addition, lakes may form in the craters or calderas of extinct volcanoes. The best-known lake of this type is Crater Lake in the Cascade Mountains of southwestern Oregon. The lake, which occupies a caldera, is about six miles wide, 2000 feet deep, and is surrounded by cliffs 500 to 2000 feet high. Because of its great natural beauty and geologic interest, Crater Lake has been set aside as a National Park.

Glaciation. Large numbers of lakes have been formed by glacial action. Such lakes may form in surface depressions scooped out by glacial erosion, or in basins developed behind natural dams of ice-deposited material.

Lakes formed at the head of glacial valleys are called **tarns** (see Chapter 11) and these are fairly common in certain mountainous regions. In other areas glaciers have scoured out depressions which have become filled with water to form lakes. The Finger Lakes of New York owe their origin to glacial scour as do many of the lakes of Minnesota, Maine, and Canada. The basins of the Great Lakes of North America are also believed to be of glacial origin.

Mass Movements or Gravity. Lakes are sometimes created when earth debris from a landslide plunges down into a stream valley, blocking the course of the stream. The natural dam formed in this manner may cause the water to back up, creating a natural lake. An example of this type of lake is Lake San Cristobal of southwestern Colorado. The lake was formed behind a large mudflow known as Slumgullion Flow.

Streams. Lake basins can also result from the erosional and depositional work of streams. They may develop when cut-off meanders form oxbow lakes (see Chapter 9), such as those along the flood plain of the Mississippi River. They may also develop on deltas—Lake Pontchartrain on the Mississippi delta is a good example.

Ground Water. We have already learned that ground water may form sinkholes and caverns in areas underlain by soluble rocks such as limestone and dolomite. If the sinkholes become choked with debris they may become filled with water, thus forming a lake. There are numerous lakes of this type in certain parts of Florida, Tennessee, Kentucky, and Indiana.

Waves and Currents. Lakes are not uncommon along coastal plains or near certain lake and ocean shorelines. These are generally formed when waves and currents deposit sand bars across the mouth of a bay or lagoon. Originally salty or brackish, the water of these shoreline lakes may eventually be replaced by fresh water.

Other Causes. Humans have built many artificial lakes or reservoirs by building dams across the path of streams. One of the largest of these, Lake Mead above Hoover Dam on the Colorado River, is more than 125 miles long. In addition, beavers' dams across streams, swamp vegetation, and log jams have been known to form lakes.

A few lakes have developed in craters created by meteorites. Water-filled craters of this type are known in northern Quebec and northern Siberia.

TYPES OF LAKES

Lakes are generally classified as **freshwater** or **saline**, depending upon the composition of their waters.

Freshwater Lakes. Lakes that have outlets are called freshwater lakes. The outlet is normally a surface stream, but some water may escape by seepage. The water in a freshwater lake is derived from rain, melting snow, ground water, and river water. The composition of the water in the lake will depend largely upon the composition of the rocks over or through which the water has passed.

Although some of the dissolved material brought in by streams may be deposited in the lake, most of it leaves by way of the outlet. This, plus the addition of rain and snow, tends to keep the lake water fresh.

Most of the earth's lakes are of the freshwater type. The largest of these, Lake Superior, has an area of 31,820 square miles.

Saline or Salt Lakes. Lakes that have no outlet will become saline or salt lakes. These are normally developed in dry climates where lakes lose their water by evaporation. As the water evaporates, the mineral salts become highly concentrated and may eventually be deposited on the lake bottom by precipitation. As noted above, the mineral composition of the water is determined by the type of rock with which the waters have been in contact. Thus, the type of salt present will differ according to the type of rock in and around the lake basin.

Some salt lakes, like the Caspian Sea, have been formed when portions of the sea became blocked off and isolated. In these cases, the waters were, of course, originally salty. Others, for example Great Salt Lake in Utah, started as freshwater bodies. This famous lake is but a small remnant of Lake Bonneville, a great freshwater lake which once covered about 30 percent of Utah. Increasing aridity in the area hastened evaporation of Lake Bonneville's waters with a resulting concentration of sodium chloride (common salt). Today the water of Great Salt Lake is almost seven times saltier than that of the Atlantic Ocean!

Alkaline Lakes. These are characterized by large amounts of sodium carbonate or potassium. The alkaline materials are commonly derived from high-sodium-content igneous rocks such as granite. Mono Lake in east central California is an example of an alkaline lake.

Playa Lakes. Usually developed in the lowest part of a desert basin, playa lakes are shallow temporary lakes formed after heavy rains. Playas disappear during dry periods, leaving behind a deposit of silt or clay that may be covered with salts. These salt-covered dry lake beds are called **alkali flats** or **salinas.** Present in arid and semiarid regions in many parts of the world, good examples of playas may be seen in Death Valley, California.

DESTRUCTION OF LAKES

Lakes are relatively temporary features, and the same geologic processes that create lakes may also bring about their destruction. Some lakes are destroyed because their basins become filled with sediments or because the adjacent high land is removed by erosion. Lakes will also disappear when they lose their water through excessive evaporation, seepage from below, or diversion of the streams that flow into them.

Some lakes become filled with organic material. Vegetation such as mosses, ferns, and swamp grass which grow along the borders of the lake may gradually spread toward the center. The remains of animals may also be mixed with the plant material, and this organic debris may ultimately turn the lake into a **swamp.**

In addition, landslides, clay deposited by melting glacial ice, and wind-blown sand and volcanic ash may also contribute to the destruction of lakes.

SWAMPS

Depressions that are partially or completely filled with living and decomposed plant materials, sediments, and water are called swamps. Many swamps have been formed from the lake-filling processes described above; others are simply areas of low, soft, boggy ground which do not have proper surface drainage.

Known also as **bogs,** swamps commonly occur on the flood plains of old rivers, such as the Mississippi. They are also found on coastal plains, where they are commonly referred to as **marshes** or **tidal marshes.** Many of these occur on the Gulf and Atlantic coasts of the United States; some, like the Everglades in Florida, cover many hundreds of square miles.

Certain swamps are characterized by great thicknesses of partially carbonized plant material called peat. The material dug from these peat bogs has a high carbon content and when dry can be used as fuel. The process by which the swamp vegetation is converted into peat is called carbonization (see Chapter 17), and the development of peat is the first step in the formation of coal. (Coal formation is discussed in Chapter 17.)

Swamps also occur in glaciated regions. Here streams have been blocked by glacial deposits which have created both lakes and swamps (as in northeastern Canada and the Great Lakes region of the United States).

In areas where the ground is permanently frozen at shallow depths, swamps may develop on the upper surface during times of thaw. This spongy, waterlogged upper surface is known as the **tundra** and is well developed in the arctic regions of North America, Europe, and Asia.

CHAPTER 15

EARTHQUAKES AND THE INTERIOR OF THE EARTH

Earthquakes, natural vibrations within the earth's crust, provide indisputable evidence that crustal movements are still taking place today. Some of these earth tremors are quite violent and are responsible for large-scale death and destruction. Most, however, are too small to be felt by man and must be detected by means of delicate recording instruments called **seismographs** (see Fig. 107).

CAUSES OF EARTHQUAKES

Although **seismology** (the study of earthquakes) has provided us with much information about earthquakes, their ultimate cause is not known with certainty. It is known, however, that man has speculated about their origin for centuries. The ancients explained earthquakes as evidence of God's displeasure with the world, or the restlessness of some animal upon whose back the earth was resting.

We do know that earth tremblings are initiated by a sudden jar or shock and that most such shocks appear to be associated with faulting. The sudden fracture and displacement of the rocks along the fault plane generates a wavelike motion in the rocks. One way to explain how these ruptured rocks react is provided by the **elastic rebound theory.** According to this theory, subsurface rock masses subjected to prolonged pressures from different directions will slowly bend and change shape. Continued pressures set up strains so great that the rocks will eventually break and suddenly snap back into their original unstrained state. It is the elastic rebound (snap-

ping back) that generates the seismic (earthquake) waves (Fig. 105).

Unfortunately, the elastic rebound theory does not completely explain the cause of all earthquakes. Recent research suggests that the pressure holding the fault blocks together is actually stronger than the rock itself. Consequently, the rock tends to fracture elsewhere rather than slip along the fault. In addition, there is evidence that in some places fault movement takes place **after** earthquakes rather than before. Despite the above objections, faults do exist and movement occurs along them from time to time. Thus, many investigators believe that elastic rebound is useful in explaining shallow earthquakes and, with some modifications, certain deeper earthquakes as well.

More recently, the cause of earthquakes has been explained by the motion of crustal plates and sea-floor spreading. It is known that shallow quakes occur in places where plates are colliding or moving apart. Intermediate and deep earthquakes appear to be limited to areas where individual plates are colliding (see Chapter 2). For example, California's San Andreas fault marks the place where two huge crustal blocks are sliding past each other. Many shallow earthquakes occur along the San Andreas fault and are caused by the relative motions of the Pacific and North American plates.

Earthquakes caused in the manner described above are called **tectonic** earthquakes and are the largest and most destructive of all. Earthquake waves may also be generated by volcanic activity. These may be caused by violent explosions (see

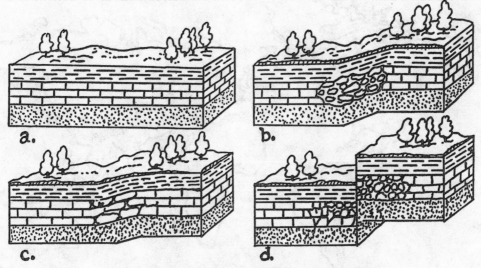

Fig. 105. A normal section of rocks (a) may be subjected to such great stress (b and c) that it may
eventually break (d), releasing energy that causes an
earthquake.

Chapter 4) or by sudden movements of molten rock below the surface. Minor causes of earth tremors include rapid mass movements such as landslides or avalanches, and the sudden collapse of caverns.

DISTRIBUTION OF EARTHQUAKES

Although earthquakes may occur at any place over the entire earth, most of them originate in areas of crustal unrest and are associated with mountain-building movements. Earthquakes, like volcanoes, occur in rather well-defined seismic belts (Fig. 106). About 80 percent of the world's earthquakes originate in the Circum-Pacific belt—a belt of young mountain ranges and chains of volcanic mountains. This belt extends from Chile along the western borders of South and North America, northward to the Aleutians, Alaska, Japan, the Philippines, Indonesia, New Zealand, and certain Pacific islands. The second major seismic belt, the Mediterranean and Trans-Asiatic belt, extends from the Caribbean area through the Himalayas and Alps and includes Spain, Italy, Greece, and northern India. Approximately 15 percent of the earth's seismic energy is released in the Mediter-

ranean and Trans-Asiatic zone; the remaining 5 percent is released in other parts of the world.

Most of the earthquakes occurring in the United States are located in the Pacific Coast region. The majority of these occur in California and are associated with movements along the San Andreas fault—a great rift which extends for hundreds of miles along the western border of California. Montana, Utah, and Nevada are also commonly shaken by earthquakes.

Not all American earthquakes are confined to the Pacific Coast. New England, Chicago, and New York have experienced earthquakes of varying intensities. It is significant, however, that of the several disastrous earthquakes in the history of the United States only two have occurred in regions other than the Pacific Coast. These were the New Madrid, Missouri, quakes of 1811–12, and the Charleston, South Carolina, earthquake of 1886.

EFFECTS OF EARTHQUAKES

The destructive effects of earthquakes are familiar to almost everyone: shattered buildings, displaced roads and railways, collapsed bridges, great cracks in the ground, and changes in sea

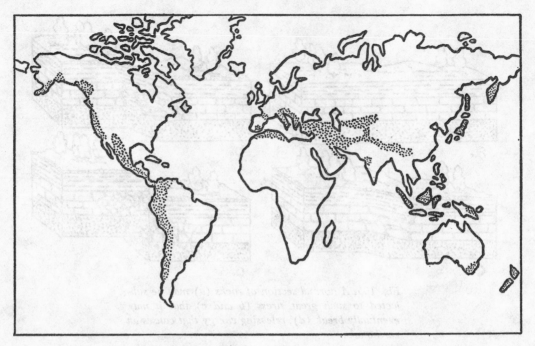

Fig. 106. Shaded areas designate the world's major seismic belts.

level. These are but a few of the physical changes that may be brought about by earthquakes. In some earthquake-stricken cities there has been more damage from fire than from seismic waves. Disrupted gas and electrical lines and overturned stoves may start numerous fires. Attempts to extinguish such fires are usually handicapped by loss of fire-fighting equipment and broken water mains and communication lines.

The loss of life accompanying a major earthquake may be staggering. For example, the great earthquake that occurred in north central China in 1556 is said to have killed about 830,000 people. Because they normally occur rapidly and unexpectedly, there is little time for precautionary measures. The death toll may also be raised by complicating factors such as disease, flood, fire, and famine.

In addition to the loss of life and property, an earthquake will usually produce numerous geologic changes in an area. These include landslides, avalanches and mudflows, disruption of ground water circulation, and sunken and fissured ground.

Earthquakes that occur beneath the ocean often generate great waves of water called **tsunamis** or **seismic sea waves**. These waves, which

have been known to be as much as 200 feet high and travel at speeds of up to 500 miles per hour, are capable of producing tremendous destruction. One such wave, associated with the great Lisbon, Portugal, quake of 1755, attained an estimated height of fifty feet and washed inland for more than one-half mile. Another, occurring north of Tokyo along the Pacific coast of Japan in 1896, reached heights of up to 100 feet and was responsible for the deaths of more than 27,000 persons.

DETECTING AND RECORDING EARTHQUAKES

Earthquake waves are detected and recorded by means of a **seismograph** (Fig. 107). Basically, the seismograph consists of a spring-suspended weight or pendulum, free to swing in the direction of the waves to be recorded, and a recording device operated by clockwork. The pendulum is attached to a frame which is embedded in bedrock. Because of its inertia the free-swinging pendulum is not affected by vibrations in the bedrock but the rest of the instrument, which is rigidly attached, will be moved by such vibrations. A pen attached to the pendulum re-

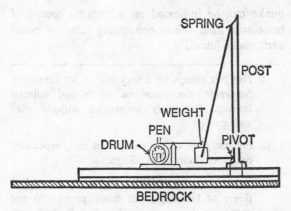

Fig. 107. Seismograph, an instrument for recording earth tremors.

cords the vibrations on a clock-operated revolving drum which contains the recording paper. (Some seismographs record on photographic paper which is exposed by means of a spot of light reflected from a mirror.) The resulting records, called **seismograms,** show both the duration and severity of the shock. When the crust is at rest the record will appear as a straight line; earthquake waves will activate the pendulum, producing a wavy line (Fig. 108).

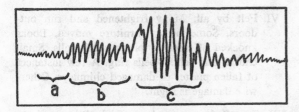

Fig. 108. Seismogram, a recording made by a seismograph.

> *a—Primary or P waves*
> *b—Secondary or S waves*
> *c—Long or L waves*

LOCATING EARTHQUAKES

If satisfactory seismograms have been obtained during an earthquake, these can be used to ascertain where the disturbance occurred. The seismologist wishes to know, for example, the **focus** of the earthquake (the point within the earth from which the shocks originated) and the location of the **epicenter,** the point on the earth's surface directly above the focus. He determines this by making a comparative study of the behavior of the various types of earthquake waves.

When an earthquake occurs, seismic waves spread out in all directions from the focus, decreasing in intensity with distance. These waves, which vary greatly in amplitude (size) and velocity (speed), are of three basic types. Primary waves, also called **P waves,** are compressional waves that travel through the earth at speeds of from 3.4 to 8.6 miles per second. P waves move faster at depth and are the first to be detected by the seismograph. **S waves,** or secondary waves, travel through the earth's interior at speeds of from 2.2 to 4.5 miles per second. These, the second set of waves to arrive at the seismograph station, will not pass through gases or liquids. Long waves, or **L waves,** are complex waves of considerable amplitude which travel near the earth's surface. They originate at the epicenter and are generated from energy produced by P and S waves. L waves travel relatively slowly (about 2.2 miles per second), are the last to be recorded, and cause most of the earthquake damage.

A study of the relative arrival times of the various types of waves at a single station can be used to determine the distance to the epicenter. If records from at least three rather widely separated seismograph stations are available, the seismologist can determine the exact location of the epicenter. To do this, circles are drawn for three stations with the station as the center of the circle. The point at which the three circles intersect is the epicenter (Fig. 109).

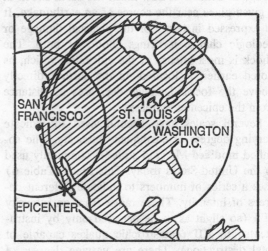

Fig. 109. Locating epicenter of earthquake by using seismograph records from different seismograph stations.

SIZE OF EARTHQUAKES

The size of an earthquake is directly related to the amount of energy released at the focus. This, in turn, is related to the amount of damage caused by the quake. These two parameters—energy released and damage caused—are measured in terms of **magnitude** and **intensity**, respectively.

Magnitude. Devised by the American seismologist Charles F. Richter, the **Richter scale** measures the total amount of energy released by an earthquake as recorded by seismographs. The scale is both objective and quantitative and measures a quake independently of its effects on people and civilization.

The Richter scale uses numbers from 1 on up to describe earthquake magnitude. Each number indicates an earthquake ten times stronger than the next lower number. An earthquake with a magnitude of 5 is ten times stronger than an earthquake with magnitude 4. An earthquake with magnitude 7 or higher is considered a major quake.

The Richter scale is an open-ended scale. That is, there is no fixed upper limit of magnitude. Nobody knows how strong an earthquake might be in the future. The strongest earthquake on record had a magnitude of 9.5 on the revised Richter scale.

Intensity. The intensity of an earthquake is a rough indication of how much the earth shook at a given place near the source of an earthquake. It is expressed in terms of the physical damage or geologic change it brings about, or both. The shock is most intense at the epicenter, which, as noted earlier, is located on the surface directly above the focus. Damage decreases as distance from the epicenter increases.

Several scales have been devised to indicate varying degrees of earthquake intensity. The so-called **modified Mercalli scale,** is commonly used in the United States today. This scale (Table 6) uses a series of numbers to indicate different degrees of intensity. These range from an intensity of I (so slight as to be detected only by instruments) to XII (catastrophic quakes capable of total destruction). There are varying degrees of destruction between these two extremes. When the epicenter is known, the intensity of an earthquake can be indicated on a map by means of **isoseismal lines**—lines connecting areas of equal earthquake intensity.

I. Not felt except by a very few under especially favorable circumstances. Birds and animals uneasy. Delicately suspended objects may swing.

II. Felt only by a few persons at rest, especially on upper floors of buildings.

III. Felt noticeably indoors, especially on upper floors of buildings, but many people do not recognize it as an earthquake. Parked cars may rock slightly. Vibrations like the passing of light trucks. Duration of shaking can be estimated.

IV. Felt indoors by many, outdoors by few. If at night, some awakened. Dishes, windows, doors disturbed. Walls creak. Sensation like the passing of heavy trucks. Parked cars rock noticeably.

V. Felt by nearly everyone. Some dishes, windows, etc., broken. A few instances of cracked plaster. Unstable objects overturned. Disturbances of trees, poles, and other tall objects sometimes noticed. Pendulum clocks may stop.

VI. Felt by all. Many frightened and run outdoors. Some heavy furniture moved. Books knocked off shelves, pictures off walls. Small church and school bells ring. A few instances of fallen plaster or damaged chimneys. Otherwise damage is slight.

VII. Everybody runs outdoors. Difficult to stand up. Negligible damage in buildings of good design and construction; slight to moderate in well-built ordinary structures; considerable in poorly built or badly designed structures; some chimneys broken. Noticed by persons driving cars.

VIII. Damage slight in specially designed structures; partial collapse in ordinary buildings; great damage to poorly built structures. Panel walls thrown out of frame structures. Chimneys, factory stacks, columns, monuments, and walls fall. Heavy furniture overturned. Small amounts of sand and mud ejected from cracks in the ground. Changes in well water.

IX. Damage considerable in specially designed structures; well-designed frame structures thrown out of plumb; partial collapse of substantial buildings. Buildings shifted off foundations, ground cracked. Serious damage to reservoirs and underground pipes. General panic.

X. Some well-built wooden structures destroyed; most masonry and frame structures destroyed. Ground badly cracked. Rails bent slightly. Considerable landslides from river banks and steep slopes. Shifted sand and mud. Water splashed over banks.

XI. Few masonry structures remain standing. Bridges destroyed. Broad fissures in ground. Underground pipelines out of service. Earth slumps and land slips in soft ground. Rails bent severely.

XII. Damage total. Waves seen on ground surfaces. Lines of sight and level distorted. Objects thrown upward into the air.

TABLE 6. The modified Mercalli scale of earthquake intensity.

EARTHQUAKE PREDICTION

When and where will the next earthquake strike? How large will it be? The answers to such questions could be vital to people living in "earthquake country." But can they be answered? A few earthquakes, especially in the People's Republic of China, have been predicted with some degree of accuracy. But most such forecasts have proved to be relatively unreliable.

Recent laboratory studies suggest that there may be changes in rock behavior prior to an earthquake. For example, rocks subjected to deforming stresses may swell and increase in volume before they finally rupture. This dilatancy is caused by microscopic fractures and tiny voids that open in the rock prior to the quake. It is believed that changes in ground level, emission of radon (a radioactive gas), and changes in the electrical conductivity of the rocks are clues to dilatancy.

Pre-earthquake changes in rock behavior can also affect the velocity of seismic waves. In some places observers have noticed that the strained rock in a fault zone was deformed in such a way that seismic waves slowed down as they passed through the zone. Other earthquake precursors include unexpected tilting of surface rocks, changes in magnetic and electrical fields, small

local quakes, and fluctuations in subsurface fluid pressure.

Attention is also being directed to the way in which animals behave prior to an earthquake. Dogs, chickens, cattle, catfish, and other animals have been known to behave strangely immediately before certain quakes. It is possible that these creatures can sense minute earth changes that humans are unable to detect.

Although progress is being made by Soviet, Japanese, Chinese, and American seismologists, the results of their studies are generally inconclusive at this time. Hence, the accurate forecasting of earthquakes is still a goal for the future.

SOME FAMOUS EARTHQUAKES

History contains numerous accounts of earthquakes, some of which go back before the birth of Christ. A few of these are briefly described below.

Lisbon, Portugal (1755). There occurred in Lisbon, on November 1, 1755, what was perhaps the strongest earthquake in recorded history. Although the initial seismic shock lasted for only six or seven minutes, it destroyed about one-half of the city and was felt over an area of about 1,250,000 square miles. The first tremor was followed by two other severe shocks; one twenty minutes after the first, and another some two hours later. The giant seismic sea wave accompanying this quake advanced inland for more than one-half mile, destroying almost everything in its path. Widespread fires added to the great property damage (about $100,000,000) and the death toll has been estimated as high as 60,000 people.

New Madrid, Missouri (1811–12). This series of seismic shocks was felt from the Atlantic Coast to the Rocky Mountains and from Canada to the Gulf of Mexico. The first shock, which occurred in the region of New Madrid, Missouri, at about 2 A.M. on December 16, 1811, was followed by a series of aftershocks which continued for days. Another very severe shock occurred in late January 1812; the third shock, which was the most severe of all, took place in early February. During this three-month period of seismic disturbance as many as 1874 shocks were recorded in Louisville, Kentucky, two hundred miles away. Fortunately, this part of the United States was sparsely settled during the early nineteenth century, so there was little loss of life or property. The region did, however, undergo considerable geologic change which caused landslides, drastically affected the topography, and even changed land boundaries. Areas that were originally swamps were uplifted and drained, other areas sank from three to ten feet to form new swamps and lakes, and the course of the Mississippi River was changed. Reelfoot Lake in northwestern Tennessee was one of the larger lakes thus formed; it is about eighteen miles long and several miles wide.

Charleston, South Carolina (1886). This disturbance, like the New Madrid quakes described above, took place in an area which is generally considered to be stable. During the earthquake, the seismic waves increased in intensity until the ground seemed to rise and fall in visible waves. This earthquake, which did considerable damage and killed twenty-seven persons, was felt over most of the eastern part of the United States.

San Francisco, California (1906). This well-known and severe earthquake occurred in the early morning of April 18, 1906, in San Francisco, California. The earthquake, which lasted only sixty-seven seconds, was caused by horizontal earth movements along the San Andreas fault. During this short space of time about 700 persons were killed and many buildings were wrecked. The great fire that followed the earthquake did hundreds of millions of dollars in damage and destroyed a large part of the city. There were landslides in the mountains, great fissures were opened in the ground, and fences and railroads were offset by as much as twenty feet.

Sagami Bay, Japan (1923). This earthquake, one of the greatest disasters of modern time, resulted in the loss of almost 100,000 lives and billions of dollars in property. Although the quake originated in Sagami Bay, seventy miles from Tokyo and fifty miles from Yokohama, both of these cities were heavily damaged. A huge tsunami generated by the submarine earthquake did extensive damage along the coast, and an outbreak of fires consumed about 70 percent of Tokyo and completely destroyed the city of Yokohama.

Hebgen Lake, Montana (1959). On August 17, 1959, a series of earthquakes struck the Hebgen Lake area on the Montana-Wyoming border in Yellowstone National Park. Much damage was done by landslides which buried an estimated twenty-eight campers in the Madison River canyon. The Madison River slide, estimated to contain between thirty and fifty million cubic yards of rock, formed a natural dam and created a new lake about seven miles below Hebgen Dam.

Chile (1960). In May of 1960, there began a series of earthquakes along the coast of Chile that were among the most destructive to be recorded in this century. So violent were these shocks that most of the man-made buildings in the area were destroyed, trees and telephone poles were snapped like matchsticks, great fissures opened in the ground, and soils flowed like liquid. Further damage was inflicted by seismic sea waves. Ranging from twelve to thirty feet in height, these tsunamis destroyed several Chilean villages and drowned hundreds of people. So great was their force that they crossed the Pacific Ocean at speeds up to 450 miles per hour and destroyed villages in Hawaii and in Japan. The original earthquake of May and subsequent shocks which occurred for a period of several months caused billions of dollars in property damage and killed more than 5000 people.

Alaska (1964). One of the most severe earthquakes ever to affect North America occurred in the vicinity of Anchorage, Alaska, on the afternoon of Good Friday, March 27, 1964. This earthquake did millions of dollars' worth of property damage, and in places the surface rocks were displaced upward more than thirty feet. In addition to damage produced by the earth tremors, the earthquake set off great seismic sea waves in the ocean. These tsunamis wiped out many man-made structures along shorelines in the area. Because the region affected is sparsely populated, only 115 lives were lost in the Good Friday earthquake. This is a relatively small number considering the magnitude or amount of energy released by this earthquake.

San Fernando Valley, California (1971). Southern California was rocked by a very strong earthquake on February 9, 1971. One of the most destructive quakes in the state's 200-year history of earthquakes, it struck the northwestern edge of Los Angeles and directly affected a population of more than 1 million people. The earthquake measured 6.5 on the open-ended Richter scale and resulted in 64 deaths. Propertywise it was the third most devastating quake yet recorded in California—damage exceeded $500 million.

Tangshan, People's Republic of China (1976). Although details were not forthcoming for more than four years, the worst natural disaster of the twentieth century hit the People's Republic of China on July 28, 1976. The epicenter of this killer quake was located in the industrial city of Tangshan, a coal-mining center 94 miles east of Peking. Rated at 8.2 on the Richter scale, this devastating earthquake killed 242,000 of Tangshan's inhabitants and left most of the city in rubble. The majority of casualties was due to the collapse of buildings made of concrete slabs. But unlike many large quakes, there were no tragic aftereffects such as fires or tsunamis.

INTERIOR OF THE EARTH

Although the seismograph's most dramatic work has been in reporting earthquakes, it has also been an important source of information about the interior of the earth. Data obtained from seismograms indicate that the lithosphere (see Chapter 1) may be divided into three zones: the **crust, mantle,** and **core** (Fig. 110).

Crust. The outermost and thinnest layer of the lithosphere is called the crust. The thickness of the crust varies greatly between the ocean basins (as little as four miles in places) and continents (possibly twenty to thirty miles thick under certain mountains). The specific gravity of the crust ranges from 2.5 to 3.4. Crustal rocks vary not only in thickness and density but in composition. Those beneath the ocean basins are heavier than those which underlie the continents. They have

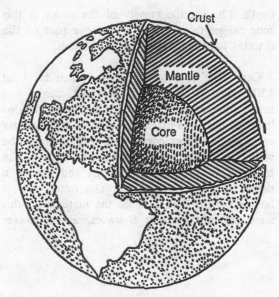

Fig. 110. Diagrammatic cross section showing three major zones of the earth.

been called **sima** because they are rich in iron, silicon, and magnesium (**si** for silicon, **ma** for magnesium). The rocks are primarily of the basaltic type.

The material comprising the continental crust appears to occur in two rather distinct layers. The upper layer is essentially granitic in nature. Because these rocks contain a high percentage of silicon and aluminum, they are often referred to as **sial.** Evidence derived from the velocities of S and P waves suggests that this sialic layer is from ten to fifteen miles thick. The lower layer, also about ten to fifteen miles thick, appears to be composed of simatic rocks similar to those underlying the ocean basins.

The base of the crust is marked by a rather clearly defined break called the **Mohorovicic discontinuity** or the **moho.** This sharp boundary, first noted in 1909 by Andrija Mohorovicic, a Yugoslav seismologist, lies twenty to thirty miles beneath the surface. Here the travel speeds of S and P waves are somewhat accelerated, implying a change in density in the rocks below the moho.

Mantle. Beneath the Mohorovicic discontinuity there is an eighteen-hundred-mile thick intermediate zone called the mantle. The velocities of S and P waves increase gradually upon entering this zone; their behavior suggests that the mantle is essentially solid and increases in density with depth. The specific gravity of the rocks in this zone ranges from 3.5 (in the upper part of the mantle) to as much as 8.0 at the bottom.

Core. The core of the earth, which is about 4300 miles in diameter, is very hot, dense, and under tremendous pressure. It has been divided into two parts: an exterior, probably liquid, **outer core,** and an **inner core** which is believed to be solid. The outer core begins at the base of the mantle (about 1800 miles down) and reaches a depth of about 3160 miles. The outer core is believed to be fluid because the material in this zone will not transmit S waves, and P waves travel at reduced velocity. The outer core is believed to be about 1300 miles thick; the materials composing this zone have specific gravities of 12.0 or more.

The inner core, with a diameter of approximately 1700 miles, is believed to be solid. This is suggested by the fact that there is an abrupt increase in the speed of P waves deep within the core. It has also been suggested that the inner core may be composed largely of nickel and iron. These rocks are presumed to be quite heavy; some may have a specific gravity of more than 17.

CHAPTER 16

PLAINS, PLATEAUS, AND MOUNTAINS

In Chapter 1 we learned that the surface of the earth is very irregular. The earth's major relief features, the continents and ocean basins, are said to be relief features, or landforms, of the **first order.** These have been discussed in earlier chapters. We shall now direct our attention to relief features of the **second order:** plains, plateaus, and mountains.

PLAINS

Plains, like plateaus (which are discussed below), are underlain by flat-lying, layered rocks. Plains and plateaus differ, however, in their relative elevation above sea level and in the amount of relief present. Most, but not all, plains are relatively near sea level; their relief is seldom more than a few hundred feet.

There are several different types of plains. They are usually classified according to the origin of the rock materials which form them.

Marine or Coastal Plains. Interior marine plains, such as the Interior Plains of the upper Mississippi River Valley, have been created by uplift with little or no folding or warping. Coastal plains, such as the Atlantic Coastal Plain, have been formed as a result of emergence of shallow sea floors.

Lake Plains. Known also as **lacustrine** plains, lake plains have been formed by the emergence of a lake floor. Exposure of a lake floor may come about as a result of evaporation, uplift, or, more commonly, drainage. The largest plain of

this type in North America represents the bottom of Lake Agassiz. This large lake, which was present during the last great ice age (see Chapter 22) covers more than 100,000 square miles of North Dakota, Minnesota, and the Canadian provinces of Manitoba and Saskatchewan.

Alluvial Plains. River plains, or alluvial plains, may be formed as flood plains in river valleys; delta plains, at the mouths of rivers; or piedmont alluvial plains—a series of alluvial fans (see Chapter 9) formed at the foot of mountains. (Alluvial means "composed of mud, sand, or other deposits.")

Glacial Plains. Glaciers may produce plains in two different ways. In some areas, the surface of the underlying horizontal rocks has been leveled by glacial erosion. In other places, outwash plains (see Chapter 11) are deposited in front of glaciers.

Lava Plains. Plains formed by widely spreading lava flows from quiet volcanoes, or from great fissure flows, are called lava plains. Good examples of this type of plain are found in Iceland and Hawaii.

PLATEAUS

Plateaus are large, essentially level areas of considerable elevation which are underlain by horizontal rock strata. Unlike plains, plateaus are regions of high relief; their surfaces are normally trenched with canyons and gorges. Most plateaus are more than 2000 feet above sea level; some, for example, the Colorado Plateau, are more than a mile above sea level.

Fault Plateaus. In some areas, former plains have been subjected to continuous vertical faulting, which has raised them well above sea level. The fault plateaus thus formed consist of a series of high, nearly horizontal fault blocks. The Colorado Plateau of the southwestern United States was formed primarily by faulting.

Warped Plateaus. Some plateaus have been raised by slow uplift, accompanied by little or no faulting. The Appalachian Plateau of the eastern United States is an example of a plateau formed in this manner.

Lava Plateaus. Lava plateaus may be formed when successive horizontal lava flows accumulate to produce a region of high elevation. The Columbia Plateau of the northwestern United States is a lava plateau that covers an area of about 200,000 square miles to a depth of several thousand feet.

MOUNTAINS

Mountains are regions of considerable relief and high elevation; they have a small summit area and rise conspicuously above the surrounding country. However, some geologists are of the opinion that mountains should include only those areas in which the rocks have been disturbed or deformed. This would exclude the so-called "erosional" mountains which have been formed on highly dissected plateaus. Mountains grouped in a series of related ridges to form a continuous unit form a mountain **range.** A mountain **system** is a group of mountain ranges with a common geologic history. A mountain **chain** is an elongate unit composed of several mountain systems, regardless of similarity of form or age relationships.

ORIGIN OF MOUNTAINS

Mountains may form in a number of ways. Some, such as **volcanic mountains,** consist of ac-

cumulations of ashes, cinders, and lava. Others, called **block** or **fault-block mountains,** are elevated segments of the crust bounded by faults. But the truly great mountain ranges have a more complex history. Mountains such as the Alps, Appalachians, and Rockies involve sedimentation, folding, faulting, igneous activity, and subsequent uplift and erosion. These are the **fold** or **complex mountains.**

In one way or another all mountains are formed from the movements of lithospheric plates. Rocks buckle, fold, and eventually break as huge plates grind against, slide past, or move away from one another. Along the borders of the continents, oceanic plates may be subducted (see Chapter 2) beneath continental margins, giving rise to magma, which may result in volcanic activity. However, a few mountain chains originate in the interior of plates; these seem to be associated with faulting or volcanism. In other words, although the theory of plate tectonics cannot explain fully the origin of all mountains, this revolutionary idea has shed much light on mountain building in general and the formation of long, narrow, arcuate, young mountain belts in particular.

Volcanic Mountains. Mountains which have been created as a result of extrusive igneous activity are called volcanic mountains (Fig. 111a). These may consist of volcanic plugs (Shiprock, New Mexico); conical layers of fragmented igneous material around a central vent (Mayon, Philippine Islands); accumulations of lava flows about a central vent (Mauna Loa, Island of Hawaii); and volcanic domes (Lassen Peak, California).

Some of the world's greatest and best-known mountains owe their origin to volcanic activity. These include Mount Shasta, Mount Hood, Mount St. Helens, and Mount Rainier in the northwestern United States, Mount Etna and Mount Vesuvius in Italy, Fujiyama in Japan, and Popocatepetl in Mexico. In addition, the Hawaiian and Aleutian islands are formed from great volcanic mountain ranges which rise from the ocean floor.

Fold Mountains. Crustal disturbances may cause rock strata to become tightly folded and bent upward for thousands of feet (Fig. 111b).

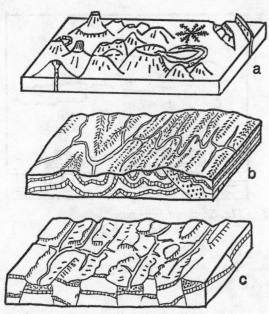

Fig. 111. Types of mountains
a–Volcanic   b–Fold   c–Fault-block or block

Folding, which normally results from compression of the rock strata, may be accompanied by faulting. Mountain ranges thus formed consist of alternating upfolds (anticlines) and downfolds (synclines). The Jura Mountains of France and Switzerland are a classic example of folded mountains. The Appalachian Mountains are a good example of mountains that were created by the folding of great thicknesses of rocks that accumulated in an ancient geosyncline. Uplift and folding were accompanied by faulting. Mountains of this type are sometimes called **complexly folded** mountains. Other fold (or possibly complex) mountains include the Coast Ranges, Alps, Himalayas, Andes, and the Rocky Mountains. (Some of the theories advanced to explain the origin of the compressive forces of folding are discussed in Chapters 2 and 7.)

Rock strata may be uplifted by igneous intrusions to form broad **domes.** This kind of mountain may be formed when molten rock material invades the bedrock, forcing the overlying strata to be lifted upward. The type of igneous intrusion most commonly responsible for doming is a laccolith (see Chapter 4). The Henry Mountains of Utah are considered to be laccolithic domes. However, not all domal mountains are associated with laccoliths. Some, like the Black Hills of South Dakota, have a broad domal struc-

ture and a granitic core, but are not believed to be laccolithic in origin.

Fault-block or Block Mountains. Faulting may cause large blocks of the earth's crust to be lifted upward and tilted at various angles (Fig. 111c). The block-faulted mountains thus formed have a short steep slope on one side and a long, more gentle slope on the other side. The Sierra Nevada of eastern California was formed by a resistant block almost 400 miles long and 75 miles wide. This great block was uplifted and tilted toward the west; the steep front of the range is a great fault scarp which faces east. The Wasatch Range of Utah was formed in a similar manner.

Complex Mountains. Many of the earth's well-known mountain ranges have been created by a combination of igneous activity and tectonism. Because of their complicated geologic history, they have been called complex mountains. They may show evidence of folding, faulting, volcanic activity, igneous intrusions, and doming. Some complex mountains consist almost wholly of igneous rocks, others are composed of metamorphic rocks or greatly deformed sedimentary rocks. Mountains of this type in the United States include the Blue Ridge Mountains of Virginia, the White Mountains of New Hampshire, the Adirondacks of New York, and much of the Rocky Mountains of the western United States.

EROSIONAL REMNANTS

Mention should be made here of certain topographic features which "rise conspicuously above the surrounding country" but are not composed of disturbed or deformed rocks. Some earth scientists classify these as erosional mountains or residual mountains because they are remnants of highlands that have undergone continuous and prolonged erosion.

Features of this sort commonly develop on high, deeply dissected plateaus. They include **mesas** (Fig. 112a) broad flat-topped hills, and **buttes** (Fig. 112b) smaller steep-sided hills, with narrow tops. These are rather common in the southwestern United States, where they may be called "mountains" because they are prominent topographic features. They are, however, composed of essentially horizontal and undisturbed strata. Likewise, the Catskill Mountains of eastern New York and the Allegheny Mountains in West Virginia and Pennsylvania have developed on the surface of a mature, highly dissected plateau.

There are certain erosional remnants that were originally part of a mountain. Devils Tower in Wyoming, for instance, is all that remains of what many geologists believe to be a laccolithic dome. Certain **monadnocks** (isolated erosional remnant rocks left standing above a peneplain) are also remains of old mountain ranges. Examples are Stone Mountain, Georgia, and Mount Monadnock, New Hampshire. (Monadnocks derived their name from the latter.)

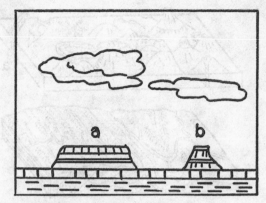

Fig. 112. Erosional remnants.
a—Mesa   b—Butte

CHAPTER 17

MINERALS AND ENERGY RESOURCES

As the science of geology has matured, we have learned to use geologic products and geologic knowledge in many ways. Preceding chapters have reviewed some of the more theoretical or scientific aspects of earth science. Now let us briefly consider some of the more practical applications of geology.

One of the geologist's major goals is the exploration, development, and conservation of our **nonrenewable mineral resources.** These rapidly dwindling, irreplaceable materials include metallic minerals such as iron, lead, and gold, and the equally important nonmetallic minerals such as salt and sulfur. The fossil fuels—coal and petroleum—are basic to the utilization of the above minerals, for they provide the energy needed to convert raw mineral products into usable goods.

Why "nonrenewable" mineral resources? These natural raw materials are a one-time "crop," for once they are gone they will not grow back. When the coal has been stripped from the ground and sent to the furnace, all that remains is an ugly scar on the landscape. Unlike a fruit tree that will bloom and produce fruit the following season, the coal is gone—forever. And so it is with the other minerals that we extract from the earth's crust. The geologist is acutely aware of our shrinking supply of minerals and knows that new mineral products will not appear in their place for thousands of years—if ever.

The health of the world's industrial economy depends, to a large degree, on the availability and utilization of these different kinds of earth materials. The ever-increasing need for more mineral resources, coupled with the expanding world population, have placed growing demands on geology and earth scientists.

MINERAL RESOURCES

Thanks to recent developments in science and technology, it is now possible to find and recover mineral resources that were unattainable a decade or two ago. But increased availability has brought about increased demand as engineers and scientists have put these earth materials to new and unforeseen uses. Thus, geology achieves one of its most important goals in the discovery, development, and conservation of the earth's natural mineral resources. These include energy-producing materials such as fossil fuels and nuclear (or radioactive) fuels, metallic minerals, and nonmetallic or industrial rocks and minerals.

FOSSIL FUELS

The **fossil fuels,** coal and petroleum, are among the most valuable and necessary products of modern industry. They derive their name from the fact that they are formed from the remains of past life.

Coal. A fossil fuel of plant origin, coal occurs in certain types of sedimentary rocks. It consists largely of carbon, hydrogen, oxygen, and nitrogen, but usually has a certain amount of sulfur, silica, and aluminum oxide as impurities. Coal is formed by carbonization, a process by which

MINERAL RESOURCE	PRINCIPAL SOURCE
Metals:	
Copper	Rare igneous concentrations of native copper and copper-bearing sulfide minerals
Lead	Rare igneous concentrations of lead-bearing sulfide minerals
Zinc	Rare igneous concentrations of zinc-bearing sulfide minerals
Iron	Sedimentary concentrations of hematite, magnetite, goethite; less common igneous or metamorphic concentrations of magnetite or hematite
Manganese	Sedimentary concentrations of uncommon manganese oxide minerals
Aluminum	Sedimentary aluminum oxide ("bauxite") deposits
Magnesium	Extracted directly from seawater; also from sedimentary dolomites
Nonmetals:	
Halite (common salt)	Sedimentary evaporite deposits
Sulfur	Native sulfur formed by alteration of sulfate minerals in sedimentary evaporite deposits
Potassium	Sedimentary evaporite deposits
Phosphorus	Phosphorus-rich sedimentary rocks associated with limestones, dolomites
Sand and gravel	Sedimentary deposits of quartz sand or pebbles
Brick clay	Sedimentary deposits of mud, shale
Limestone	Sedimentary limestones
Gypsum	Sedimentary evaporite deposits
Building stone	Sedimentary limestones, sandstones, igneous granites; metamorphic schists, marbles

TABLE 7. Principal metallic and nonmetallic mineral resources and their major source.

decaying plant material loses water and volatile substances with a resulting concentration of carbon (see also Chapter 19). The various kinds of coal and their method of formation are discussed in Chapter 5.

Coal is not only plentiful, it is widely distributed over the earth. Germany, the United States, and Great Britain are the major coal-producing countries of the world. In the United States, West Virginia, Pennsylvania, Illinois, Kentucky, and Ohio are the leading coal-producing states (Fig. 113). Although petroleum has replaced coal in many phases of industry, hundreds of millions of tons of coal are mined in the United States each year, and it remains the most important solid fuel in the world.

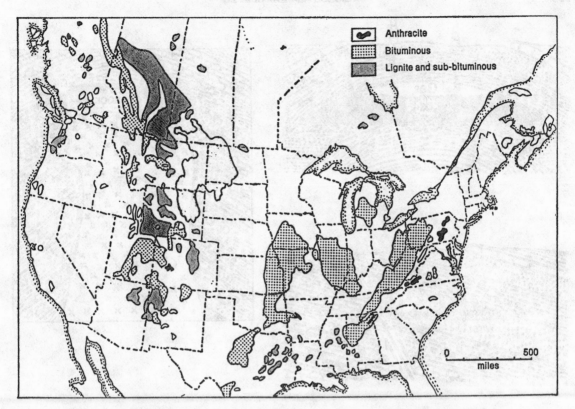

Fig. 113. Location of coalfields and various grades of coal produced in the United States and southern Canada.

Despite coal's abundance and relative ease of recovery, oil and natural gas are more widely used as fuels. When burned, high-sulfur coals pollute the atmosphere and can be the cause of "acid rain," which is detrimental to life. Not only is petroleum a cleaner fuel, it is less expensive to transport and store. Even so, as our rapidly dwindling supplies of petroleum become scarcer, coal may once again become our prime energy-producing mineral resource.

Petroleum: Oil and Natural Gas. It is generally believed that petroleum (oil and natural gas) originated from the remains of microscopic marine plants and animals. These remains, which were buried in the mud and sand of shallow prehistoric seas, underwent slow decomposition by bacteria, leaving a residue of hydrogen and carbon. These **hydrocarbon** compounds commonly occur mixed with smaller amounts of sulfur, nitrogen, and other elements.

Although the processes by which organic material was finally converted to petroleum are not thoroughly understood, they appear to have required vast amounts of time, accompanied by increases in temperature and compression of the sediments.

After its formation, the petroleum moved from the muds and shales in which it was formed into more porous rock. It then migrated to rock structures favorable for petroleum concentration. The sediments in which the oil and gas were formed are called **source rocks.** These are typically dark clays and shales of high organic content. The porous and permeable rocks through which the oil migrates are known as **reservoir rocks.** Sands, sandstones, and porous limestones and dolomites make effective reservoir rocks. **Structures** (or **traps**) are areas in the reservoir rock which will stop oil and gas migration and cause it to accumulate. Anticlines, faults, salt domes, and various types of stratigraphic traps are all effective traps (Figs. 114 and 115). Thus, in order to

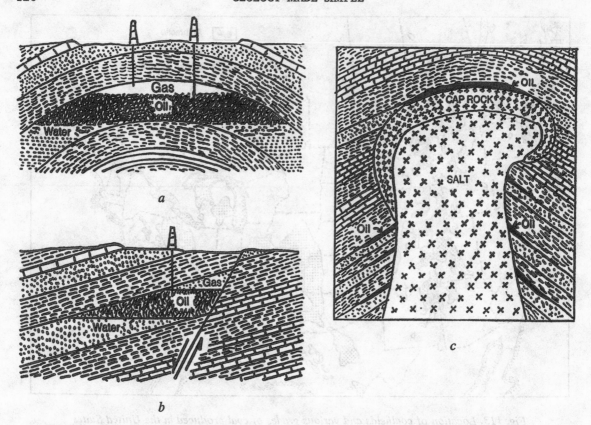

Fig. 114. Cross sections showing typical structural oil traps. (a) Anticline, (b) Fault,
(c) Salt dome showing oil trapped on flanks where the salt plug has pierced oil-bearing
sands and in the cap rock that has formed on top of the salt plug.

have an oil pool (a porous bed or rock saturated with oil) we must have (1) a source bed, (2) reservoir rocks, and (3) traps or structures.

The main task of the petroleum geologist is to locate traps that are suitable for stopping the migration of oil and gas. This search is carried on in a number of ways. The geologist may study and map rocks which are exposed at the surface or he may examine rock fragments brought to the surface when exploratory or wildcat wells are drilled. In addition, many oil companies employ geophysical methods in their search for oil. This kind of exploration requires a special type of seismograph similar to that used to record earth-

quakes. This technique, known as **geophysical prospecting**, is carried on by producing small artificial "earthquakes" by means of explosives. The seismograph records the path of the shock waves as they travel through the rocks; seismic records secured in this manner give some indication as to the type of rocks present, their relative depth, and whether or not a suitable trap may be present.

Petroleum is found in many parts of the world and in rocks ranging from Cambrian to Late Tertiary in age. In some areas it is produced a few feet beneath the surface; in others it must be taken from rocks several miles down. Texas is

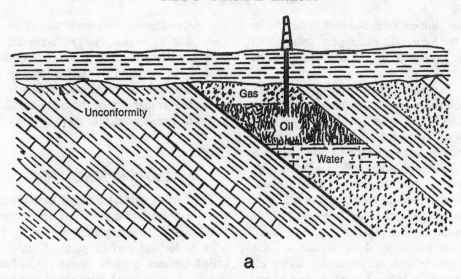

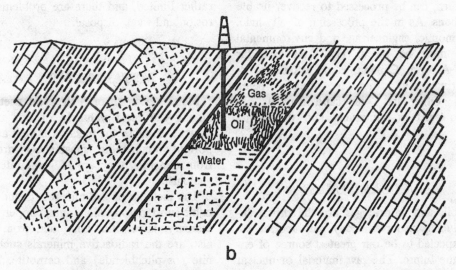

Fig. 115. Cross sections showing typical stratigraphic oil traps. (a) Tilted oil-bearing sandstone overlain by impervious shale in an angular unconformity. (b) Facies change or pinch out in which oil-bearing sandstone grades into a nonporous and impermeable shale which traps the hydrocarbons.

the leading oil-producing state, but Louisiana, Alaska, California, Oklahoma, Kansas, Illinois, and Wyoming also produce large quantities of petroleum. Russia, Rumania, the Middle East (Saudi Arabia, Iran, and Iraq), the East Indies (Borneo and Sumatra), certain South American countries (such as Venezuela and Colombia), Canada, and Mexico are some of the more important oil-producing areas outside the United States.

In addition to the oil and natural gas produced from conventional wells, there are other sources of petroleum. **Oil shale** is a very fine-grained, laminated, sedimentary rock which contains organic material called kerogen. Oil shale consists of sediments which accumulated as layers of organic ooze and mud on the bottoms of ancient lakes and shallow seas where plant and animal life were abundant.

If oil shale is heated to about 900 degrees Fahrenheit, much of the kerogen melts and gases are released. When the resulting liquid is heated to still higher temperatures, some of these can be condensed to form oil, while part remains as hydrocarbon gas. Oil shale can also be burned as a solid fuel.

Although located in many parts of the world, the richest oil shale deposits cover parts of Utah, Colorado, and Wyoming in the Rocky Mountain region. Pilot oil-extraction plants are now operating in this region in an attempt to produce commercial quantities of shale oil. Unfortunately, many environmental, economic, and technological problems must be solved before oil shale can be utilized as a major energy source.

Tar sands are another possible source of crude oil. The sand grains in these formations are cemented together with very viscous, sticky oil called tar or asphalt. When heated, tar can be extracted from these oil-impregnated sandstones. This, in turn, can be processed to recover usable hydrocarbons. As in the processing of oil shale, many economic, engineering, and environmental problems must be faced. The Athabasca tar sands in Alberta, Canada, is an extensive asphalt-bearing rock that is already being processed. Other large tar sand deposits are known to exist in Venezuela and the Soviet Union.

NUCLEAR FUELS

Coal, oil, and natural gas are the prime energy-producing resources today, but **nuclear energy** is expected to be our greatest source of energy for the future. The raw material of nuclear energy is found in uranium ore, which contains the radioactive isotope known as uranium-235 (^{235}U). Formed by igneous activity, the principal ore of uranium is the mineral **uraninite.** This uranium oxide (also called pitchblende) occurs in parts of Colorado, Wyoming, New Mexico, Utah, and Texas, as well as in Zaire, Canada, and Czechoslovakia. **Carnotite,** a more complex uranium oxide, is found associated with weathered sandstones of Colorado, New Mexico, Arizona, and Utah.

Nuclear energy is released by the process of **fission,** which occurs when ^{235}U atoms are bombarded by neutrons and broken down into other isotopes. The fission process produces enormous amounts of energy: one gram of ^{235}U releases energy equivalent to two metric tons of oil. But despite this apparent energy "bonanza," serious questions remain to be answered about nuclear energy. In addition to technological, political, and health-related problems, there are concerns about the availability of the nonrenewable radioactive materials needed to serve as fuel.

GEOTHERMAL ENERGY

The earth's natural internal heat produces energy in some areas. Derived from steam, hot water, and hot rock, **geothermal energy** is widely used in Iceland and in parts of Italy. The so-called Geysers area in northern California also produces commercial amounts of geothermal energy. The potential of geothermal energy is rather limited, and there are problems with corrosion and water disposal.

METALLIC MINERALS

Metals, because of their great usefulness, are among the most valuable of our mineral resources. Because the metals (as well as many important nonmetallic substances) are obtained from minerals, they are of great interest to the geologist.

The metallic or ore minerals include such valuable substances as aluminum, copper, gold, lead, mercury, silver, tin, zinc, and iron. Important also are the radioactive minerals such as uraninite (or pitchblende) and carnotite. The occurrence, use, and physical and chemical characteristics of the more important metallic minerals have been discussed in Chapter 3.

Metallic minerals may occur in either igneous, sedimentary, or metamorphic rocks. The ores of many metals commonly occur in **veins.** Some veins are formed when circulating ground water picks up metallic compounds and deposits them in crevices in the rock. Others, associated with igneous activity, occur as a result of magma being injected into the country rock. The latter deposits are commonly associated with contact metamorphic zones (see Chapter 4) along the periphery of igneous intrusions.

In some areas there are residual concentrations of ores which are the product of chemical weathering. Thus, the valuable aluminum ore bauxite may be formed as the result of the weathering of certain clays, granites, or syenites of high aluminum content. Some of our larger deposits of iron ore are believed to have been formed in a similar manner.

Metallic minerals also occur in natural mechanical concentrations called **placer deposits.** Ore accumulations of this type have been found in sands and gravels in the beds of streams that eroded the rocks in which the metals were originally formed. The initial discovery of the famous California gold field in 1849 was a placer deposit in the bed of the Sacramento River.

Some ore deposits appear to be the result of deposition of minerals in prehistoric lakes and seas. These include some of the larger iron ore deposits of the United States and France, and the enormous manganese deposits in Russia.

Again, it is the geologist, working in many parts of the world, who must find new and larger supplies of the metals we must have to continue our industrial and scientific progress. Today the well-trained mining geologist employs a host of geophysical and geological techniques and instruments that have been developed to replace the screening pan and pick of the prospector of 1849.

NONMETALLIC OR INDUSTRIAL ROCKS AND MINERALS

In addition to the fossil fuels and metallic minerals, there is an important group of rocks and minerals that are utilized, not for any metals they may contain, but for some other purpose. Included here are such valuable materials as asbestos, quartz, sand, clay, cement, plaster, mineral fertilizers, salt, and sulfur. These were discussed in Chapter 3.

Building stones such as sandstone, granite, limestone, and marble are other nonmetals of considerable economic importance. They, like the metallic minerals, have been discussed in earlier chapters.

PART II—HISTORICAL GEOLOGY

CHAPTER 18

THE ORIGIN AND AGE OF THE EARTH

The first part of this book is concerned primarily with the physical aspects of the earth and the geologic processes that are working on it. In this and succeeding chapters we shall discuss the origin and age of the earth, and attempt to reconstruct some of the more important events of the geologic past.

THE ORIGIN OF THE EARTH

The earth, as we learned in Chapter 1, is but one of nine planets which make up our solar system. But to humans Earth is by far the most important of all planets, for it is our home. It is also, so far as we know, the only planet which supports any type of life.

Whence came the earth? How and when did it all begin? People have speculated on such questions since the beginning of recorded history. This problem, one that is still unsolved, has resulted in the development of a number of hypotheses—none of which is entirely satisfactory.

The Nebular Hypothesis. This hypothesis suggests that the solar system developed from a **nebula**—a vast disc-shaped cloud of gas. This idea was first proposed in 1755 by the German philosopher Immanuel Kant. Later, in 1796, the French mathematician Pierre Laplace developed this theory more fully and stated it in more scientific terms. It is interesting to note that these men arrived at similar conclusions, although Laplace was not aware of Kant's earlier work.

This hypothesis assumes, in brief, that at some period in the distant past, a great nebula—its diameter reaching beyond the orbit of Pluto (our most distant planet)—was slowly rotating in space. As this gaseous mass cooled, it shrank and rotated more and more rapidly. Eventually the outermost part of the nebula rotated so fast that centrifugal force overcame gravitational force and a ring of gas separated itself from the equatorial region of the parent body. The nebula continued to contract and the speed of rotation increased until a total of ten rings had been thrown off. Nine of these rings slowly condensed to form our planets. The sixth ring, rather than condensing into a single body, broke up into many small masses. These small bodies formed the planetoids, and the central mass of the nebula later condensed to form the sun (Fig. 116).

The Laplacian hypothesis was quite popular and gained much scientific support in the nineteenth century. Unfortunately, later research proved this theory to be untenable and it was abandoned in the early twentieth century. There are numerous objections to this hypothesis, but the most important is that this mechanism would not work because the sun rotates too slowly in comparison with the rest of the planets.

The Planetesimal Hypothesis. The planetesimal hypothesis was proposed in 1900 by Thomas C. Chamberlin, a geologist, and Forest R. Moulton, an astronomer, both from the University of Chicago. According to this hypothesis, the sun was originally a star which existed without planets.

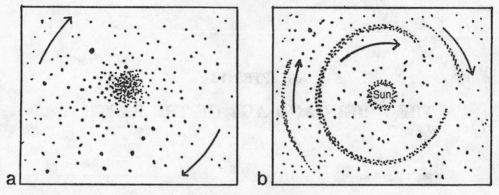

Fig. 116. Early nebular hypotheses to explain the origin of the solar system suggest that a large, slowly rotating cloud of dust and gas (a) gradually contracted and flattened. Rings of material were left behind (b) and the planets condensed from these.

At some time in the remote past, another star passed very close to the sun, exerting a gravitational force great enough to tear great masses of material from opposite sides of the sun. As the matter pulled out from the sun it cooled and condensed into solid particles called **planetesimals.** The largest of these planetesimals acted as nuclei which attracted other planetesimals, and by accretion the planets slowly grew to their present size—each pursuing its own orbit around the sun. It is believed that the five major planets were produced from the sun matter torn from the side closest to the passing star, and the minor planets and planetoids were formed from smaller masses of sun material derived from the opposite side. The satellites formed from small clusters of planetesimals located near the nuclei from which the planets originated.

Although this hypothesis was rather widely accepted for several decades, a number of geological and astronomical objections have been raised to this idea. For example, much of what we know of the structure of the earth suggests that it was originally in a molten condition. However, Chamberlin and Moulton postulated an originally solid planet. In addition, there is some doubt that the planetesimals could have gathered together by accretion—the collision of these particles in outer space would probably have destroyed them.

The Tidal or Gaseous Hypothesis. This hypothesis, like the planetesimal hypothesis which preceded it, also involves an original sun that had a close encounter with a passing star. Known also as the **tidal disruption** or **tidal filament** hy-

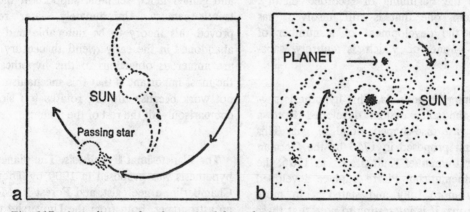

Fig. 117. According to the planetesimal hypothesis, a passing star pulled large masses of gas from the sun; these gases later condensed to form the planets (a). In (b) we see a stage in solar system development when planetesimals are accumulating around the larger nuclei. Some of these have attained the size of planets.

pothesis, this conception of how our solar system formed was proposed in 1918 by two British scientists, Sir James Jeans and Sir Harold Jeffreys. Jeans, an astronomer, and Jeffreys, a geophysicist, offered this proposal to counteract some of the objections that had been raised to the planetesimal hypothesis. They accepted the supposed near-collision between the sun and another star but believed that the material pulled out of the sun came out as a long spindle or cigar-shaped filament of solar gases. This gaseous filament later broke up into units which condensed to a molten and finally a solid stage, thus forming the planets. Astronomers have shown that a gaseous filament of this sort would not form solid bodies such as our planets; it would instead simply disappear in space. For this and many other reasons, this hypothesis is no longer acceptable to most scientists.

The Protoplanet Hypothesis. Within recent years scientists have taken a closer look at a possible nebular origin of the earth and devised a new theory in the light of newer findings. This idea has replaced the original nebular hypothesis of Kant and Laplace as well as the later planetesimal hypothesis. The revised theory, known as the protoplanet hypothesis, was first proposed in 1944 by C. F. von Weizsäcker and modified by Gerald P. Kuiper. It has been found that rapidly rotating nebulas will develop large whirlpools or **vortexes** at various places on the disk of nebular material.

Each of these great whirlpools might then have collected the surrounding material by gravitational attraction, thus forming a **protoplanet** (Fig. 118). It is believed that nine protoplanets —one for each of the present-day planets—were formed, and these were originally much larger than the finished planet. Smaller whirlpools developed inside some of the larger vortexes, and these gave rise to spinning discs that became the satellites, or moons, of the planets. Many astronomers support this theory because observations through large telescopes have revealed numerous true nebulas between the stars. Equally significant is the fact that some of these massive swirls of gas and dust are actually condensing to form new stars. The protoplanet hypothesis is generally acceptable to most scientists because it explains many of the known facts about the solar system. It is nonetheless far from complete, and the origin of the solar system and Earth is still largely in the realm of speculation.

THE AGE OF THE EARTH

Now that we have speculated as to *how* the earth was formed, we should give some thought as to *when* it was formed. Estimates of the earth's age have ranged from as few as 6000 years (by early theologians) to as many as 10 billion years (by astronomers and physicists). However, the latest scientific evidence indicates that the earth is probably closer to 4½ billion years old.

How do we know? Before attempting to an-

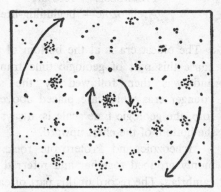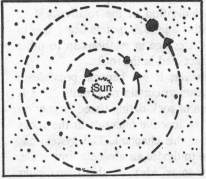

Fig. 118. A more recent nebular theory assumes that large condensations called "proto-planets" condensed from the flattened, rotating nebulas around the central sun.

swer this question we should become familiar with the geologic time scale; this will help us more fully to understand the great antiquity of our earth.

THE GEOLOGIC COLUMN AND GEOLOGIC TIME SCALE

The **geologic column** refers to the total succession of rocks, from the oldest to the most recent, that are found in the entire earth or in a given area. Thus, the geologic column of a given state would include all rock divisions known to be present in that state. By referring to the geologic column previously determined for a specific area, the geologist knows what kind of rocks one might expect to find in that particular region.

The **geologic time scale** (Fig. 119) is composed of named intervals of geologic time during which the rocks represented in the geologic column were deposited. These intervals of time bear the same names that were originally used to distinguish the rock units in the column. For example, one can speak of Ordovician time (referring to the geologic time scale) or of Ordovician rocks (referring to the geologic column).

Both the geologic column and the geologic time scale are based upon the principle of **superposition.** This important principle states that unless a series of sedimentary rock has been overturned, a given rock will be older than all the layers above it and younger than all the layers below it. The field relationship of the rocks plus the type of fossils (if present) give the geologist some indication of the relative age of the rocks. Relative age does not indicate age in years; rather, it fixes age in relationship to other events that are recorded in the rocks.

Recently, however, it has become possible to assign ages in years to certain rock units. This is done by a system of rock dating based largely on the presence of radioactive minerals in the rocks (described later in this chapter). This system has made it possible to devise an absolute time scale, which gives us some idea of the tremendous amount of time that has passed since the oldest known rocks were formed. It has also been used to verify the previously determined relative ages of the various rock units.

Units of the Time Scale. The largest unit of geologic time is an **era,** and each era is divided into smaller time units called **periods.** A period of geologic time is divided into **epochs,** which in turn may be subdivided into still smaller units. The geologic time scale might be roughly compared to the calendar, in which the year is divided into months, months into weeks, and weeks into days. It should be emphasized, however, that, unlike years, geologic time units are arbitrary and of unequal duration, and the geologist, dealing with relative time, cannot be positive about the exact amount of time involved in each unit. The time scale does, however, provide a standard by which he can discuss the relative age of the rocks and the fossils they contain. For instance, by referring to the time scale, it is possible to state that a certain event occurred in the Paleozoic Era in the same sense that one might say that something happened during the American Revolution.

There are five eras of geologic time, and each has been given a name that is descriptive of the degree of life development that characterizes it. Hence, Paleozoic means "ancient-life," and the era was so named because of the relatively simple and ancient stage of life development of that time.

The eras and the literal translation of each name are shown below.

> Cenozoic—"recent-life"
> Mesozoic—"middle-life"
> Paleozoic—"ancient-life"
> Proterozoic—"fore-life"
> Archeozoic—"beginning-life"

The oldest era is at the bottom of the list because this part of geologic time transpired first and was then followed by the successively younger eras which are placed above it. Therefore, the geologic time scale is always read from the bottom of the chart upward.

Archeozoic and Proterozoic rocks are commonly grouped together and referred to as **Precambrian.** The record of this part of earth history contains very few fossils, and is most difficult to interpret. It has been estimated that Precambrian time may represent as much as 85 percent of all geologic time.

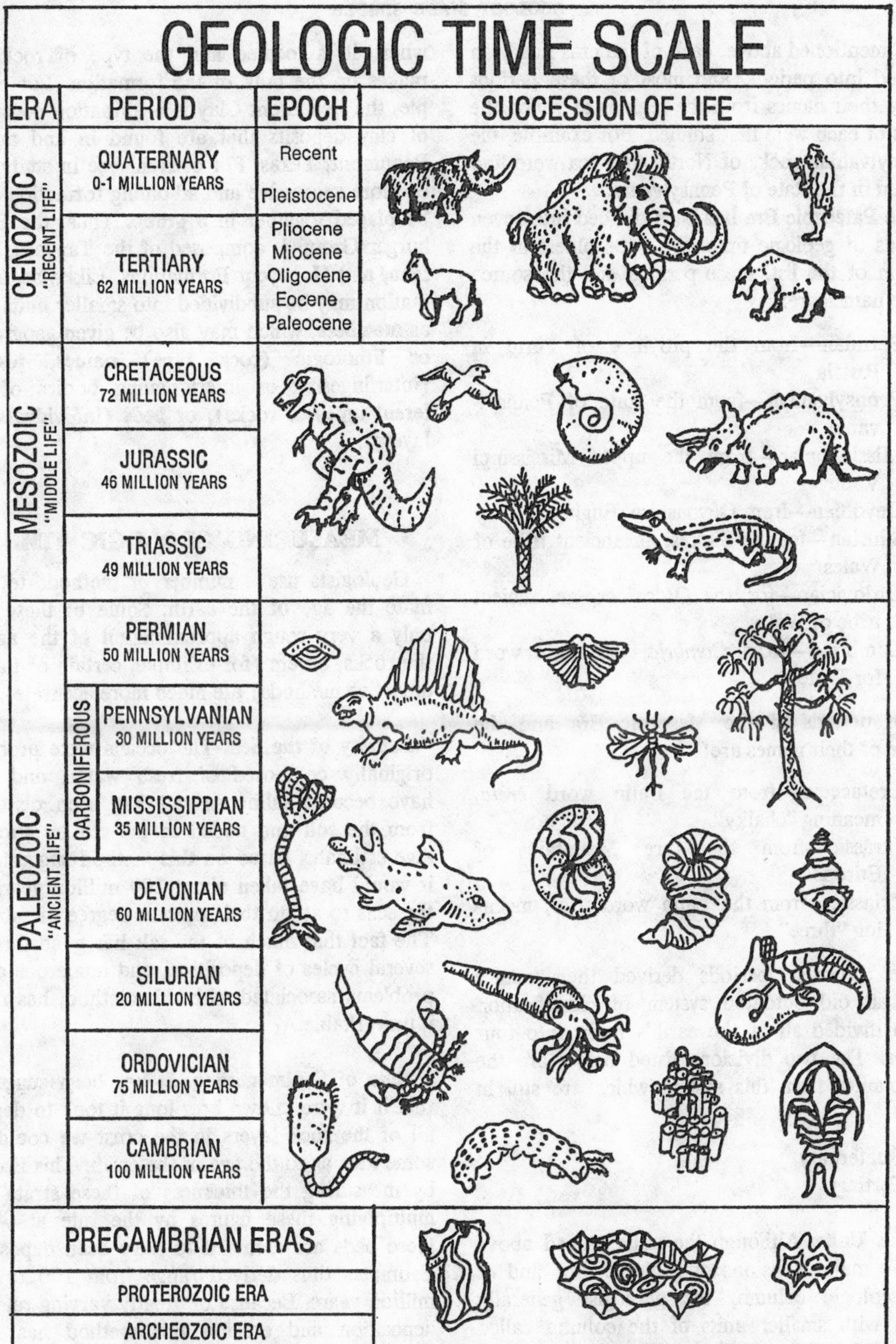

GEOLOGIC TIME SCALE

ERA	PERIOD	EPOCH	SUCCESSION OF LIFE
CENOZOIC "RECENT LIFE"	QUATERNARY 0-1 MILLION YEARS	Recent / Pleistocene	
	TERTIARY 62 MILLION YEARS	Pliocene / Miocene / Oligocene / Eocene / Paleocene	
MESOZOIC "MIDDLE LIFE"	CRETACEOUS 72 MILLION YEARS		
	JURASSIC 46 MILLION YEARS		
	TRIASSIC 49 MILLION YEARS		
PALEOZOIC "ANCIENT LIFE"	PERMIAN 50 MILLION YEARS		
	CARBONIFEROUS: PENNSYLVANIAN 30 MILLION YEARS		
	CARBONIFEROUS: MISSISSIPPIAN 35 MILLION YEARS		
	DEVONIAN 60 MILLION YEARS		
	SILURIAN 20 MILLION YEARS		
	ORDOVICIAN 75 MILLION YEARS		
	CAMBRIAN 100 MILLION YEARS		
PRECAMBRIAN ERAS	PROTEROZOIC ERA		
	ARCHEOZOIC ERA		
APPROXIMATE AGE OF THE EARTH MORE THAN 4 BILLION 550 MILLION YEARS			

Fig. 119. Geologic time scale. (Reprinted by permission from Fossils: An Introduction to Prehistoric Life, by William H. Matthews III, Barnes & Noble, Inc., New York.)

As mentioned above, each of the eras has been divided into periods, and most of these periods derive their names from the regions in which the rocks of each were first studied. For example, the Pennsylvanian rocks of North America were first studied in the state of Pennsylvania.

The Paleozoic Era has been divided into seven periods of geologic time. With the oldest at the bottom of the list, these periods and the source of the names are:

Permian—from the province of Perm in Russia

Pennsylvanian—from the state of Pennsylvania

Mississippian—from the upper Mississippi Valley

Devonian—from Devonshire, England

Silurian—for the Silures, an ancient tribe of Wales

Ordovician—for the Ordovices, an ancient tribe of Wales

Cambrian—from *Cambria,* the Latin word for Wales

The periods of the Mesozoic Era and the source of their names are:

Cretaceous—from the Latin word *creta,* meaning "chalky"

Jurassic—from the Jura Mountains of Europe

Triassic—from the Latin word *trias,* meaning "three"

The Cenozoic periods derived their names from an old outdated system of classification which divided all of the earth's rocks into four groups. The two divisions listed below are the only names from this system which are still in use:

Quaternary
Tertiary

Rock Units. Although the units named above are the major divisions of geologic time and of the geologic column, the geologist generally works with smaller units of the column called **geologic formations.** A geologic formation is a unit of rock that is recognized by certain physical and chemical characteristics. A formation is generally given a double name which indicates both where it is located and the type of rock that makes up the bulk of the formation. For example, the Beaumont Clay is a formation consisting of clay deposits that are found in and around Beaumont, Texas. For convenience in study, two or more successive and adjoining formations may be placed together in a **group.** Thus, the Ellenburger Group is composed of the Tanyard, Gorman, and Honeycut Formations. Likewise, a formation may be subdivided into smaller units such as **members,** which may also be given geographic or lithologic (rock type) names, **tongues** (interfingering or intertonguing bodies of different types of rocks), or **beds** (individual rock layers).

MEASURING GEOLOGIC TIME

Geologists use a number of methods to estimate the age of the earth. Some of these give only a very rough approximation of the age of the rocks, others (for example, certain of the radioactive methods) are much more accurate.

Salinity of the Sea. The oceans were probably originally composed of fresh water, and they have become saline as salt has been dissolved from the soil and added to the sea by streams. Age estimates based on this method suggest that it would have taken about 100 million years for the seas to attain their present degree of salinity. The fact that much of the salt has gone through several cycles of deposition, and numerous other problems associated with this method, has made it unworkable.

Rate of Sedimentation. It has been suggested that if it were known how long it took to deposit all of the rock layers in the crust we could get some idea as to the age of the earth. This is done by measuring the thickness of these strata and multiplying these figures by the rate at which these beds are assumed to have been deposited. Estimates thus derived range from 100 to 600 million years. Because of greatly varying rates of deposition and erosion this method has little scientific value.

Radioactive Methods. This is the most recent and accurate method yet devised. Certain radioactive elements, for example thorium and uranium, undergo slow spontaneous disintegration. This rate of disintegration is constant, and is not affected by changes in temperature, pressure, or other natural conditions. Helium is released as the mineral disintegrates, and a new series of elements is formed. The last element formed in this series is lead. By calculating the ratio between the radioactive lead and the remaining amount of uranium present in a given specimen, it is possible to determine the age of the radioactive mineral. This method is limited, of course, to those rocks containing radioactive minerals. Similar methods based on the rate of decay of rubidium to strontium and potassium to argon are also being used with some accuracy. The oldest rocks dated by radioactive methods indicate that the earth is approximately four and one-half billion years old.

The **Carbon-14 method** of dating has proved successful in dating objects less than 50,000 years old. Briefly, this method is based on the fact that all organisms contain a constant amount of Carbon-14, a radioactive **isotope** (isotopes are atoms of the same atomic number, but of different atomic weights). When an organism dies, Carbon-14 (or radiocarbon) is gradually lost, and the decay of this radioactive carbon proceeds at a known rate. This rate is such that one-half of the Carbon-14 has disintegrated at the end of about 5568 years. The approximate age of the specimen may be determined by comparing the amount of radiocarbon remaining in the specimen to the amount present in most living things. This method has been extremely useful in dating both geological and archeological materials.

CHAPTER 19

THE RECORD IN THE ROCKS

How do historical geologists know what happened to this planet millions—or even billions—of years ago? They learn by studying the record of the rocks, a record which indicates that both the earth and its inhabitants have undergone many changes throughout the long life span of our planet. What does this record consist of? By what means does the geologist interpret it? These are some of the questions that will be considered in this chapter.

KEYS TO THE PAST

As pointed out in the preceding chapter, it is now believed that the earth is at least four and one-half billion years old. There is, moreover, evidence which suggests that life may have been present on our planet as long as 3 billion 300 million years ago. In addition, there are many indications that the earth's physical features have not always been as they are today. For instance, mountains now occupy the sites of ancient seas and coal is being mined where swamps existed millions of years ago. Furthermore, plants and animals have undergone great change. The trend of this organic change is, in general, toward more complex and advanced forms of life. However, some life forms have remained virtually unchanged and others have become extinct.

In order to interpret earth history, the geologist must study the rocks and gather evidence of the great changes in geography, climate, and life that took place in the geologic past. To do this he has developed several methods or principles which act as keys to the more important events of prehistoric time.

The Doctrine of Uniformitarianism. This important geologic principle states that the geologic processes of the past operated in essentially the same manner and at the same rate as they do today. Or, more simply stated, *the present is the key to the past*. This means, in effect, that the earth features of today have been formed as the result of present processes acting over long periods of time.

The Law of Superposition. In an undisturbed sequence of sedimentary rocks, the rocks at the bottom of the sequence are older than any of the rocks which overlie them (Fig. 120). This fundamental geologic concept, the law of superposition, is basic to an understanding of geologic history. It should be noted that in areas where the rocks have been greatly disturbed, it is necessary to determine the tops and bottoms of beds before the normal sequence can be established.

Relative Age of Igneous Rocks. Extrusive rocks, such as lava flows, are obviously younger than the rocks on which they rest. Intrusive rocks, for example dikes, sills, batholiths, etc., are younger than the rocks into which they have been injected.

Organic Succession. This principle assumes that fossil **faunas** (assemblages of animals that lived together at a given time and place) follow

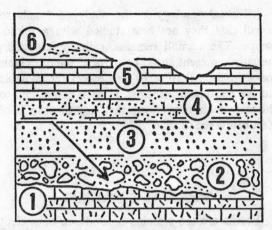

Fig. 120. Geologic section illustrating law of superposition. Bed 1, eroded metamorphic rock, is the oldest; a disconformity (arrow) separates it from Bed 2. The beds become progressively younger as they ascend; Bed 6 is the youngest.

each other in a definite and determinable order. These faunas are distinctive for each portion of earth history, and by comparing them the geologist is able to recognize deposits of the same age. This succession of life is such that older rocks may be expected to yield the remains of more primitive organisms, while the remains of more advanced life forms would be confined to the younger rocks.

Correlation. Correlation, the process of determining the relative ages of the rocks exposed in different areas (or from rock cuttings from different wells), is one of the most important tools of the geologist. It is an especially valuable technique because no single area can provide a rock section containing a record of all geologic time. But since deposition has always been continuous in one place or another we can correlate widely scattered outcrops to compile a composite record of all geologic time.

Although there are numerous methods of correlation, those most frequently used are:

Continuity of Outcrops—Rock layers that may be traced without interruption are the easiest to correlate. This method is usually limited to use in relatively small areas, however.

Lithologic Similarity—Some formations are relatively consistent in their rock characters, and this uniformity may be used in tracing the formation from one area to another. This method should be used with caution, however, as many rock units undergo some change in texture or composition from one outcrop to another. On the other hand, some formations are marked by the presence of such diagnostic features as unusual weathering patterns, distinctive mineral associations, peculiar concretions, and the like.

Similarity of Sequence—The geologist often correlates by comparing the positions in which certain strata appear in widely separated vertical sections. If, for example, a red sandstone is known to occur normally between a very coarse conglomerate and black shale, this sequence will be relatively easy to recognize in the field. Unconformities (Chapter 7), if present, may be used in a similar manner.

Similarity of Fossils—If fossils are present in the rocks, they are especially useful for purposes of correlation. Those fossils having a limited vertical range but a rather wide geographic distribution are particularly useful and are called **guide** or **index** fossils. Correlation by means of fossils is discussed in some detail later in this chapter.

Paleogeography. This branch of historical geology is concerned with the distribution and relationships of ancient seas and landmasses. "Ancient geography" (which is what paleogeography literally means) is reconstructed through an interpretation of the sedimentary rocks of a certain age. Fossils, if present, are also valuable in determining past geographic conditions.

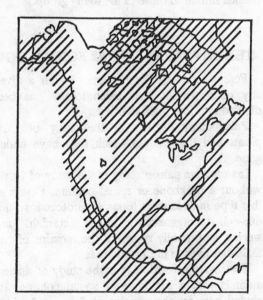

Fig. 121. Simplified paleogeographic map showing extent of lands and seas during the Cambrian Period.

If in a given area, for example, we find sedimentary rocks containing marine fossils of Late Cretaceous age, this would indicate the presence of seas in this area in Late Cretaceous time. Restorations of these ancient geographic features are shown on **paleogeographic maps** (Fig. 121).

FOSSILS: THE RECORD OF LIFE ON EARTH

Paleontology—the study of fossil plant and animal remains—has done much to advance our knowledge of prehistoric life. The paleontologist has traced the development of life from its first clear and continuous record—some 600 million years ago—through its evolution into the more advanced forms of later geologic time and today.

Because it is concerned with the record of life, paleontology is closely related to the science of biology. In studying fossils, the paleontologist relies heavily on uniformitarianism, the principle that states that "the present is the key to the past." Because of the great amount of time involved in earth history, we are not always certain of the life habits or environments of extinct plants and animals. However, when we discover a fossil group whose members closely resemble the members of a living group, it is usually safe to infer that the fossil organisms lived under conditions similar to those of the living group.

THE DIVISIONS OF PALEONTOLOGY

Fossils represent the remains of such a diversity of organisms that paleontology has been divided into four main divisions.

Paleobotany deals with the study of fossil plants and the changes which they have undergone.

Invertebrate paleontology is the study of fossils without a backbone or spinal column. Fossils of this type include such forms as protozoans (tiny one-celled organisms), clams, starfish, and worms, and usually represent the remains of animals that lived in prehistoric seas.

Vertebrate paleontology is the study of ancient animals with a backbone or spinal column. Included here are the remains of fish, amphibians, reptiles, birds, and mammals.

Micropaleontology is the study of fossils so small that they are best studied with a microscope. These small remains, called **microfossils**, usually represent shells or parts of minute plants or animals. Microfossils are especially valuable to the petroleum geologist, as they enable him to identify rock formations that are thousands of feet below the surface.

WHAT ARE FOSSILS?

Fossils are the remains or evidence of ancient plants or animals that have been preserved in the rocks of the earth's crust. Most fossils represent the hard parts of prehistoric organisms that lived in the area in which their remains were collected.

With the aid of fossils the paleontologist is able to form a reasonably accurate picture of life of past ages. He does this by studying bones, teeth, shells, footprints, or any other indication of the presence of past life.

Fossils have undoubtedly attracted man since his earliest history, for they have been found in association with the remains of prehistoric men. In later times, certain of the early Greek and Roman philosophers noticed the remains of fossil sea shells far from the ocean. One of these ancient scholars reported fossil fish high above sea level and concluded that they were the forerunners of all life. Aristotle (384–322 B.C.) explained fossils as the result of mysterious plastic forces within the earth. One of his students, Theophrastus, believed that fossils represented some type of life, but stated that they had developed from seeds or eggs that had been planted in the rocks.

Herodotus, in 450 B.C., noticed marine fossils in the Egyptian desert and correctly concluded that the Mediterranean Sea had once been in that area. During the "Dark Ages," fossils were alternately explained as freaks of nature, the remains of attempts at special creation, or devices of the devil placed in the rocks to lead men astray. Such superstitious beliefs hindered the development of paleontology for hundreds of years. But in the last hundred years, fossils have been accepted without question as the remains of ancient life, and have become increasingly important to the earth scientist.

HOW FOSSILS ARE FORMED

The majority of fossils are found in marine sedimentary rocks. Such rocks were formed when salt-water sediments such as lime muds, sands, or shell beds were compressed and cemented together to form rocks. Only rarely do fossils occur in igneous and metamorphic rocks.

But even in the sedimentary rocks only a minute fraction of prehistoric plants and animals have left any record of their existence. This is not difficult to understand if we are aware of the rather rigorous requirements of fossilization.

Requirements of Fossilization. There are many factors which ultimately determine whether an organism will be fossilized, but the three basic requirements are:

1. The organism should possess hard parts. These might be shell, bone, teeth, or the woody tissue of plants. However, under unusually favorable conditions of preservation it is possible for even such fragile objects as a jellyfish or an insect to become fossilized.

2. The organic remains must escape immediate destruction after death. If the body parts of an organism are crushed, decayed, badly weathered, or otherwise greatly changed, this may result in the alteration or complete destruction of the fossil record of that particular organism.

3. Rapid burial must take place in a material capable of retarding decomposition. The type of material burying the remains usually depends upon where the organism lived. The remains of marine animals are common as fossils because they fall to the ocean bottom after death, and here they are covered by soft muds which are converted into the shales and limestones of later geologic ages. The finer sediments are less likely to damage the organic remains, and certain fine-grained Jurassic limestones in Germany have faithfully preserved such delicate specimens as birds, insects, and jellyfishes.

Ash falling from nearby volcanoes has been known to cover entire forests. Some of these fossil forests have been found with the trees still standing and in excellent state of preservation. Good examples of such trees can be seen at Yellowstone National Park, Wyoming.

Quicksand and tar have also been responsible for the rapid burial of animals. The tar acts as a trap to capture the beasts and as an antiseptic to retard the decomposition of their hard parts. The Rancho La Brea tar pits at Los Angeles, California, are famous for the large number of prehistoric animal bones that have been recovered from them. These include such forms as the saber-tooth cat, giant ground sloths, and other creatures that are now extinct. Under special conditions, the remains of certain animals that lived during the Ice Ages have been incorporated into the ice or frozen ground, and some of these frozen remains, especially the great woolly mammoths, are famous for their remarkable degree of preservation.

GAPS IN THE FOSSIL RECORD

Although untold numbers of organisms have inhabited this planet in past ages, only a minute fraction of these have left any record of their existence. Even if the basic requirements of fossilization have been fulfilled, there are still other reasons why some fossils may never be found.

For example, large numbers of fossils have been destroyed by erosion or their hard parts have been dissolved by underground waters. Others were buried in rocks that were later subjected to great physical change, and fossils found in these rocks are usually so damaged as to be unrecognizable.

Then, too, many fossiliferous rocks cannot be studied because they are covered by water or great thicknesses of sediments, and still others are situated in places that are geographically inaccessible. These and many other problems confront the geologist as he attempts to describe the plants and animals of the past.

The gaps in the fossil record become more numerous and more obvious in the older rocks of the earth's crust. This is because the more ancient rocks have had more time to be subjected to physical and chemical change or to be removed by erosion.

THE DIFFERENT KINDS OF FOSSIL REMAINS

There are numerous ways in which plants and animals may become fossilized, but most paleontologists recognize four major types of preservation. Each of these is based upon the composition of the remains or the changes which they have undergone since their burial.

ORIGINAL SOFT PARTS OF ORGANISMS

To be preserved in this manner, the organism must be buried in a medium capable of retarding decomposition of the soft parts. Materials known to have produced this type of fossilization are frozen soil or ice, oil-saturated soils, and **amber** (fossil resin). It is also possible for organic remains to become so desiccated (dried out) that a natural mummy is formed. This is apt to occur only in arid or desert regions and in situations where the remains have been protected from predators and scavengers.

The best-known examples of preserved soft parts of prehistoric animals have been discovered in Alaska and Siberia. The frozen tundra of these areas has yielded the remains of large numbers of frozen woolly mammoths—an extinct elephant-like animal. The bodies of these huge beasts, many of which have been buried for as long as 25,000 years, are exposed as the frozen earth begins to thaw. Some of these giant carcasses have been so well preserved that their flesh has been eaten by dogs and their tusks sold by ivory traders.

Original soft parts have also been recovered from oil-saturated soils in eastern Poland. The well-preserved nose-horn, a foreleg, and part of the skin of an extinct rhinoceros were collected from these deposits.

The natural mummies of ground sloths have been found in caves and volcanic craters in New Mexico and Arizona. The extremely dry desert atmosphere permitted thorough dehydration of the soft parts before decay set in, and specimens with portions of the original skin, hair, tendons, and claws have been discovered.

Another interesting and unusual type of fossilization is preservation in amber. This type of preservation was made possible when ancient insects became trapped in the sticky gum that exuded from certain coniferous trees. With the passing of time this resin hardened, leaving the insect encased in a tomb of amber, and some insects and

spiders have been so well preserved that even fine hairs and muscle tissues may be studied under the microscope.

The preservation of original soft parts has produced some interesting and spectacular fossils. However, this type of fossilization is relatively rare, and the paleontologist usually finds it necessary to study remains that have been preserved in stone.

ORIGINAL HARD PARTS OF ORGANISMS

Almost all plants and animals possess some type of hard parts which are capable of becoming fossilized. Such hard parts may consist, for example, of the shell material of clams, oysters, or snails, the teeth or bones of vertebrates, the exoskeletons (outer body coverings) of crabs, or the woody tissue of plants. These hard parts are composed of various materials which are capable of resisting weathering and chemical action, and fossils of this sort are relatively common.

Calcareous Remains. Hard parts composed of calcite (calcium carbonate) are quite common among the invertebrates. This is especially true of the shells of clams, snails, and corals, and many of these shells have been preserved with little or no evidence of physical change. (See Fig. 122.)

Fig. 122. Fossil snail composed of calcium carbonate.

Phosphatic Remains. The bones and teeth of vertebrates and the exoskeletons of many invertebrates contain large amounts of calcium phosphate. This compound is particularly weather-resistant. Hence, phosphatic remains are found in an excellent state of preservation.

Siliceous Remains. Many organisms having skeletal elements composed of silica (silicon dioxide) have been preserved with little noticeable change. The siliceous hard parts of many microfossils and certain types of sponges have become fossilized in this manner.

Chitinous Remains. Some animals have an exoskeleton composed of chitin, a material that is similar in composition to our fingernails. The fossilized chitinous exoskeletons of arthropods and other organisms are commonly preserved as thin films of carbon because of their chemical composition and method of burial.

ALTERED HARD PARTS OF ORGANISMS

The original hard parts of an organism normally undergo great change after burial. Such changes take place in a variety of ways, but the type of alteration is usually determined by the composition of the hard parts and where the organism lived. Some of the more common processes of alteration are described below.

Carbonization. This process, known also as **distillation,** takes place as organic matter slowly decays after burial. During the process of decomposition, the organic matter gradually loses its gases and liquids, leaving only a thin film of carbonaceous material. Coal is formed by this same process, and carbonized plant fossils are not uncommon in many coal deposits. In addition, some unusual preservations of fish, graptolites, and reptiles have been preserved by carbonization.

Petrifaction or Permineralization. Large numbers of fossils have been permineralized or petrified—literally turned to stone. This type of preservation occurs when mineral-bearing ground waters infiltrate porous bone, shell, or plant material. These underground waters deposit their mineral content in the empty spaces of the hard parts, thereby making them heavier and more resistant to weathering. Some of the more common minerals deposited in this manner are calcite, silica, and various compounds of iron.

Replacement or Mineralization. Preservation of this type takes place when the original hard parts of organisms are removed after being dissolved by underground water. This is accompanied by almost simultaneous decomposition of other substances in the resulting voids. Some replaced fossils will have the original structure destroyed by the replacing minerals. Others, as in the case of certain silicified tree trunks, may be preserved in minute detail.

Although more than fifty minerals have been known to replace original organic structures, the most frequent replacing substances are calcite, dolomite (a calcium magnesium carbonate), silica, and certain iron compounds.

TRACES OF ORGANISMS

Fossils consist not only of actual plant and animal remains but of any trace or evidence of their existence. Although the latter type of fossil reveals no direct evidence of the original organism, there is some definite indication of the former presence of an ancient plant or animal. This type of fossil may provide much information as to the identity or characteristics of the organism responsible for it.

Molds and Casts. Shells, bones, leaves, and other forms of organic matter are commonly preserved as molds and casts. If a shell pressed down into the ocean bottom before the sediment hardened into rock, it may have left the impression of the exterior of the shell. This impression is known as a mold. If at some later time this mold was filled with another material, this produced a cast. A cast formed in this manner will show the original external characteristics of the shell. Such objects are called external molds if they show the external features of the hard parts, and internal molds if the nature of the inner parts is shown.

Molds and casts are likely to be found in most fossiliferous (fossil-bearing) rocks. It is particularly common to find fossil clams and snails preserved by this method. This is primarily because their shells are composed of minerals that are relatively easy to dissolve, and the original shell material is often destroyed.

Tracks, Trails, and Burrows. Many animals have left records of their movements over dry land or the sea bottom. Some of these, for example footprints (Fig. 123) indicate not only the type of animal that left them but may also furnish valuable information about the animal's environment.

Thus the study of a series of dinosaur tracks may not only indicate the size and shape of the dinosaur's foot but also give some indication as to the weight and length of the animal. Moreover, the type of rock containing the track would probably help determine the conditions under which the animal lived.

Fig. 123. Fossil reptile tracks preserved in stone.

Invertebrates also leave tracks and trails of their activities, and markings of this type may be seen on the surfaces of many sandstone and limestone beds. These may be simple tracks, left as the animal moved over the surface, or the burrows of crabs or other burrowing animals. Markings of this sort provide some evidence of the manner of locomotion of these organisms and of the type of environment that they inhabited.

Coprolites. These objects are fossil dung or body waste (Fig. 124). Coprolites may provide valuable information as to the food habits or anatomical structure of the animal that made them.

Fig. 124. Coprolite.

Gastroliths. These highly polished well-rounded stones (Fig. 125) are believed to have been used in the stomachs of reptiles for grinding

their food into smaller pieces. Large numbers of these "stomach stones" have been found with the remains of certain types of dinosaurs and other extinct reptiles.

Fig. 125. Gastrolith.

THE CLASSIFICATION OF FOSSILS

There are such vast numbers of organisms, both living and extinct, that some system of classification is needed to link them all together. Many fossils bear distinct similarities to plants and animals that are living today, and for this reason paleontological classification is similar to that used to classify modern organisms. This system, known as the system of **binomial nomenclature,** was proposed in 1758 by Linné (or Linnaeus), an early Swedish naturalist.

Scientific names established in accordance with the principles of binomial nomenclature consist of two parts: the **generic** (or **genus**) name and the **specific,** or **trivial (species)** name. These names are commonly derived from Greek or Latin words descriptive of the organism or fossil being named. They may, however, be derived from the names of people or places, and in such instances the names are always latinized. Greek or Latin is used because they are "dead" languages and not subject to change. They are also "international" languages in that scientists all over the world can use the same names regardless of what language they write in. The system of binomial nomenclature has led to the development of the science of **taxonomy,** the systematic classification of plants and animals according to their relationships.

THE UNITS OF CLASSIFICATION

The world of organic life has been divided into the plant and animal kingdoms. These kingdoms have been further divided into larger divisions called **phyla** (from the Greek word *phylon,* "a race"). Each phylum is composed of organisms with certain characteristics in common. For example, all animals with a spinal cord (or notochord) are assigned to the phylum Chordata.

The phylum is reduced to smaller divisions called **classes;** classes are divided into **orders;** orders into **families;** families into **genera;** and each genus is divided into still smaller units called **species.** A species may be further reduced to subspecies, varieties, or other subspecific categories.

The following table illustrates the classification of man, a dog, and a clam:

UNIT	MAN	DOG	CLAM
Kingdom	Animalia	Animalia	Animalia
Phylum	Chordata	Chordata	Mollusca
Class	Mammalia	Mammalia	Pelecypoda
Order	Primates	Carnivora	Eulamellibranchia
Family	Hominidae	Canidae	Veneridae
Genus	*Homo*	*Canis*	*Venus*
Species	*sapiens*	*familiaris*	*mercenaria*

The generic name and the trivial name constitute the **scientific name** of a species, and according to this system of classification the scientific name of all living men is *Homo sapiens.* It is obvious that there are many variations among individual men, but all men have certain general characteristics in common and are therefore placed in the same species.

When writing a scientific name, the generic name should always start with a capital letter and the trivial name with a small letter. Both names must be italicized or underlined.

HOW FOSSILS ARE USED

Fossils are useful in a number of different ways, for each specimen provides some information about when it lived, where it lived, and how it lived.

We use fossils, for example, in tracing the development of the plants and animals of our earth. They are useful for this purpose because the fossils in the older rocks are usually primitive and relatively simple. However, a study of similar specimens that lived in later geologic time reveals that the fossils become progressively complex and more advanced in the younger rocks.

Certain fossils are valuable as environmental indicators. For example, the reef-building corals appear to have always lived under much the same conditions as they live today. Hence, if the geologist finds fossil reef corals *in place* (that is, where they were originally buried), he can be reasonably sure that the rocks containing them were formed from sediments deposited in warm, fairly shallow salt water. A study of the occurrence and distribution of such marine fossils makes it possible to outline the location and extent of prehistoric seas. The type of fossils present may also provide some indication as to the depth, temperature, bottom conditions, and salinity of these ancient bodies of water.

One of the more important uses of fossils is for purposes of correlation—the process of demonstrating that certain rock layers are closely related to each other. By correlating or "matching" the beds containing specific fossils, it is possible to determine the distribution of a geologic formation in a given area. Certain fossils have a very limited vertical or geologic range and a wide horizontal or geographic range. In other words, they lived but a relatively short time in geologic history but were rather widely distributed during their relatively short lives. Fossils of this type are known as **index fossils** or **guide fossils.** They are especially useful in correlation because they are normally associated only with rocks of one particular age.

Microfossils are especially valuable as guide fossils for the petroleum geologist. The **micropaleontologist** (one who specializes in the study of microfossils) washes the well cuttings from the drill hole and separates the tiny fossils from the surrounding rocks. The specimens are then mounted on special slides and studied under the microscope. Information derived from these minute remains may provide valuable data on the age of the subsurface formation and the possibilities of oil production. Microfossils are particularly useful in the oil fields of California and in the Atlantic and Gulf coastal regions of the United States. In fact, some of the oil-producing zones of Texas and Louisiana have even been named for certain key genera of Foraminifera (see Chapter 20). Other microfossils, such as fusulinids, ostracodes, spores, and pollens, are also used to identify subsurface formations in many other parts of the United States.

Although plant fossils are very useful as cli-

matic indicators, they are not very reliable for purposes of correlation. They do, however, provide much information about the development of plants throughout geologic time.

CHAPTER 20

LIFE OF PAST AGES

The preceding chapter, which deals with the geologic record of life on earth, suggested that there were many different types of plants and animals inhabiting our earth during prehistoric time. Some of these organisms are surprisingly similar to those living today. Others attained tremendous size, assumed bizarre shapes, and were quite unlike any of our modern organisms.

The purpose of this chapter is to give you an introduction to the diversity of life forms of both the past and the present. Although no attempt is made to introduce a highly technical classification, the taxonomy presented here is up-to-date and compares favorably with those of recent textbooks of paleontology and historical geology. It should be noted, however, that the classification used in this book may differ in some respects from that of certain other (especially older) publications. Because of this, it has seemed advisable to list alternative taxonomic names for a few of the groups that will be considered.

The emphasis in this chapter is largely on **morphology** (the study of structure or form). This will enable you to visualize the identifying characteristics of each group studied. It should also make it possible for you to recognize some of the more common forms if you should find them as fossils. Included also are comments on the habitat, most common method of preservation, and geologic range (the known duration of an organism's existence throughout geologic time), of each group.

PROTISTS: PLANTS, ANIMALS, OR IN-BETWEENS?

The members of Kingdom Protista are complex one-celled organisms that do not always have the distinguishing characteristics of plants or animals. Hence, **protists** include organisms that were once classified as either plants or animals. One group of protists, the green algae, are believed to be the forerunners of plants. In fact, protists as a group are generally assumed to be the common ancestors of both plants and animals, and are counted among the first life forms to inhabit the earth.

Phylum Protozoa. Members of this phylum are simple one-celled organisms, most of which have no hard parts. Some species, however, have external hard parts that are capable of fossilization. Many protozoans are microscopic in size, and for this reason are important as microfossils.

Included in this phylum is **class Sarcodina,** of which two orders, the Foraminifera and Radiolaria, are useful as fossils.

Members of the **order Foraminifera** (commonly called **forams**) are predominantly marine animals that secrete tiny many-chambered shells —or **tests**—of chitin, silica, or calcium carbonate (Fig. 126). Forams are abundant in many marine sedimentary rocks and range from Cambrian to Holocene in age. Because of their wide distribution and great numbers, the forams are probably the most useful of all microfossils.

Fig. 126. *Fossil foraminifers (greatly enlarged).*
a–Fusulina *(Pennsylvanian)*
b–Lenticulina *(Cretaceous)*

The radiolarians secrete delicate, spine-covered, siliceous tests (Fig. 127) and their remains are very abundant in certain marine sediments. They range from Cambrian to Holocene in age but are not commonly found as fossils.

PLANTS OF THE PAST

To review briefly what we have already discussed: Plant fossils are usually fragmental and not well preserved. They have, nevertheless, left an adequate fossil record which has provided us with much information about plant evolution. In addition, certain types of plant fossils are useful as indicators of ancient climatic conditions, and they are important in the formation of coal.

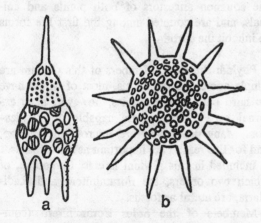

Fig. 127. *Fossil Radiolarians (greatly enlarged).*
a–Podocyrtis *(Tertiary)*
b–Trochodiscus *(Mississippian)*

PLANT CLASSIFICATION

Only the larger taxonomic groups will be considered in the following plant classification. Even so, you will be able to appreciate the great variety of forms which make up the plant kingdom. You will notice that the term *division* has been used in place of the term *phylum* as used in the animal kingdom. This usage is now preferred by many botanists and paleobotanists.

Subkingdom Thallophyta. The thallophytes comprise the simplest of all plants. They do not form embryos, possess roots, stems, or leaves, and include such forms as the fungi, algae, lichens, and diatoms. The latter are commonly found as microfossils in marine sedimentary rocks (Fig. 128). Certain species of algae secrete calcium carbonate in such quantities as to build large limestone masses called reefs. Such algal reefs are fairly common in certain Precambrian rocks, and are among the oldest fossils known. Thallophytes range from Precambrian to Holocene in age.

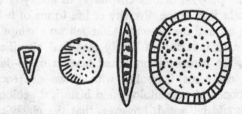

Fig. 128. *Diatoms (greatly enlarged).*

Subkingdom Embryophyta. Plants of this subkingdom are embryo-forming plants that show considerable advance over the thallophytes. Included here are members of the division **Bryophyta,** the mosses and liverworts. Although they range from Devonian to Holocene in age, bryophytes are rarely found as fossils.

Among the more important embryophytes are the plants that have been assigned to the division **Tracheophyta.** The tracheophytes, or vascular plants, have been divided into four subdivisions, among which are many of our more important living and fossil plants. These include such important forms as the ferns, evergreens, flowering plants, and hardwood trees. Among the better-known fossil tracheophytes are the cycads, ferns, and ginkgoes, in addition to such important "coal plants" as the club mosses, scouring rushes, and scale trees (Fig. 129). Tracheophytes range from Silurian to Holocene in age.

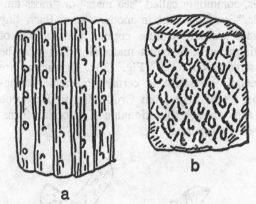

Fig. 129. Fossil "Coal Plants."
a–Lepidodendron *b*–Sigillaria

Fossilized seeds, spores, and pollen have also been found. Because of their small size, certain of these are valuable as microfossils.

ANCIENT ANIMAL LIFE

The fossilized remains of animals are quite common in many sedimentary rocks. Such remains are of many different kinds and represent the fossils of such diverse organisms as the shells of microscopic one-celled animals and the bones of huge dinosaurs. The fossils most commonly found, however, are the remains of invertebrate animals such as corals, clams, and snails.

ANIMAL CLASSIFICATION

The fundamentals of taxonomy have already been presented in Chapter 19 and it is the system of binomial nomenclature explained there that will be followed.

Phylum Porifera. These are the sponges—the simplest of the many-celled animals. Living sponges secrete a skeleton which may be composed of chitin, silica, calcium carbonate, or

spongin. These substances typically occur as spicules—small needle-like hard parts (Fig. 130) which help to support the soft tissues of the sponge.

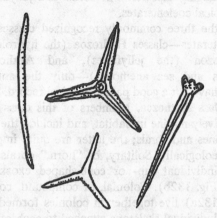

Fig. 130. Sponge spicules (greatly enlarged)

Although not abundant as fossils, a few sponges (Fig. 131) are fairly common in certain Paleozoic rocks. In addition, the spicules of some species are occasionally found as microfossils. Members of phylum Porifera were probably present during Precambrian time, and certain sponges and spongelike forms were abundant during the Cambrian Period.

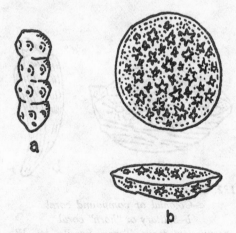

Fig. 131. Fossil sponges.
a–Girtyocoelia (*Pennsylvanian*)
b–Astraeospongium (*top and side view*)
(*By permission from* Fossils by W. H. Matthews III, *Barnes & Noble, Inc., New York.*)

Phylum Coelenterata. The coelenterates include a large group of aquatic (water-dwelling) multicelled animals. Although more complex than the sponges, they are rather primitive. The living animal is characterized by a saclike body cavity, a well-defined mouth, and tentacles which bear stinging capsules. The corals and jellyfishes are typical coelenterates.

Of the three commonly recognized classes of coelenterates—classes Hydrozoa (the hydroids), Scyphozoa (the jellyfishes), and Anthozoa (corals and sea anemones)—only the anthozoans have left a good paleontological record.

Class Anthozoa. Members of this class are exclusively marine in habitat, and include the sea anemones and corals; the latter are quite important geologically. Solitary, or "horn," corals secrete individual cup- or cone-shaped exoskeletons (Fig. 132b). Colonial, or compound, corals (Fig. 132a) live together in colonies formed by many individual skeletons attached to each other. The reef-building corals are colonial forms that commonly build calcareous masses called coral reefs. These reef-building animals typically live in warm, clear, relatively shallow seas, and are good indicators of ancient climates. Although a questionable Cambrian form has been found, corals are definitely known to range from Ordovician to Holocene in age and are one of the more important groups of fossils—especially for rocks of Paleozoic age.

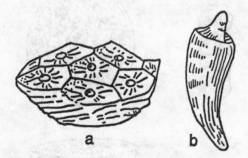

Fig. 132. Corals.
a–Colonial or compound coral
b–Solitary or "horn" coral
(*By permission from* Texas Fossils *by W. H. Matthews III, Bureau of Economic Geology, The University of Texas, Austin.*)

Worms. As used here, the "worms" include a large group of diverse animals which have been assigned to three phyla: the Platyhelminthes (flatworms), Nemathelminthes (roundworms),

and Trochelminthes (rotifers). Because of their lack of hard parts, these animals have left little or no fossil record. This is not the case with the annelid worms which will be discussed later.

Phylum Bryozoa. These small colonial animals, commonly called "sea mats" or "moss animals," are abundant in modern seas. Each tiny animal secretes a little cuplike exoskeleton of chitinous or calcareous material which may be preserved as a fossil (Fig. 133). Bryozoans are especially abundant in certain Paleozoic formations. They range from Ordovician to Holocene in age, though questionable Cambrian forms have been reported.

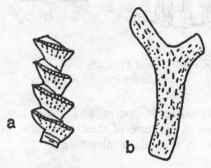

Fig. 133. Fossil bryozoans.
a–Archimedes (Mississippian)
b–Lioclema (Pennsylvanian)

Phylum Brachiopoda. The brachiopods (or "lamp shells") are a large group of exclusively marine animals with shells composed of two pieces called **valves** (Fig. 134). These valves, typically composed of calcareous or phosphatic material, enclose and protect the soft parts of the animal.

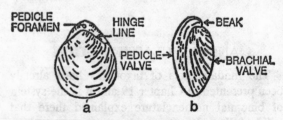

Fig. 134. Morphology and principal parts of articulate brachiopods. (By permission from Fossils *by W. H. Matthews III, Barnes & Noble, Inc., New York.)*

The typical adult brachiopod is attached to the ocean floor by means of the **pedicle**—a soft fleshy stalk. The pedicle is usually extruded through the **pedicle foramen,** a hole in the pedicle, or ventral, valve. The other valve of the shell, called the brachial or dorsal valve, is usually the smaller of the two.

The phylum has been divided into two classes: the Inarticulata and Articulata.

Class Inarticulata. The inarticulate brachiopods are rather primitive forms with a long geologic history (Early Cambrian to Recent). Most are oval to tongue-shaped and lack a pedicle foramen. Their valves are held together by muscles and are not provided with hinge teeth (see below). *Lingula* (Fig. 135) is a typical inarticulate brachiopod.

Class Articulata. The members of this class have a well-defined hinge, and one valve has well-developed teeth which articulate with sockets in the opposing valve. Articulate brachiopods are characterized by calcareous and phos-

Fig. 135. Lingula.

phatic shells, which are typically of unequal size and assume a wide variety of shapes (Fig. 136). They range from Early Cambrian to Holocene in age, and are especially abundant in fossiliferous strata of Paleozoic age.

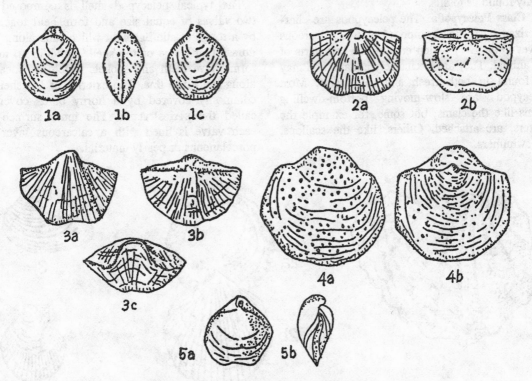

Fig. 136. Typical Fossil Articulate Brachiopods.
1–Kingena wacoensis (Cretaceous)
2–Chonetes (Pennsylvanian)
3–Neospirifer cameratus (Pennsylvanian)
4–Juresania (Pennsylvanian)
5–Composita subtilita (Pennsylvanian)
(By permission from Fossils by W. H. Matthews III,
Barnes & Noble, Inc., New York.)

Phylum Mollusca. The mollusks are a large group of aquatic and terrestrial (land-dwelling) animals. Members of this phylum include such familiar forms as the snails, slugs, clams, oysters, squids, and octopuses. Most mollusks possess a calcareous shell that serves as an exoskeleton, and these hard parts are well adapted for preservation as fossils. But there are some mollusks, for example the slugs, which have no shells, and others (the squids) which have internal shells. Because of their relative abundance, great variety, and long geologic history, mollusks are especially common as fossils.

The phylum Mollusca has been divided into five classes: Amphineura (chitons or "seamice"), Scaphopoda ("tusk-shells"), Pelecypoda (clams and oysters), Gastropoda (snails and slugs), and Cephalopoda (squids, octopuses, and the extinct ammonoids). Only the classes Gastropoda, Pelecypoda, and Cephalopoda are commonly found as fossils.

Class Pelecypoda. The pelecypods are characterized by a shell composed of two calcareous valves (Fig. 137) which enclose the soft parts of the animal. They are exclusively aquatic and may be found in both fresh and salt water. Most pelecypods are slow-moving bottom-dwelling forms like the clams, but some, for example the oysters, are attached. Others, like the scallops, are swimmers.

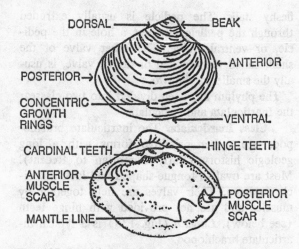

Fig. 137. Morphology and principal parts of typical pelecypod shell. (By permission from Texas Fossils *by W. H. Matthews III, Bureau of Economic Geology, The University of Texas, Austin.)*

The typical pelecypod shell is composed of two valves of equal size and form held together by a tough elastic **ligament** which runs along the **dorsal** (top) side of the shell. In addition, most forms have teeth and sockets which are located along the **hinge line.** The exterior of the shell is commonly covered by a horny outer covering called the **periostracum.** The inner surface of each valve is lined with a calcareous layer of porcelaneous or pearly material.

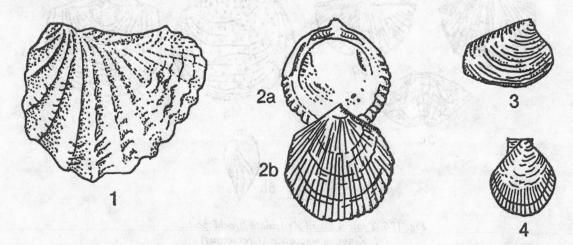

Fig. 138. Typical fossil pelecypods.
1–Trigonia (Cretaceous) 2–Glycymeris (Tertiary)
3–Astartella (Pennsylvanian) 4–Pecten (Tertiary)
(By permission from Fossils *by W. H. Matthews III, Barnes & Noble, Inc., New York.)*

Although the shell form may vary considerably (Fig. 138), most pelecypods are clamlike. The beak, which represents the oldest part of the shell, is located on the anterior (front) end of the shell and the end of the shell opposite this is designated posterior (the rear). The lower margin of the shell (where the valves open) is called the ventral margin. As noted earlier, the dorsal margin is the top side along which the hinge and ligament are located.

The interior of the valve may be marked by such structures as teeth, sockets, muscle scars, and other diagnostic features. The exterior of many shells is marked by concentric growth lines, as well as nodes, spines, ribs, and other types of ornamentation.

Fossil pelecypods are commonly preserved as casts and molds, but many are found with original shell material that appears to have undergone little change.

The first pelecypods appeared in the Cambrian Period and were especially abundant during Late Paleozoic, Mesozoic, and Cenozoic time.

Class Gastropoda. The typical gastropod has a spirally coiled, single-valved, unchambered shell. Most gastropods have gills and live in shallow marine waters, but some inhabit fresh water. Others are land dwellers and breathe by means of lungs.

Gastropods range from Early Cambrian to Recent and both fossil and recent gastropods exhibit a variety of shapes, sizes, and ornamentation (Fig. 139). Such shells may be flat, spirally coiled, cone-shaped, turreted, or cylindrical. The closed, pointed end of the shell is known as the **apex,** and each turn of the shell is called a **whorl** (Fig. 140). The largest and last-formed whorl is called the body whorl, and the opening of the shell—the **aperture**—is in this whorl. The spire is composed of the combined whorls exclusive of the body whorl. The inner and outer margins of the aperture are designated the inner lip and the outer lip respectively. Some snails close the aperture by means of the **operculum**—a horny or calcareous plate attached to the foot of the animal. This plate effectively seals the aperture when the animal is withdrawn into its shell.

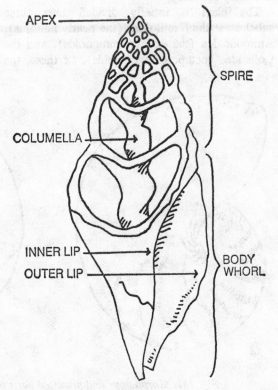

Fig. 140. Morphology and principal parts of gastropods. (By permission from Texas Fossils by W. H. Matthews III, Bureau of Economic Geology, The University of Texas, Austin.)

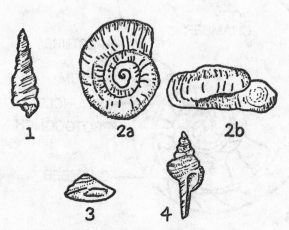

Fig. 139. Typical fossil gastropods.
1–Turritella (Tertiary) 2–Straparolus (Pennsylvanian) 3–Trepospira (Pennsylvanian) 4–Fusus (Tertiary)
(By permission from Fossils by W. H. Matthews III, Barnes & Noble, Inc., New York.)

Large numbers of gastropods, especially certain Mesozoic and Paleozoic forms, have been preserved as internal or external molds. Internal molds are formed after the animal dies and its soft parts have decomposed. This enables the shell to become filled with sediment, which later becomes solidified. The outer shell of the snail may eventually be removed by weathering or solution, freeing the internal mold. This type of mold is called a **steinkern** and normally does not reflect any external shell characteristics.

Class Cephalopoda. The cephalopods are marine mollusks with or without shells. When a shell is present, it may be internal or external, chambered or solid. They are exclusively marine, carnivorous (meat-eating), free-living animals with a high degree of body organization. Cephalopods are among the most advanced of all mollusks and include the squid, octopus, pearly nautilus, and the extinct ammonoids. Their geologic range is from Cambrian to Holocene, but they were much more abundant in ancient seas than they are today.

The class is usually divided into three subclasses: the Nautiloidea (the pearly nautilus), Ammonoidea (the extinct ammonoids), and the Coleoidea (octopuses and squids). Of these, the nautiloids and ammonoids constitute important fossil groups.

Subclass Nautiloidea. The nautiloids are cephalopods with external chambered shells in which the **septa** (dividing partitions) are simple and have smooth edges. This subclass is represented by a single living form, *Nautilus,* and a large number of fossil species.

Nautilus has a shell composed of calcium carbonate, which is coiled in a flat spiral (Fig. 141). The interior of the shell is divided into a series of chambers by calcareous partitions called **septa.** The juncture of the septum and the inner surface of the shell forms the suture. These suture lines (Fig. 142) cannot be seen unless the outer shell has been removed, but they are visible on the internal molds of many fossil cephalopods and are important in nautiloid and ammonoid classification. Nautiloids are characterized by simple smoothly curved suture patterns (Fig. 142a) but ammonoids display more complex and wrinkled sutures (Fig. 142d).

Although the shell of the only living nautiloid is coiled, many of the earlier forms had uncoiled, cone-shaped shells (Fig. 143-2). Some of the early Paleozoic forms measured as much as fifteen feet long (see Chapter 22).

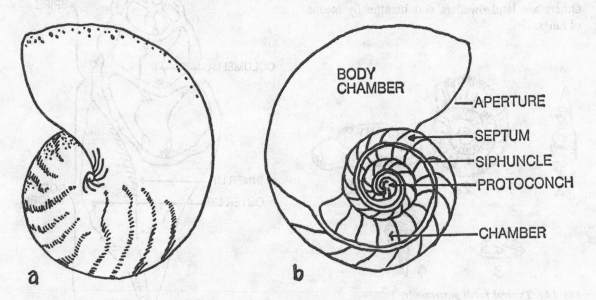

Fig. 141. Morphology and principal parts of pearly nautilus.
a–Exterior view of a recent shell
b–Sectioned view of same shell

(*By permission from* Fossils *by W. H. Matthews III, Barnes & Noble, Inc., New York.*)

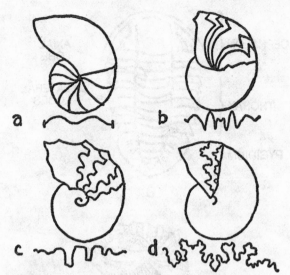

Fig. 142. Characteristic cephalopod suture.
  a–Nautiloid   b–Goniatite
  c–Ceratite   d–Ammonite
(*By permission from* Fossils *by W. H. Matthews III,*
Barnes & Noble, Inc., New York.)

The earliest known nautiloids have been collected from Lower Cambrian rocks, and they were much more abundant during the Paleozoic Era than they are today.

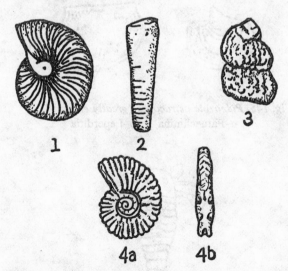

Fig. 143. Typical fossil cephalopods.
1–Cymatoceras, *a Cretaceous nautiloid. 2*–Orthoceras, *a Pennsylvanian nautiloid. 3*–Turrilites, *a spirally coiled Cretaceous ammonoid. 4*–Dufrenoyia, *a Cretaceous ammonoid. (By permission from Fossils by W. H. Matthews III, Barnes & Noble, Inc., New York.)*

Subclass Ammonoidea. Members of this subclass are extinct cephalopods which are related to the nautiloids but characterized by more complex suture patterns. Ammonoids have an external partitioned shell which is straight, curved, or spirally coiled (Fig. 143). They appeared first in Devonian time, were abundant and varied during the Mesozoic, and were extinct by the end of the Cretaceous Period.

Ammonoids exhibit three types of sutures: (1) **goniatitic** (a curved and angular pattern), (2) **ceratitic** (curved and crenulated—marked in places by a series of toothlike indentations), and (3) **ammonitic** (a very complexly subdivided pattern). Cephalopods with ammonitic sutures range from Pennsylvanian to Cretaceous in age and were the most abundant cephalopods of the Mesozoic.

Subclass Coleoidea. These are cephalopods that are characterized by an internal shell or no shell at all. Included here are the squids, octopuses, cuttlefish, and the extinct belemnoids. The belemnoids (also called belemnites) appear to represent the fossil remains of a living animal that was similar to the modern cuttlefish. Their characteristic shape has caused them to be called "finger stones" or "fossil cigars." They range from Mississippian to Cretaceous in age, and certain species are valuable guide fossils for Jurassic and Cretaceous rocks.

Phylum Annelida. The annelid worms are segmented worms such as the common earthworm. They are marine, freshwater, or terrestrial in habitat and have apparently been common throughout much of geologic time. Because of their lack of hard parts, annelids have left little direct evidence of their activities in the geologic past. Some have, however, left calcareous tubes, chitinous jaws and teeth called **scolecodonts,** and burrows and borings.

Undoubted fossil annelid remains have been found in rocks ranging from Cambrian to Holocene in age. However, the presence of wormlike tracks and burrows in certain Precambrian rocks suggests that annelids probably lived prior to Cambrian time.

Phylum Arthropoda. The arthropods are one of the more advanced groups of invertebrates, and they are known from the Cambrian to the

Holocene. Modern representatives of this group
include the crabs, shrimps, crayfish, insects, and
spiders. Arthropods vary greatly in size and
shape and are among the most abundant of all
animals.

They have adapted themselves to a variety of
habitats and live on land, in the water, and in the
air. Although of great importance in nature
today, only a few groups are important to the
paleontologist. Three of these—the trilobites, ostracodes, and eurypterids—are discussed below.

Trilobites. These are members of class Trilo-
bita of subphylum Trilobitomorpha. The trilobites are exclusively marine arthropods, which
derive their name from the typical three-lobed
appearance of their bodies. The body of the animal is encased in a chitinous exoskeleton and is
divided into a central or axial lobe, and two lateral or pleural lobes (Fig. 144a). The body is
also divided, from front to back, into the **ceph-
alon** or head, the **thorax** or abdomen, and the
pygidium or tail. Some species have the body
segments of the thorax arranged in such a manner as to permit the trilobites to roll up into a
ball, and many trilobites are found in this position (Fig. 144b). Trilobites range from Cambrian to Permian in age, and were especially
abundant during some of the earlier Paleozoic
periods.

Ostracodes. These minute bivalved arthropods belong to class Ostracoda of the subphylum
Crustacea—the same subphylum to which the
crabs, shrimp, crayfish, and lobsters have been
referred. The ostracodes are small aquatic crusta-
ceans which externally resemble small clams
(Fig. 145). However, the animal that inhabits
the shell possesses all of the typical arthropod
characteristics. Fossil ostracodes range from Ordovician to Holocene in age, and because of their
small size they are especially useful as microfossils.

Eurypterids. These extinct arthropods have
been assigned to class Merostomata of subphylum Chelicerata. The scorpions, spiders,
mites, ticks, and "king crabs" have also been assigned to this subphylum. Eurypterids are scorpion-like aquatic forms characterized by broad
winglike appendages (Fig. 146) and some are
believed to have possessed a poison gland and
stinger.

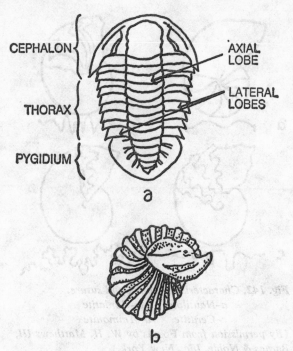

*Fig. 144. Morphology and principal parts of trilo-
bites.*
*a–Top view, b–Side view of enrolled form. (By per-
mission from* Fossils *by W. H. Matthews III, Barnes
& Noble, Inc., New York.)*

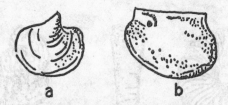

Fig. 145. Paleozoic ostracodes (greatly enlarged).
   a–Paraechmina   b–Leperditia

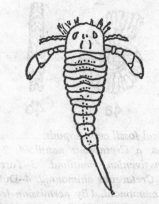

*Fig. 146. Eurypterid, an early Paleozoic scorpion-
like arthropod.*

Although not common as fossils, they occur locally in certain Silurian and Devonian formations. Their geologic range is from Early Ordovician to Permian.

Phylum Echinodermata. The echinoderms are a large group of exclusively marine animals, most of which exhibit a marked fivefold symmetry. The typical echinoderm is a relatively complex organism with a skeleton composed of numerous calcareous plates which are intricately fitted together and covered by the **integument**—a leathery outer skin. Many echinoderms have a typical star-shaped body, but some types may be heart-shaped, biscuit-shaped, or cucumber-shaped.

Geologic range of the Echinodermata is from Cambrian to Holocene, and members of the phylum are abundant as fossils in marine sedimentary rocks of all ages.

The phylum has been divided into two subphyla: the Pelmatozoa (attached echinoderms), and Eleutherozoa (unattached echinoderms).

Subphylum Pelmatozoa. These are echinoderms which are more or less permanently attached to the sea bottom by means of a stalk composed of slightly movable, calcareous, disc-like segments. They range from Cambrian to Holocene in age and are particularly common as fossils in Paleozoic rocks.

Although the Pelmatozoa has been divided into several classes, only three of these, the Cystoidea, Blastoidea, and Crinoidea will be discussed here. With the exception of the Crinoidea, all of the pelmatozoans are extinct.

Class Cystoidea. These are primitive, extinct, attached echinoderms which were relatively common during the early Paleozoic. Cystoids are characterized by a globular or saclike **calyx** (the main body skeleton) which is made up of numerous irregularly arranged calcareous plates (Fig. 147b). The animal was attached to the sea floor by a short stem.

Ranging from Cambrian to Devonian in age, cystoids were especially numerous during the Ordovician and Silurian periods.

Class Blastoidea. Members of this extinct class are short-stemmed echinoderms with a small, symmetrical, budlike calyx. The mouth is located near the center of the calyx and is surrounded by five openings called **spiracles.** Five

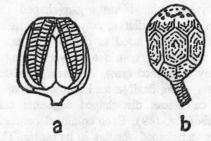

Fig. 147. Fossil attached echinoderms.
a–Pentremites (Mississippian)
b–Caryocrinites (Silurian)

distinct **ambulacral** or **food grooves** radiate outward from the mouth (Fig. 147a).

Blastoids range from Ordovician to Permian in age and were especially abundant during the Mississippian Period.

Class Crinoidea. The crinoids, commonly called "sea lilies" because of their flower-like appearance, are the only attached echinoderms living today. The crinoid calyx is composed of numerous symmetrically arranged plates, and most crinoids have a long stem or **stalk** (Fig. 148). Other crinoids are free-swimming in the adult stage and are attached only during the earlier phases of their development.

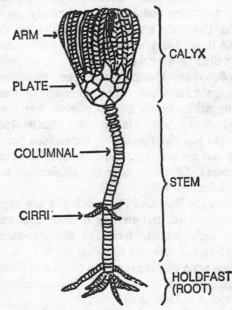

Fig. 148. Typical modern crinoid or "sea lily" showing principal parts. (By permission from Fossils by W. H. Matthews III, Barnes & Noble, Inc., New York.)

The typical crinoid has a cup-shaped calyx with five grooves radiating outward from its center. These grooves, used as channels to convey food to the mouth, continue outward along the complexly segmented arms. The stem consists of a relatively long flexible stalk composed of numerous calcareous disc-shaped segments called **columnals** (Fig. 149). Each columnal contains a round or star-shaped opening in its center. These columnals become separated when the animal dies and certain Paleozoic limestones contain such great numbers of columnals that they are called crinoidal limestones.

Fig. 149. Fossil crinoid columnals.

The crinoid stalk is attached to the sea floor by means of the **holdfast.** This structure branches out into the surrounding sediments and serves to anchor the animal to the bottom.

Crinoids range from Ordovician to Holocene in age, and their remains are particularly abundant in Paleozoic strata. The majority of the crinoids living today are stemless free-swimming forms called "feather stars."

Subphylum Eleutherozoa. The eleutherozoans are unattached, free-swimming, bottom-dwelling echinoderms. The subphylum has been divided into three classes, the Stelleroidea (starfishes and "brittle stars"), Echinoidea (sand dollars and sea urchins), and Holothuroidea (sea cucumbers). Of these, only the Echinoidea are useful as fossils.

Class Stelleroidea. The stelleroids are typically star-shaped, free-moving echinoderms and include such familiar forms as the star-fishes (Fig. 150) and "serpent stars" or "brittle stars." Although none of this group is a particularly useful fossil, they do have a long geologic history (Ordovician to Holocene).

Class Echinoidea. The echinoids are a group of unattached echinoderms with bodies consisting of numerous calcareous plates and spines. They do not possess the radiating arm-like extensions

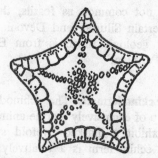

Fig. 150. Fossil starfish.

which characterize the stelleroids; instead, their bodies are disc-shaped, heart-shaped, biscuit-shaped, or globular (Fig. 151). Modern representatives of the Echinoidea include such familiar forms as the sand dollars, heart urchins, and sea urchins.

The test (exoskeleton) of the echinoid is composed of many intricately fitting calcareous plates which enclose and protect the animal's soft parts. The outside of the test is commonly covered with large numbers of spines. These spines vary in size and are used to aid in locomotion, support the test, and for purposes of protection.

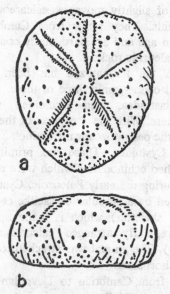

Fig. 151. Hemiaster, *a cretaceous heart urchin.*
a–Top view   b–Side view

Echinoids range from Ordovician to Holocene in age, but flourished during the Mesozoic, and were especially abundant during the Cretaceous.

Class Holothuroidea. The sea cucumbers are

characterized by a rather elongate, saclike, cucumber-shaped body. With the exception of small calcareous rods or plates called **sclerites**, or **ossicles**, holothuroids do not possess any hard parts and are thus seldom fossilized. Sclerites as old as Mississippian have been reported, and impressions of supposed sea cucumber-like forms have been described from Middle Cambrian rocks in Canada. The sea cucumbers make up only a small part of our modern-day marine faunas.

Phylum Chordata. Members of this phylum are characterized by the presence of a well-developed nervous system and a body supported by a bony or cartilaginous notochord or spinal column.

Only two of the several chordate subphyla are of paleontological significance—the Hemichordata (which includes the extinct graptolites) and the Vertebrata (including all animals with backbones).

Subphylum Hemichordata. Hemichordates do not possess a true backbone; rather, they are characterized by a well-defined notochord which runs the length of the body. Only the class Graptolithina is of paleontological importance.

Class Graptolithina. The graptolites are a group of extinct colonial animals that were very abundant during Early Paleozoic time. They are characterized by a chitinous exoskeleton consisting of rows of cups, or tubes, which housed the living animal. These grew along single or branching stalks (Fig. 152) which were attached to rocks, seaweeds, or other foreign objects. Some graptolites were attached to floats and attained wide distribution in this manner.

There has been considerable uncertainty about the exact taxonomic position of these animals, and earlier classifications have considered them to be members of the classes Hydrozoa, Scyphozoa, and Graptozoa of phylum Coelenterata. In addition, certain of the earlier paleontologists placed them in the phylum Bryozoa. Recent research, however, suggests that the graptolites are some type of extinct chordate.

Graptolites are recorded in rocks ranging from Cambrian to Mississippian in age. They are especially useful as guide fossils in certain black shales of the Ordovician and Silurian ages, where

Fig. 152. Lower Paleozoic graptolites.
a–Diplograptus *b*–Phyllograptus
(By permission from Texas Fossils *by W. H. Matthews III, Bureau of Economic Geology, The University of Texas, Austin.)*

their remains are commonly preserved as a flattened carbon residue.

Subphylum Vertebrata. The vertebrates, the most advanced of all chordates, are characterized by a **skull**, a bony or cartilaginous **internal skeleton**, and a **vertebral column** of bone or cartilage.

The subphylum is commonly divided into two superclasses, the Pisces (fishes and their relatives) and the Tetrapoda (the "four-footed" animals including snakes which have vestigial limbs).

Although the geologist makes most paleontological correlations with invertebrate fossils, the remains of vertebrates have provided the historical geologist with much-needed and valuable paleontological information. Furthermore, such unusual fossils as the remains of dinosaurs, giant fishes, mammoths, saber-tooth cats, and other unusual vertebrates are among the most interesting and fascinating fossils known.

Superclass Pisces. The Pisces, commonly called fishes, are the simplest of the vertebrate animals. They are aquatic, free-moving, cold-blooded (their blood maintains the temperature of the surrounding water), and most forms breathe by means of gills. (The unusual lungfishes of Australia and Africa are exceptions for they breathe by means of a primitive lung developed from the swim bladder.)

The four classes recognized in most recent fish classifications are briefly considered below.

Class Agnatha. These are primitive jawless fishes, represented by such living forms as the lampreys and hagfishes. The earliest agnathans, the ostracoderms, first appeared in the Cambrian and were extinct by the end of the Devonian. These early fishes, which were armored by a bony covering on the front part of their bodies, are believed to represent the earliest known vertebrates.

Class Placodermi. Placoderms are primitive jawed fishes, most of which were heavily armored. These creatures were sharklike in appearance and some grew to be as much as thirty feet in length. They first appeared in the Silurian and were extinct by the end of the Permian.

Class Chondrichthyes. Members of this class are characterized by a skeleton composed of cartilage. Included here are the sharks, skates, and rays. They first appeared in Devonian time and have been relatively common up to the present. Fossil shark teeth (Fig. 153) are relatively abundant in certain Mesozoic and Cenozoic formations.

Fig. 153. Fossil shark teeth (about natural size).

Class Osteichthyes. These are the true bony fishes—the most highly developed and abundant of all fishes. They are typified by well-developed jaws, an internal bony skeleton, an air bladder, and, typically, an external covering of overlapping scales. Fish fossils are commonly found in the form of teeth, bones, scales, and an occasional well-preserved skeleton. They range from Middle Devonian to Holocene in age.

Conodonts. These small, amber-colored, toothlike fossils (Fig. 154) are believed to be the hard parts of some type of extinct fish.

Although paleontologists are not certain what type of animal these strange fossils represent, their small size and rather limited stratigraphic occurrence makes them useful as microfossils.

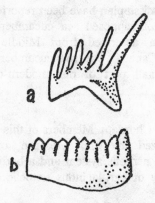

Fig. 154. Conodonts (enlarged about 30 times).
a–Metalonchodina (*Pennsylvanian*)
b–Spathognathodus (*Silurian*)
(*By permission from* Fossils *by W. H. Matthews III, Barnes & Noble, Inc., New York.*)

Superclass Tetrapoda. These are the most advanced chordates, and characteristically possess lungs, a three- or four-chambered heart, and paired appendages. Four classes, the Amphibia (frogs, toads, and salamanders), Reptilia (lizards, snakes, and turtles), Aves (birds), and Mammalia (including the mammals, such as men, dogs, bats, whales) are recognized.

Class Amphibia. The amphibians are represented by such common forms as the toads, frogs, and salamanders. They are cold-blooded animals that breathe primarily by lungs and spend most of their life on land, but during their early stages of development they live in the water where they breathe by means of gills.

The amphibians were the earliest developed four-legged animals and appeared late in Devonian time. They were relatively abundant in the Pennsylvanian, Permian, and Triassic periods (Fig. 155a).

Class Reptilia. The reptiles evolved from the amphibians and have become adapted to permanent life on land and need not rely on an aquatic environment. They are cold-blooded and are normally characterized by a scaly skin. Reptiles were formerly much more abundant than they are today, and they assumed many

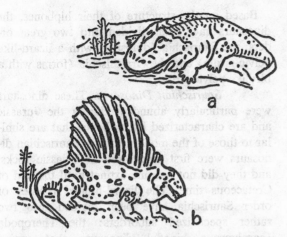

Fig. 155. a–Eryops, *a Permian amphibian.* b–Dimetrodon, *a Permian pelycosaur. (By permission from* Texas Fossils *by W. H. Matthews III, Bureau of Economic Geology, The University of Texas, Austin.)*

different shapes and sizes in the geologic past. Modern classifications recognize a large number of reptilian groups, but only the more important ones are briefly reviewed here.

Cotylosaurs. These primitive reptiles although retaining some amphibian characteristics, became adapted to an exclusively terrestrial mode of life. They lived during the Pennsylvanian and Permian periods, and apparently became extinct during Triassic time.

Turtles and Tortoises. The bodies of these reptiles are more or less completely encased by bony plates. They range from Late Triassic to Holocene in age, although there is questionable evidence of a Late Permian turtle-like reptile. Some of the Cenozoic tortoises were three to four feet long, and certain of the Cretaceous sea turtles attained lengths of as much as twelve feet.

Pelycosaurs. These are a group of Late Paleozoic reptiles, some of which were characterized by the presence of a sail-like fin on their back (Fig. 155b).

Therapsids. The therapsids constitute a mammal-like group of reptiles which were well adapted to a terrestrial existence. Although this group is not especially important as fossils, study of their remains has provided much information about the origin of the mammals. They range from Middle Permian to Middle Jurassic in age.

Ichthyosaurs. The so-called "fish-lizards" were short-necked marine reptiles which were definitely fishlike in appearance (Fig. 167a). They resembled the modern dolphins and some of them attained lengths of twenty-five to thirty feet, though the average was much less. Ichthyosaurs first appeared in Middle Triassic time and were extinct by the end of the Cretaceous.

Mosasaurs. The mosasaurs, another group of extinct marine lizards, grew to be as much as fifty feet long. They were apparently vicious carnivores, as attested by their great, gaping, tooth-filled jaws (Fig. 167b). These giant reptiles lived only during the Cretaceous Period.

Plesiosaurs. The plesiosaurs were marine reptiles which were characterized by a broad turtle-like body, paddle-like flippers, and a long neck and tail (Fig. 167c). Although these reptiles were not as streamlined or well equipped for swimming as the ichthyosaurs or mosasaurs, their long serpent-like necks were probably quite useful in catching fish and other small animals for food. Plesiosaur remains range from Middle Triassic to Late Cretaceous in age.

Phytosaurs. The phytosaurs were a group of crocodile-like reptiles, which ranged from six to twenty feet in length. Although they resembled crocodiles both in appearance and in their mode of life, this similarity is only superficial, for the phytosaurs and crocodiles are two distinct groups of reptiles. The phytosaurs lived only during Triassic time.

Crocodiles and Alligators. These reptiles, which are common today, adapted themselves to the same type of habitat as that occupied by the phytosaurs, which preceded them. Crocodiles and alligators were much larger and more abundant during Cretaceous and Cenozoic time than they are today. The crocodiles first appeared in the Cretaceous and the alligators in the Tertiary.

Pterosaurs. These were Mesozoic reptiles with batlike wings supported by arms and long thin "fingers" (Fig. 156). The pterosaurs were well adapted to life in the air, and their lightweight bodies and wide skin-covered wings enabled them to soar or glide for great distances. The earliest known pterosaurs were collected from Lower Jurassic rocks, and the group had become extinct by the end of the Cretaceous. During the Cretaceous Period, certain of these creatures attained a wingspread of as much as fifty feet, but their bodies were small and light.

Dinosaurs. The collective term "dinosaurs" (which literally means "terrible lizards") has been given to that unusual group of reptiles that dominated the life of the Mesozoic for some 165 million years. These unusual reptiles ranged from as little as a few feet to as much as eighty-five feet in length and from a few pounds to perhaps forty-five tons in weight. Some dinosaurs were carnivorous, but most were herbivorous (plant-eaters). Some forms were bipedal (walked on their hind legs), while others were quadrupedal (walked on all fours), and although most of the dinosaurs were land-dwelling forms, aquatic and semiaquatic species were also present.

Based on the structure of their hipbones, the dinosaurs have been divided into two great orders: the Saurischia (dinosaurs with a lizard-like pelvic girdle) and the Ornithischia (forms with a birdlike pelvic girdle).

Saurischian Dinosaurs. These dinosaurs were particularly abundant during the Jurassic and are characterized by hipbones that are similar to those of the modern lizards. Saurischian dinosaurs were first discovered in Triassic rocks, and they did not become extinct until the end of Cretaceous time. The lizard-hipped reptiles of order Saurischia have been divided into two rather specialized suborders: the Theropoda (carnivorous bipedal dinosaurs that varied greatly in size) and the Sauropoda (herbivorous, quadrupedal, semiaquatic, usually gigantic dinosaurs).

Theropods. These saurischian dinosaurs walked on birdlike hind limbs, and they were exclusively meat-eating forms. Some of the theropods were exceptionally large and were undoubtedly vicious beasts of prey. This assumption is borne out by such characteristics as the small front limbs with long sharp claws for holding and tearing flesh, and the large strong jaws which were armed with numerous sharp teeth. The largest of all known theropods was *Tyrannosaurus rex* which, when standing on his hind limbs, was almost twenty feet tall (Fig. 157). Some individuals were as much as fifty feet long, and *Tyrannosaurus* is believed to have been among the most vicious animals ever to inhabit our earth.

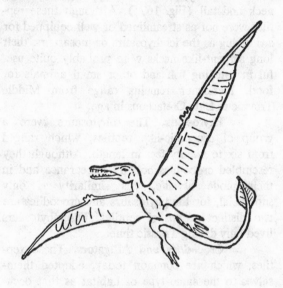

Fig. 156. Pterosaurs, Mesozoic flying reptiles.
a–Rhamphorhynchus (Jurassic)
b–Pteranodon (Cretaceous)
(By permission from Fossils *by W. H. Matthews III, Barnes & Noble, Inc., New York.)*

Fig. 157. Tyrannosaurus rex, *mighty Cretaceous carnivore.*

Fig. 158. Representative dinosaurs of the Mesozoic
Era
a–Brontosaurus   b–Trachodon (or Anatosaurus)
c–Ankylosaurus   d–Triceratops
(By permission from Texas Fossils by W. H.
Matthews III, Bureau of Economic Geology, The
University of Texas, Austin.)

Sauropods. Members of the Sauropoda were the largest of all dinosaurs. Some were as much as eighty-five feet long and probably weighed forty to fifty tons (see *Brontosaurus,* Fig. 158a). The sauropods were primarily herbivorous dinosaurs which had become adapted to an aquatic or semiaquatic way of life, and they probably inhabited lakes, rivers, and swamps.

Ornithischian Dinosaurs. The ornithischian, or bird-hipped dinosaurs, were herbivorous reptiles which were quite varied in form and size. They appear to have been more highly developed than the saurischians. Included in this order are the duckbilled dinosaurs (suborder Ornithopoda), the plate-bearing dinosaurs (suborder Stegosauria), the armored dinosaurs (suborder Ankylosauria), and the horned dinosaurs (suborder Ceratopsia).

Ornithopods. The ornithopods were unusual dinosaurs which were predominantly bipedal, semiaquatic, and some (like *Trachodon,* the duckbilled dinosaur) were highly specialized (Fig. 158b).

Stegosaurs. These were herbivorous, quadrupedal ornithischians with large projecting plates along their backs and heavy spikes on their tails. *Stegosaurus,* a Jurassic form, is most typical of the plate-bearing dinosaurs (Fig. 159). This great beast weighed about ten tons, was some thirty feet long, and stood approximately ten feet tall at the hips. *Stegosaurus* was characterized by a double row of large, heavy, pointed plates which ran along the animal's back. These plates began at the back of the skull and stopped near the end of the tail. The tail was also equipped with four or more long curved spikes which were probably used for purposes of defense. The animal had a very small skull which housed a brain that was about the size of a walnut, and it is assumed that these, and all other dinosaurs, were of very limited intelligence.

Ankylosaurs. The ankylosaurs were four-footed, plant-eating, Cretaceous reptiles characterized by relatively flat bodies. The skull and back of the dinosaur were protected by bony armor, and the clublike tail was armed with spikes. *Ankylosaurus* (Fig. 158c), a typical ankylosaur, also had spines projecting from along the sides of the body and tail. The armored spiked back and the heavy clublike tail probably provided the animal with much-needed protec-

Fig. 159. Stegosaurus, *plate-back dinosaur.*

tion from the predatory dinosaurs of the Cretaceous.

Ceratopsians. The horned dinosaurs, or ceratopsians, are another group of dinosaurs that are exclusively Cretaceous in age. These herbivorous dinosaurs had beaklike jaws, a bony neck frill which extended back from the skull, and one or more horns. *Triceratops* (Fig. 158d) is the largest of the horned dinosaurs (some forms were as much as thirty feet long), and the skull measured as much as eight feet from the tip of the parrot-like beak to the back of the neck shield.

Class Aves. Birds, because of the fragile nature of their bodies, are seldom found as fossils. Nevertheless, some interesting and important fossil birds have been described.

The oldest bird yet discovered was collected from rocks of Late Jurassic age in Germany. Named *Archaeopteryx,* this primitive bird was little more than a reptile with feathers and was about the size of a pigeon. It possessed a lizard-like tail, toothed beak, and certain other definitely reptilian characteristics.

Birds underwent numerous changes during Cretaceous time, and most of our present-day forms had developed by the end of the Tertiary.

Class Mammalia. The mammals, animals that are born alive and fed with milk from the mother's breast, are warm-blooded, air-breathing creatures characterized by a protective covering of hair. They are the most advanced of all vertebrates. The characteristics noted above are the more typical mammalian features, but exceptions to these are found in certain mammals.

First appearing in Triassic time, mammals

were probably derived from some form of mammal-like reptile. They were rare during the Mesozoic, but underwent rapid development and expansion during the Cenozoic, and during this era certain types of mammals became extremely large and assumed many bizarre shapes. The majority of these unusual forms were doomed to early extinction but are well known from their fossils.

Recent mammalian classification recognizes several subclasses and numerous orders and suborders, but the treatment of the mammals in a publication of this nature must of necessity be somewhat brief. No attempt at detailed classification will be made, but two of the subclasses will be discussed, as will the more important orders of each of these groups. These two subclasses are the Allotheria, containing a group of primitive early mammals, and the Theria, which contains the **placental** animals (mammals which are born in a relatively advanced stage of development).

Subclass Allotheria. The allotherians first appeared during the Jurassic and underwent considerable development in the Late Cretaceous and Early Tertiary. Included here are the **multituberculates**, a group of small, rodent-like animals that were probably the earliest of the plant-eating mammals. These animals were probably never very numerous, and they became extinct during the early part of Eocene time.

Subclass Theria. Therians are first known from rocks of Jurassic age, and constitute the largest group of mammals that are living today. They undergo considerable development before they are born and at birth usually resemble their parents. This subclass has been divided into several orders, but only the more important ones will be discussed here.

Order Edentata. A rather primitive group of mammals, the edentates are represented by such living forms as the armadillos, tree sloths, and anteaters. Members of this order were common in the southern part of the United States in Pleistocene and Pliocene time, and fossil edentates are fairly common in certain Cenozoic rocks. One such form was *Mylodon* (Fig. 160) one of the extinct giant ground sloths. These huge sloths were quite heavy, and some of them stood as much as fifteen feet tall. These great creatures were the forerunners of the modern tree sloths of South America.

Fig. 160. Mylodon, *giant ground sloth.*

The glyptodont was another interesting representative of this order. These peculiar mammals, which were ancestral to the present-day armadillos, lived at about the same time as the ground sloths. *Glyptodon,* a typical Pleistocene glyptodont, is quite characteristic of this group. This armadillo-like beast had a solid turtle-like shell that in some forms was as much as four feet high. From the front of the bone-capped head to the tip of its tail a large individual might measure as much as fifteen feet long. There was a series of bony rings on the thick heavy tail, and in some species the end of the tail was developed into a bony, heavily spiked club.

Order Carnivora. The carnivores are characterized by clawed feet and by teeth which are adapted for tearing and cutting flesh. The carnivores, or meat eaters, were first represented by an ancient group of animals called **creodonts**, a short-lived group that first appeared in the Paleocene Epoch and was extinct by the end of the Eocene. The creodonts ranged from the size of a weasel to that of a large bear, and their claws were sharp and well developed.

Fig. 161. Smilodon, *a saber-tooth cat.*

These early meat eaters were followed by more specialized carnivores which developed throughout Cenozoic time. Some examples of these are the saber-tooth cat *Smilodon* (Fig. 161) and the dire wolf *Canis dirus*.

Order Pantodonta. The pantodonts, known also as **amblypods**, were primitive, hoofed, plant-eating animals. They were distinguished by a heavy skeleton, short stout limbs, and blunt spreading feet. The pantodonts appeared first during the Paleocene and had become extinct by the end of Oligocene time.

Order Dinocerata. The members of this order are an extinct group of gigantic mammals commonly called uintatheres. *Uintatherium*, which is typical of the group, had three pairs of blunt horns, and the males had dagger-like upper tusks. Some of the uintatheres were as large as a small elephant and stood as much as seven feet tall at the shoulders. The size of the brain in relation to the size of the body suggests that these animals were not as intelligent as most mammals. Uintatheres are known from rocks ranging from Paleocene to Eocene in age.

Order Proboscidea. The earliest proboscideans, the elephants and their relatives, were collected from Upper Eocene rocks of Africa. These early forms were about the size of a small modern elephant, but had larger heads and shorter trunks. Proboscidean development is marked by an increase in size, change in skull and tooth structure, and elongation of the trunk. Two of the better-known fossil proboscideans are the **mammoth** and the **mastodon**, both of which inhabited North America and other parts of the world during Pleistocene time. The mastodons resembled the elephants, but the structure of their teeth was quite different. In addition, the mastodon skull was lower than that of the elephant and the tusks were exceptionally large— some reaching a length of nine feet.

There were several types of mammoths, and the woolly mammoth is probably the best known of these. This animal lived until the end of the Pleistocene Epoch and, like the woolly rhinoceros discussed below, is known from ancient cave paintings and frozen remains. Information gathered from these sources indicates that this great beast had a long coat of black hair with a woolly undercoat (Fig. 162b).

Order Perissodactyla. The perissodactyls (odd-toed animals) are mammals in which the central toe on each limb is greatly enlarged.

The horses, rhinoceroses, and tapirs are typical living members of this order. Extinct members of the Perissodactyla include the titanotheres, chalicotheres, and baluchitheres, all of which grew to tremendous size and took on many unusual body forms.

Fig. 162. Pleistocene mammals.
a–Woolly rhinoceros   b–Woolly mammoth
(*By permission from* Texas Fossils *by W. H. Matthews III, Bureau of Economic Geology, The University of Texas, Austin.*)

Horses—Hyracotherium (also called *Eohippus*) was one of the first perissodactyls. This small animal was about one foot high and his teeth indicate a diet of soft food. Following the first horse, there is a long series of fossil horses which provide much valuable information on the history of this important group of animals.

Titanotheres—This group of odd-toed mammals appeared first in the Eocene, at which time they were about the size of a sheep. By Middle Oligocene time, they had increased to gigantic proportions, but still had a small and primitive brain. *Brontotherium* bore a slight resemblance to the rhinoceros and is believed to be the largest land mammal that ever inhabited the North American continent. This huge beast was about eight feet tall at the shoulders. A large bony growth protruded from the skull and this was extended into a flattened horn which was divided at the top.

Although the titanotheres underwent rapid development during the Early Tertiary, these queer beasts became extinct during the middle of the Oligocene Epoch.

Chalicotheres—The chalicotheres were in some ways like the titanotheres, but they also exhibited many peculiarities of their own. The head and neck of *Moropus,* a typical chalicothere, were much like that of a horse, but the front legs were longer than the hind legs, and the feet resembled those of a rhinoceros except that they bore long claws instead of hoofs. The chalicotheres lived in North America from Miocene until Pleistocene time, but were probably never very numerous.

Rhinoceroses—The rhinoceroses are also odd-toed animals, and there are many interesting and well-known fossils in this group. The woolly rhinoceros was a Pleistocene two-horned form that ranged from southern France to northeastern Siberia. The woolly rhinoceros (Fig. 162a) is well known from complete carcasses recovered from the frozen tundra of Siberia and from remains that were found preserved in an oil seep in Poland. These unusual specimens plus cave paintings made by early man have given us a complete and accurate record of this creature. Fossil rhinoceroses have been found in rocks ranging from Middle Oligocene to Late Pliocene in age.

Baluchitherium, the largest land mammal known to science, was a titanic hornless rhinoceros that lived in Late Oligocene and Early Miocene time. This immense creature measured approximately twenty-five feet from head to tail, stood almost eighteen feet high at the shoulder, and must have weighed many tons. Remains of these creatures have not been discovered in North America, and they appear to have been restricted to Central Asia.

Order Artiodactyla. The artiodactyls, or even-toed hoofed mammals, include such familiar forms as the pigs, camels, deer, goats, sheep, and hippopotamuses. This is a large and varied group of animals, but the basic anatomical structure of the limbs and teeth show well the relationship between the different forms. Artiodactyls are abundant as fossils in rocks ranging from Eocene to Pleistocene in age.

Entelodonts—These giant piglike artiodactyls lived during Oligocene and Early Miocene time and were characterized by a long heavy skull that held a relatively small brain. The face was marked by large knobs which were located beneath the eyes and on the underside of the lower jaw, and although these knoblike structures were blunt, they had the appearance of short horns. Certain of these giant swine attained a height of six feet at the shoulders and had skulls that measured three feet in length.

Camels—The earliest known fossils of camel were collected from rocks of Late Eocene age, and these small forms underwent considerable specialization of teeth and limbs as they developed in size. Many of the camels that lived during the Middle Cenozoic had long legs which were well adapted to running, and long necks which would have helped the animals to browse on the leaves of tall trees. Their fossilized remains are common in many parts of the United States.

CHAPTER 21

EVOLUTION: CHANGING LIFE

As mentioned earlier, the earth's inhabitants have undergone continual and gradual change throughout the geologic past. The record of this change is well documented and may be explained by the theory of **organic evolution.** This theory, which is of paramount importance to both biologists and geologists, has been defined as a process of cumulative change characterized by the progressive development of plants and animals from more primitive ancestors. Thus, a study of evolution indicates that our modern-day plants and animals have attained their present degree of development as a result of gradual and orderly changes which have taken place in the geologic past. Because of its importance to the historical geologist, a brief review of the concept of evolution is appropriate here. (For more information on organic evolution, see *Biology Made Simple,* by Ethel M. Hanauer.)

THEORIES OF EVOLUTION

The idea of organic evolution is not new, for certain of the early Greek philosophers had a rather crude concept of evolution as early as 500 B.C. It was not until the nineteenth century, however, that the first scientific theory was presented.

Although many scientists have studied the evolutionary changes undergone by plants and animals, relatively few have attempted to explain how these changes have come about. Among those who have are Jean Lamarck, Charles Darwin, and Hugo de Vries.

Theory of Inheritance of Acquired Characteristics. Proposed by Jean Baptiste Lamarck in 1809, this theory contends that an organ which is constantly used becomes highly developed, and one which is not used becomes weak and eventually disappears. Lamarck was also of the opinion that these **acquired characteristics** could be transmitted from parent to offspring. Thus, after several generations, new or changed species would be produced. Lamarck believed, for example, that a blacksmith's son would be born with larger biceps than would the son of a shopkeeper, the difference being attributed to the superior physical condition of the blacksmith. Known also as the **Theory of Use and Disuse,** this theory has little support from the scientists of today.

Theory of Natural Selection. This theory was proposed in 1859 by Charles Darwin, one of the most famous and best known of all biologists. Darwin, in his attempt to explain the cause of evolution, developed a theory based on a great deal of scientific research and experimentation.

Presented in his classic book, *The Origin of Species,* Darwin based his theory of natural selection on four factors:

1. The struggle for existence. All organisms produce far more offspring than can be expected to reach maturity. This overproduction results in a continual competition for food, water, shelter, etc. The organism must overcome these difficulties or perish.

2. Variation. No two of these offspring are alike, for there is variation even within an immediate family.

3. **Natural selection.** Only those individuals that are best adapted to survive and reproduce their kind reach maturity. This leads to the "survival of the fittest."

4. **Sexual selection.** Some individuals possess certain characteristics which give them an advantage in securing a mate and these favorable characteristics are passed along to their offspring. Individuals lacking such attractive characteristics are unable to secure mates and would not, therefore, produce offspring.

Although modern scientists accept much of Darwin's theory, several objections have been raised to some of his ideas. As a result of these objections, certain aspects of Darwinism (as his ideas are called) have been modified in the light of more recent scientific knowledge.

The Mutation Theory. Hugo de Vries, a Dutch botanist, proposed this theory in 1901. De Vries' work was based on the pioneer genetics studies of Gregor Johann Mendel, an Augustinian monk, whose original work was published in 1866. Mendel laid the foundations for the modern science of genetics.

The mutation theory is based on the belief that new species appear in nature as a result of **mutations** (sudden variations in the germ plasm of organisms) which are favorable for the survival of the organism. These helpful mutations may be inherited by offspring and passed along from one generation to the next until a new species has been developed.

This theory, which complements, rather than contradicts, the work of Darwin, suggests that new species may appear relatively suddenly rather than as a result of minor changes over long periods of time.

EVIDENCE OF EVOLUTION

Although much of the evidence supporting evolution is indirect, it is gathered from many sources and is largely indisputable. For this reason, biologists and geologists consider evolution to be more factual than theoretical. Some of the more important types of evidence are briefly discussed below.

Evidence from Comparative Anatomy. Many plants and animals which do not resemble each other and appear to be totally unrelated possess comparable anatomical structures. For example, the arm of man, the wing of a bat, the flipper of a whale, and the wing of a bird all possess basic structural similarities. They are, moreover, all organs of locomotion. Such structures, or organs, which bear fundamental structural similarities are called **homologous structures.**

Many animals also possess structures or organs recognizable as once being useful but which have since lost their function. These are called **vestigial structures** and provide further proof of organic evolution. The vermiform appendix, for example, is a useless, if not actually troublesome, organ in man. But in certain other animals (such as the rabbit or dog), this appendix is still a useful part of the digestive system.

Evidence from Embryology. A study of an organism from the time of fertilization until its birth offers considerable evidence of the close relationship between the simple and complex forms of life. It is definitely known that the early embryos of certain animals possess structures which resemble those of adult forms of less highly developed animals. Such structures may disappear as the embryo grows older, or they may remain as vestigial structures. For example, nonfunctional gill slits are present in all embryonic reptiles, amphibians, birds, and mammals. Although they disappear before the birth of the animal, these primitive gills are seen as a relic of the past and indicate a common aquatic ancestor for all of these forms.

Evidence from Classification. Taxonomy is based upon kinship of organisms. The Linnean system of animal classification begins with the most simple forms of animal life (the Protozoa) and proceeds to the most complicated (the Chordata). This classification, which is based on structural relationships, indicates a line of common descent which is most easily explained by evolutionary processes.

Evidence from Genetics. Studies in genetics (the science of heredity) have done much to favor the acceptance of evolution. Man, by means of artificial selection or controlled breeding, has been able to produce numerous varieties of plants and animals. For example, each of the many varieties of horses can be traced back to a single species of wild horse. Geneticists, in carefully controlled laboratory experiments, have been able to produce variations in organisms such as the fruit fly. Controlled breeding actually puts evolution on a practical basis.

Evidence from Geographic Distribution. The distributional relationships of certain animals is thought to be related to evolutionary change. There is evidence in some cases to suggest that species originally developed in certain central areas, but changed as they later became isolated. For example, the camel of Asia and the llama of South America had a common ancestry before the continents were completely separated. After the continents separated, evolution proceeded along two different lines. It appears then that isolation can lead to the development of new species.

Evidence from Paleontology. Evidence gathered from studies of fossils provides one of the strongest arguments supporting organic evolution. Fossils actually show the progression of evolution because the oldest rocks bear fossils representing the simplest forms of life, and the fossil remains become increasingly complex in the younger rocks. Thus, when arranged in chronological order, fossils commonly show a progressive series of change that is most logically explained as the result of organic evolution.

CHAPTER 22

EARTH HISTORY

The earth, as mentioned earlier, is not only very old, but has undergone multitudinous changes during its long history. These changes, both physical and biological, had a marked effect on the climate, geography, topography, and life forms of prehistoric times. In this chapter we shall become acquainted with some of these changes and their role in geologic history.

THE PRECAMBRIAN ERAS

The Archeozoic and Proterozoic Eras, are commonly grouped together and referred to as "Precambrian." Precambrian rocks have been greatly contorted and metamorphosed, and the record of this portion of earth history is most difficult to interpret.

The Archeozoic and Proterozoic comprise that portion of geologic time from the beginning of earth history until the deposition of the earliest fossiliferous Cambrian strata. If the earth is as old as we believe it to be, Precambrian time may well represent as much as 85 percent of all earth history.

ARCHEOZOIC ERA

The Archeozoic Era represents a vast interval of time during which the earth appeared to be virtually devoid of life. There is, nevertheless, some indirect fossil evidence in the form of carbon-bearing deposits which may be organic in origin. However, most Archeozoic rocks consist primarily of highly metamorphosed volcanic and sedimentary rocks which have been intruded by granite. Most are so greatly altered that they provide little information about their original nature. This was a time of considerable igneous activity and mountain building, marked at the end by a period of massive erosion.

For convenience in study, the Archeozoic Era has been divided into the Keewatin (Lower Archeozoic) and Timiskaming (Upper Archeozoic) periods.

PROTEROZOIC ERA

The rocks of the Proterozoic Era were formed after the long period of erosion which marked the end of Archeozoic time. Two periods, the Huronian (Lower) and Keeweenawan (Upper) are recognized.

This era is believed to have started more than two billion years ago and included periods of glaciation, volcanic activity, and marine sedimentation. In general, Proterozoic strata contain more sedimentary material and less igneous and metamorphic rocks than do those of the Archeozoic.

The end of the Proterozoic was a time of extensive orogeny. This period of mountain building, called the **Killarney-Grand Canyon revolution**, formed mountains in the Lake Superior, New York, and Arizona areas. This mountain-building activity was followed by a long period of erosion, during which the Precambrian mountains were worn away. This vast break in the geologic record is marked by a profound unconformity.

Proterozoic rocks contain the oldest known direct evidence of fossils. These consist largely of worm burrows, sponge spicules, radiolarians, and calcareous algae. Some of the marine algae secreted rather large masses of organic limestone and are the most abundant fossils of this time. There was apparently no life on the land. So far as is determinable from the poor fossil record, the climate of this time probably ranged from warm and moist to dry and cold.

Rocks of Proterozoic age contain some of the largest deposits of metallic ores known to man. Found both in Canada and the United States, they include such valuable materials as silver, gold, nickel, iron, copper, and cobalt.

PALEOZOIC ERA

The beginning of Paleozoic time marks the beginning of the first accurate records in geological history. Paleozoic rocks have not been subjected to such great physical change as have those of the Precambrian, and there is an abundance of sedimentary rocks, many of which are quite fossiliferous.

The Paleozoic Era, which began more than 600 million years ago, has been divided into seven periods of geologic time. These periods were of varying duration, some lasting as little as 20 million years, others lasting as much as 100 million years. The periods are separated on the basis of relatively brief, naturally-occurring periods of broad continental uplift. During such times, the seas were drained from the continents. These periods of uplift were followed by times of submergence, during which portions of the continents were covered by the seas and were receiving sediments.

Let us now briefly review the Paleozoic periods and learn something of the physical history, climate, life forms, and economic products of each.

THE CAMBRIAN PERIOD

The Cambrian, the oldest period of the Paleozoic Era, is the earliest period in geologic history

in which we find an abundance of well-preserved fossils. The period derives its name from *Cambria,* the Latin word for Wales. It was in Wales that these rocks were first studied.

During this period, which lasted for about 70 million years, approximately 30 percent of the North American continent was submerged. These seas deposited great thicknesses of limestone, shale, sandstone, and conglomerate, which are widely distributed over the United States. The end of Cambrian time was marked by continental uplift and withdrawal of the seas, and there was local mountain building in the form of the **Green Mountain disturbance.** This activity was confined largely to New England and the east coast of Canada.

Cambrian life was dominated by trilobites and inarticulate brachiopods. Trilobites were especially numerous, forming as much as 60 percent of the total fauna. Present also were such invertebrates as protozoans, sponges, snails, worms, and cystoids. There is no record of terrestrial or freshwater life.

We can only speculate on the climate of the Cambrian Period. It appears, however, that climatic zones were not as clearly defined as they are today, and the overall climate was probably mild and equable. The economic resources of the Cambrian rocks are meager when compared to those of other geologic systems. Some building stone (primarily marble and slate) in New England, plus some gold and lead deposits, are all that are worthy of mention.

THE ORDOVICIAN PERIOD

The Ordovician Period, which lasted approximately 65 million years, was named for the Ordovices, an ancient Celtic tribe that once inhabited Wales.

This was a time of great marine flooding, and during part of the period approximately 70 percent of North America was covered by warm shallow Ordovician seas. Thick beds of shale and limestone were deposited in these seas, and many of these marine formations are richly fossiliferous.

Near the end of the period, there was uplift in eastern North America along a line extending from New Jersey to Newfoundland. This mountain-building movement is known as the **Taconic disturbance** and marks the end of Ordovician time.

Ordovician climates were probably mild and equable over much of the world, and climatic zones, if present, are assumed to have been much less marked than those of today.

The warm, widespread Ordovician seas must have been conducive to the expansion of the marine life of the time. This is suggested by the paleontological record, which clearly indicates that these seas must have been teeming with seaweeds, protozoans, brachiopods, bryozoans, corals, gastropods, pelecypods, cephalopods, trilobites, cystoids, blastoids, crinoids, and graptolites. Especially noteworthy was the development of exceptionally large, straight, cone-shaped cephalopods, some of which attained a length of fifteen feet. Also unusually characteristic of the Ordovician Period are large numbers of carbonized graptolite remains. Fishes—which had first appeared in Late Cambrian time—were apparently the only vertebrates on earth. These were small, primitive, armored fishes (Fig. 163) whose remains consist of fragmental bony plates and scales. These primitive backboned animals are called **ostracoderms,** and their remains have been found primarily in the Rocky Mountain region.

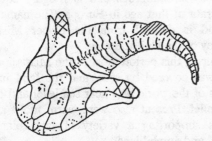

Fig. 163. Ostracoderm, a primitive jawless fish.

Mineral resources recovered from Ordovician strata include petroleum, building stone, glass sand, and ores of iron, lead, and zinc.

THE SILURIAN PERIOD

The Silurian Period also derived its name from an ancient Celtic tribe (the Silures) and was likewise first studied in Wales.

This period, which was of relatively short duration (about 40 million years), saw much of the North American continent above sea level, although there was considerable submergence in the central part of the continent. Silurian rocks are relatively widespread in the eastern United States, and the resistant Lockport dolomite of Middle Silurian age forms the cap rock of Niagara Falls. There was considerable shrinkage of the seas in Late Silurian time, and isolated landlocked bodies of salt water were left in Ontario, New York, Michigan, Pennsylvania, and Ohio. Thick salt and gypsum deposits accumulated in these evaporating seas, which apparently existed in desert-like regions.

The Silurian closed quietly in most of North America, and there is no evidence of mountain-building movements. In Europe, however, there was considerable crustal unrest created by the **Caledonian disturbance.** This resulted in the formation of the Caledonian Range which extends for some four thousand miles through the British Isles, Scandinavia, and westward to Greenland.

Silurian climates were probably warm and mild over wide areas. This assumption is based upon the presence of large numbers of reef-building corals and the thick, widespread deposits of limestone and dolomite. The great salt and gypsum deposits of the Upper Silurian suggest a period of pronounced aridity in those areas where such deposits are found.

Marine life of the Silurian is marked by an expansion of the reef-building corals, articulate brachiopods, bryozoans, echinoderms, mollusks, and graptolites. Present also were myriad invertebrates which had inhabited Cambrian and Ordovician seas. Trilobites had reached the peak of their development and were diminishing in variety and numbers. Particularly distinctive were a group of scorpion-like arthropods called eurypterids. These unusual "sea-scorpions" were the largest animals of this time. The only vertebrates recorded from the Silurian are primitive fishes similar to those of the Ordovician Period.

The earliest known land plants and animals appeared during the Silurian. These early terrestrial animals were the scorpions and millipedes which appeared in Late Silurian time. The fossilized fragments of what appear to be land-dwelling plants have been found in Upper Silurian rocks in Australia, England, and Gotland.

Economic products obtained from Silurian rocks include iron ore from the Birmingham, Alabama, area, salt from the great salt beds of Ohio, Michigan, and New York, gypsum from western New York, and petroleum in several parts of the United States.

THE DEVONIAN PERIOD

The Devonian was named from Devonshire, England, where the rocks of this system were first studied. Lasting for about 50 million years, the Devonian was a time of great change for both plant and animal life.

In the early part of the period, North America was essentially a low-lying continent. There was a rather widespread invasion of the seas in central North America during the Middle Devonian, and as much as 40 percent of the continent was submerged. The climax of the **Acadian disturbance,** which began in Middle Devonian time, marked the end of the period. This disturbance raised mountains from the Appalachian region north through New England to Newfoundland. In addition, there is evidence to indicate that this orogeny was accompanied by considerable igneous activity.

Much of Devonian time appears to have been marked by mild temperate climates, and there is no evidence of marked climatic belts throughout the world. Although there are many indications of warm humid areas, extensive anhydrite deposits suggest that at least some parts of the United States were quite arid.

Devonian life was characterized by expansion of the land plants, especially seed ferns, scale trees, and ferns. Another important plant group, the seed plants, made their initial appearance in this period.

The invertebrates were characterized by many species of reef-building corals, sponges, echinoderms (especially crinoids), pelecypods, and gastropods. Brachiopods were the dominant animals of this period; trilobites were present but still declining in numbers. A small cephalopod with a goniatitic suture pattern marked the first appearance of the ammonoids. Also appearing for the first time were the insects.

Vertebrates underwent unprecedented development and both freshwater and marine fishes were abundant. Among these were ostracoderms and the jawed, armored placoderms. The true sharks appeared, as did a group of large shark-like forms known as arthrodires. Some of the arthrodires were heavily armored and reached a length of thirty feet. However, the most important "first" among the vertebrates was the appearance of the first tetrapod (four-footed vertebrate), a primitive amphibian, which appears to have evolved from the crossopterygians, or Devonian lungfishes.

Among the economic products of Devonian rocks are glass sand, building stone, lime and cement, abrasives, and salt. In addition, Devonian rocks are among the most important of all oil-producing formations in many parts of the United States. In fact, Colonel Drake's famous well of 1859, the first to strike oil in the United States, produced from strata of Devonian age in Pennsylvania.

THE MISSISSIPPIAN PERIOD

The Mississippian is not recognized as a separate period in Europe; rather, it is combined with the Pennsylvanian (see below) to form the Carboniferous Period. For this reason the Mississippian Period has also been referred to as the Lower Carboniferous and is roughly equivalent to strata of that age in Europe. The name of the period is derived from the Upper Mississippi Valley of the United States.

During this period most of the Mississippi Valley was covered by seas, and the land in many parts of the world was near sea level and had little relief. Present also were warm moist swamplands supporting a variety of land plants, insects, and amphibians.

The end of the Mississippian was a time of widespread crustal unrest, although there is no evidence of extensive mountain-building in North America. Orogenic movements were more pronounced in Europe where the **Variscan disturbance** produced a great mountain chain. This range, the Variscan Mountains, formed an arc across England, France, and Germany.

Mississippian climates were essentially warm and humid on the land, and the widespread seas gave rise to warm temperate climates in much of the world. Arid conditions in Michigan and Newfoundland are suggested by the presence of salt and gypsum in these areas.

During the approximately 25 million years that comprised Mississippian time, there was an abundance of life on land and in the water. The seas contained the usual invertebrate hordes of which foraminifers, bryozoans, brachiopods, cephalopods, blastoids, and crinoids were especially numerous. Many of the Mississippian brachiopods were of the productid type, characterized by spiny shells. Other distinctive Mississippian invertebrates were *Archimedes,* the "corkscrew" bryozoan, and *Pentremites,* an unusually symmetrical blastoid, or "sea bud." The most characteristic vertebrates of this period were the sharks, but many types of fishes were present also.

On the land there were dense swamp-forests composed of seed ferns, ferns, and other plants closely related to those of Pennsylvanian time. There is also evidence to indicate that these swamps were inhabited by primitive insects and amphibians.

Mississippian economic products include building stone (especially the Bedford limestone of Indiana), oil and gas in the mid-continent regions, zinc and lead ores in Kansas, Oklahoma, and Missouri, salt in Michigan, and minor amounts of coal in West Virginia.

THE PENNSYLVANIAN PERIOD

The Pennsylvanian, or Upper Carboniferous, Period lasted for about 40 million years. It was named for the state of Pennsylvania, where rocks of this age are well exposed.

The interior of North America was a broad low-lying area of slight relief during Pennsylvanian time. Its warm, moist, swampy lowlands were marked by great forests of ferns, seed ferns, scale trees, giant rushes, and conifers. The remains of these plants form the bulk of the coal taken from the coal fields of West Virginia, Ohio, Indiana, Illinois, and Pennsylvania. The lands were especially low in the eastern half of the United States and the low, swampy coastlands were subjected to numerous inundations from the sea.

Although the Pennsylvanian closed relatively quietly in North America, there were localized mountain-making disturbances in Oklahoma, Arkansas, Texas, New Mexico, and Colorado.

Pennsylvanian climates were, in general, warm and moist, and the vegetation of this period suggests that it was tropical to subtropical in many areas. This was not necessarily true all over the earth, for locally there are indications of aridity, and then, as today, it must have been cold on top of the mountains.

The warm seas of the Pennsylvanian were ideally suited for habitation by all of the previously mentioned marine invertebrates. Productid brachiopods, crinoids, bryozoans, solitary corals, and the distinctive spindle-shaped forams called fusulinids were especially characteristic of this time.

The flora (plant life) of this period was composed largely of the typical coal plants mentioned above. These were so numerous that thousands of species of Pennsylvanian land plants have been described. The dense jungle-like Pennsylvanian forests were also inhabited by myriad insects, which included cockroaches as much as four inches long and dragonfly-like insects with a wingspread of twenty-nine inches!

As for the vertebrates, the amphibians continued to expand both in and out of the water. A large number of Pennsylvanian species have been described, and some attained a length of almost ten feet. But the most noteworthy event among the animals was the appearance of the first reptile. Unlike the amphibians, the reptiles can spend their entire life on land and need not go back to the water to lay their eggs.

Economic resources associated with rocks of Pennsylvanian age are numerous, but this system is best known for its vast coal deposits. In fact, 80 percent of the world's coal production is derived from Pennsylvanian strata of Europe and North America. Most of the Pennsylvanian coal fields in the United States are located in Pennsylvania, West Virginia, Ohio, Kentucky, and Alabama.

Other economic products include great quantities of oil and gas from the mid-continent fields of Texas, Oklahoma, and Kansas, as well as several other states across the nation. Pennsylvanian limestones and clays are used in cement and ceramics in the eastern part of the United States.

THE PERMIAN PERIOD

The Permian, named from the province of Perm in eastern Russia, is the last of the Paleozoic periods. Of about 55 million years' duration, Permian climates, geography, faunas, and floras were considerably different from those of preceding periods.

The Permian seas were quite restricted and exposures of Permian rocks are rare in eastern North America, for most of this part of the continent was well above sea level during this period. Among the areas submerged during this period were Mexico, southeastern New Mexico, western Texas, Kansas, Nebraska, and much of the western United States. Permian rocks have provided our nation with some of its most scenic areas. Such attractions as White Sands National Monument and Carlsbad Caverns in New Mexico, the Grand Canyon and Monument Valley in Arizona, and the Garden of the Gods in Colorado are totally or partially Permian in age.

The close of the Permian was also the close of the Paleozoic Era. The end of the period is marked by the culmination of the **Appalachian revolution**—a great orogeny which resulted in the formation of a mountain chain extending from Nova Scotia to Alabama. Included in this system are the present-day Appalachian Mountains.

The Permian is also notable for the pronounced climatic changes that occurred. Never before in geologic history had climates been so diverse; there were alternating periods of humidity and warmth, and aridity and glacial cold. The elevation of the lands and withdrawal of the seas resulted in climates that were considerably colder and drier than at any time in the Paleozoic. There is evidence of desert-like conditions in parts of the southwestern United States, swamplands in Australia and Asia, and glaciation in South Africa, South America, and Australia.

Such drastic climatic and geographic changes had a marked effect on Permian life and resulted in the extinction of several important animal groups. Among these were the once-abundant trilobites, fusulinids, cystoids, blastoids, and certain species of specialized brachiopods. On the other hand, ammonoid cephalopods underwent considerable expansion, as did certain species of pelecypods and gastropods. In addition, the Permian seas in some parts of western Texas and southeastern New Mexico contained extensive coral reefs, and large numbers of well-preserved and unusual specimens have been recovered from these fossiliferous reef deposits.

Permian plant life differed considerably from that of the Pennsylvanian. Most of the swamp-loving plants had disappeared and were replaced by the more advanced conifers or cone-bearing plants.

The amphibians and reptiles continued to establish themselves on the land and several unusual species evolved. Among the amphibians, *Eryops,* a rather sluggish, sprawling amphibian about six feet long, is characteristic. Reptiles of several types are well represented in Permian rocks, but the pelycosaurs were undoubtedly the most distinctive. These include *Dimetrodon* and *Edaphosaurus,* both of which were characterized by great fins on their backs. Present also were the peculiar mammal-like reptiles called therapsids. The tooth and skull structure of this group suggests that they were probably ancestral to the mammals.

Among the more important mineral resources associated with Permian rocks are oil and gas in the mid-continent and western states; also salt deposits in Texas, New Mexico, Kansas, and Oklahoma, and thick beds of gypsum in Texas, New Mexico, Kansas, Colorado, South Dakota, Iowa, and Oklahoma. Wyoming, Utah, and Idaho contain commercial quantities of calcium phosphate, which is used as a mineral fertilizer. Coal of Permian age has been mined in Europe, India, China, Australia, and other parts of the world, but such occurrences are not common in the United States.

THE MESOZOIC ERA

The Mesozoic, as its name implies, has been called the time of "middle-life," because it represents the transition period from the relatively primitive plants and animals of the Paleozoic to the more modern Cenozoic forms. During the approximately 160 million years encompassing Mesozoic time there was unprecedented expansion of the land animals (especially the reptiles).

Also noteworthy was the appearance of the first mammals, flowering plants, and birds.

THE TRIASSIC PERIOD

The earliest Mesozoic period, the Triassic, derives its name from the Latin word *trias,* meaning "three." This refers to the distinct threefold division displayed by Triassic rocks in central Germany where the system was first described.

The Triassic Period lasted for approximately 30 million years, and during this time there was both continental and marine deposition in western North America. Much of the continent was desert-like, and with the exception of the Atlantic and Gulf coastal plains, the North American continent looked much as it does today. The colorful Triassic continental deposits of New Mexico, Arizona, Colorado, and Utah have provided us with some remarkable scenery. Zion Canyon in Utah, and Arizona's Grand Canyon and Petrified Forest are all associated with rocks of Triassic age.

The **Palisades disturbance,** a moderate uplift which formed mountains from South Carolina to Nova Scotia, marked the end of the period. There is no evidence of mountain-making in the western part of the United States, and the period closed quietly there. The Palisades disturbance was accompanied by considerable igneous activity, and the Palisades on the western bank of the Hudson River are formed from the exposed edge of a thick basaltic sill that was associated with this activity.

The presence of reptile and amphibian remains suggests mild climates for much of Triassic time. In some areas the occurrence of fossil plants indicates warm humid climates, while arid conditions were responsible for thick deposits of salt and gypsum in other parts of the world.

Life of the Triassic was quite different from that of any of the preceding Paleozoic periods. Many new groups, both aquatic and terrestrial, appeared and there were marked changes among the invertebrates, vertebrates, and plants.

Triassic land plants were dominated by conifers, cycads, and ferns. There were, in addition, a few species of the typical coal plants still living. The trunks of the fossilized trees found in the Petrified Forest in Arizona are the remains of some of the huge coniferous trees of the Triassic.

Marine invertebrates included large numbers of cephalopods, pelecypods, gastropods, echinoids, corals, and representatives of most of the other invertebrate phyla. Brachiopods, though present, were greatly diminished in numbers. The ammonites (shelled cephalopods with frilled septa) were probably the most abundant and distinctive animals of this time. The belemnoids (Fig. 164) relatives of the modern squid, were also abundant and are useful as Triassic guide fossils. Reef-building corals, similar to Holocene species, formed coral reefs in many parts of the world.

Fig. 164. Belemnoid.

The vertebrates continued their rather rapid development and were of many different types. Sharks were still common in the seas, and the true bony fishes were increasing in numbers and species. Amphibians, though now overshadowed by the rapidly evolving reptiles, continued to thrive.

The reptiles were the dominant vertebrates of Triassic time and were represented by the turtles, phytosaurs, marine reptiles, and dinosaurs. The early dinosaurs were small when compared with the giant reptiles of the Jurassic and Cretaceous, but some of the marine reptiles attained great size. Among the latter were the streamlined, swordfish-like ichthyosaur, (Fig. 167a) and the clumsy plesiosaurs (Fig. 167c). Some of these reptiles were thirty to forty feet in length, although the average was much less. The semi-aquatic crocodile-like phytosaurs (Fig. 165) were another distinctive reptilian group of this period.

Economic products derived from Triassic rocks are of considerably less importance than those of most of the other geologic systems. Relatively minor amounts of Triassic coal occur in North Carolina and Virginia, and these deposits are not of great economic importance. In addition, there are commercial salt deposits in Europe.

Fig. 165. Phytosaur. (By permission from Texas Fossils *by W. H. Matthews III, Bureau of Economic Geology, The University of Texas, Austin.)*

THE JURASSIC PERIOD

This period derives its name from the Jura Mountains located between France and Switzerland. The Jurassic lasted for about 59 million years and is best known for the many unusual reptiles which lived during this period.

The eastern part of the United States was exposed to erosion throughout much of Jurassic time, but there was both marine and continental deposition in the west. Some Jurassic formations, for example those exposed in Zion National Park and Rainbow Bridge National Monument, Utah, are noted for their scenic beauty.

The **Nevadian disturbance** occurred at the end of the period, and the folding and igneous activity of this orogeny produced a mountain chain extending from California and Nevada to British Columbia. Included in this system are the Sierra Nevadas in California. Here igneous intrusions have formed some of the world's richest gold-producing veins.

Jurassic climates appear to have been mild and equable, but desert-like aridity is indicated for such areas as the southwestern United States.

Life flourished during Jurassic time, and plants and animals inhabited land, sea, and air in great numbers.

Jurassic floras were varied and abundant. Cycads were so abundant that the Jurassic has been called the "Age of Cycads." Forests of this period contained ferns, tree ferns, cycads, ginkgoes, scouring rushes, and conifers.

Invertebrates were remarkably abundant and reef-building corals, pelecypods, gastropods,

foraminifers, bryozoans, and a host of other invertebrates filled the seas. As in the Triassic, the ammonites and belemnoids were especially numerous, for both of these groups reached the peak of their development in this period. Shrimps, crabs, and other arthropods were also present in great numbers. Land-dwelling invertebrates included land snails and a variety of insects and other arthropods.

It was the reptiles—and more specifically the dinosaurs—that dominated the backboned animals. Fishes, largely primitive bony fishes and sharks, were numerous. Amphibians were not as abundant as in the Permian and Triassic, but their absence was compensated for by the great expansion of the reptiles.

On the land such quadrupedal plant-eating dinosaurs as *Brontosaurus* and *Diplodocus* attained lengths of up to ninety feet and weighed tens of tons. Present also were carnivores such as *Allosaurus,* a bipedal form about thirty-five feet long. *Stegosaurus,* an armored dinosaur, was another distinctive Jurassic reptile.

This period also gave rise to the first flying reptiles. Known as pterosaurs, these unusual animals had hollow bones and small light bodies. *Rhamphorhyncus,* a typical Jurassic form, had a long tail, sharp teeth, and a maximum wingspread of about two feet. Marine reptiles, such as ichthyosaurs and plesiosaurs, were still common in Jurassic seas.

An especially important event of this period was the appearance of the first bird. Known from a feather, two skeletons, and the fragments of a third, this famous discovery was made in the Solnhofen limestone quarries of Bavaria. This primitive bird, called *Archaeopteryx,* still retained such reptilian characteristics as teeth, and there were claws on the wings (Fig. 166). However, the presence of feathers definitely establishes *Archaeopteryx* as a bird.

Undoubted mammal fossils are found in Jurassic rocks, their presence being indicated by fragmental remains representing an animal about the size of a large rat. The structure of their teeth suggests that some were herbivorous while others were apparently meat-eaters.

Jurassic economic products include coal in China, Hungary, Australia, Siberia, Japan, and a few other parts of the world. Jurassic strata pro-

Fig. 166. Archaeopteryx, *a Jurassic bird.*

duce petroleum in Wyoming, Arkansas, and the Gulf coastal area of Louisiana and Texas.

As noted earlier, much gold has been mined along the western side of the Sierra Nevada in California. The gold occurs in quartz veins which are believed to be of Jurassic age.

THE CRETACEOUS PERIOD

The Cretaceous Period, which lasted for approximately 71 million years, is characterized by thick deposits of white chalky limestone. In fact, the name Cretaceous is derived from the Latin word *creta,* meaning "chalk." The rocks of the Cretaceous were first studied in the white cliffs of Dover along the English Channel.

During Cretaceous time the Atlantic and Gulf coastal plains were submerged, and a great inland sea extended from the Gulf of Mexico to the Arctic Ocean. This shallow sea represents the last great submergence of the North American continent, and in it were deposited great thicknesses of sandstone, shale, and limestone.

The Mesozoic Era ended with the **Laramide revolution,** a period of intense crustal deformation during which the Rocky Mountain system was formed. This great orogeny was accompanied by folding, faulting, and much volcanic activity.

The Cretaceous was marked by mild temperate climates, though they may have been somewhat cooler than those of the Jurassic. Evidence provided by both fossils and sediments supports this climatic interpretation. There is, however, evidence of some Early Cretaceous glaciation in Australia.

Plant life of the earlier Cretaceous consisted of cycads, conifers, and ferns, and closely resembled Jurassic floras. The angiosperms, or flowering plants, appeared in the middle of the period, and by Late Cretaceous time the vegetation was quite similar to that of today.

The warm shallow Cretaceous seas teemed with a multitude of invertebrates and, as in the preceding periods of the Mesozoic, the mollusks were the dominant forms. Foraminifers with calcareous shells contributed greatly to the building of the limestones and are useful guide fossils for Cretaceous rocks. Large numbers of pelecypods, gastropods, and cephalopods (particularly ammonites in great variety and abundance) were also present. The echinoderms were well represented by sea urchins and heart urchins and, to a lesser degree, by starfishes and "brittle stars."

The dinosaurs were the dominant vertebrates, but other reptiles, fishes, birds, and primitive mammals were quite abundant. The fishes were similar to our present-day forms and are well known from their fossils. Birds were more specialized and more abundant than they had been in the past and they have left an interesting fossil record. *Hesperornis,* a large flightless bird, is typical. Cretaceous mammals were small and possibly resembled the modern shrews or hedgehogs.

The reptiles continued to rule land, sea, and air, and developed more unusual forms than ever before. The ornithopods were well represented by such genera as *Trachodon* (known also as *Anatosaurus*) and similar duckbilled dinosaurs. The armored ankylosaurs were quadrupedal herbivorous forms that lived only during Cretaceous time. *Ankylosaurus* is typical of this group. Even more unusual were the ceratopsians, a group of horned dinosaurs. *Triceratops,* the largest of this group, was a heavy-set quadrupedal plant-eater, as much as thirty feet long. Its eight-foot skull was characterized by a parrot-like bill, and a heavy, frilled, bony shield which protected the back of the neck. *Tyrannosaurus,* the largest of the flesh-eating dinosaurs, stood twenty feet tall, was forty to fifty feet long, and weighed many tons. Its forelimbs, greatly reduced in size, were armed with sharp claws suitable for grasping and tearing prey. Its giant skull was armed with powerful jaws and dagger-like teeth—some as much as six inches long.

The flying reptiles had continued to evolve, and by Cretaceous time some new and unusual forms were present. One of the most interesting pterosaurs was *Pteranodon*. This lightweight, hollow-boned animal had a body little more than two feet long, but a wingspread of as much as fifty feet. Its tail was short but the back of the head was marked by a long triangular extension of the skull.

Cretaceous seas supported an unusual assortment of marine reptiles. Ichthyosaurs and plesiosaurs were still present, and they had been joined by the mosasaurs—giant lizard-like swimming reptiles (Fig. 167b). These huge creatures, some as much as fifty feet long, had a typical lizard-like body, a flattened tail, and large, sharp, recurved teeth, and the four limbs were modified into flippers. The giant sea-turtles were another interesting group. Some, such as *Archelon*, were as much as eleven feet long and twelve feet across the flippers.

What happened to the dinosaurs? Why did they "suddenly" (geologically speaking) become extinct? This is a question that has long perplexed both biologists and paleontologists. They did not become extinct because they were unsuccessful, for they lived for over 100 million years, attained great variety in size and shape, and successfully invaded any number of different environments. As to why, we can only speculate. Some ideas that have been advanced are: (1) the climatic and geographic changes of the Cretaceous were too drastic and the dinosaurs could not adapt to them; (2) the group was in "racial old age" and their "time was up"; (3) a widespread epidemic or "plague" wiped them out (there is little, if any, scientific support for this); (4) the mammals, who were rapidly increasing in numbers, may have been eating the dinosaur eggs; and (5) changes in the Cretaceous flora were unacceptable to herbivorous forms for they could not eat them. As the plant-eaters disappeared, the carnivores died out also.

Most scientists believe that dinosaur extinction was a result of not one, but several of the above reasons. We shall, in all probability, never really know the answer to this baffling question.

Fig. 167. *Swimming reptiles of the Mesozoic Era.*
a–Ichthyosaur b–Mosasaur
c–Plesiosaur
(*By permission from* Texas Fossils *by W. H. Matthews III, Bureau of Economic Geology, The University of Texas, Austin.*)

A wide variety of rich mineral resources have been produced from rocks of Cretaceous age. Oil and gas are produced from petroleum-bearing strata in hundreds of fields from southern Louisiana to Alaska. Cretaceous coal deposits are mined in the Rocky Mountain region, and Cretaceous clays, shales, and limestones are used in ceramics, the manufacture of Portland cement, and as building stone. Ore minerals, such as lead, copper, zinc, and silver, were formed as a result of the igneous activity which accompanied the Laramide revolution and they are mined commercially in the Rocky Mountain region.

THE CENOZOIC ERA

The Cenozoic Era has lasted for about 65 million years—a relatively short time when compared with the preceding geologic eras. The word Cenozoic literally means "recent life" and refers to the large numbers of recent plant and animal species which developed during this time.

THE TERTIARY PERIOD

The Tertiary Period, which lasted for about 63 million years, derived its name from an early and now unused classification of rocks. The period has five well-defined epochs. These epochs, with the oldest list last, and the origin of their names are:

Pliocene—"more recent"
Miocene—"less recent"
Oligocene—"little recent"
Eocene—"dawn recent"
Paleocene—"ancient recent"

The geographic features of the Tertiary were much like those of today except for intermittent submergence in California and along the Atlantic and Gulf coastal plains. Most of western North America was above sea level during the Tertiary Period, and there was continental deposition in the Great Plains and western United States. These thick deposits of terrestrial sediments have yielded a large number of Tertiary mammal remains. They are also responsible for some of our spectacular scenery—Bryce Canyon National Park, Utah, and Badlands National Monument, South Dakota, are typical.

A widespread series of crustal movements began in the western United States in Miocene time, and continued with increasing intensity until the end of the Tertiary. These mountain-making movements culminated in the **Cascadian disturbance** which elevated the Alps in Europe, the Himalayas in Asia, the Coast Ranges of California, and the Cascade Mountains of Oregon and Washington. The Colorado Plateau underwent a series of uplifts near the end of the period allowing the Colorado River to dig more deeply into the plateau. It was during the last period of uplift that the Colorado River carved out the Grand Canyon in Arizona.

There is an abundance of evidence to indicate that there was much volcanism during the Tertiary Period. Such evidence may be seen in the great lava flows of the Columbia Plateau, Craters of the Moon National Monument, Idaho, and such famous western volcanic peaks as Mount Shasta and Lassen Peak in California, Mount Rainier in Washington, and Mount Hood in Oregon.

It is believed that Tertiary climates in North America were warmer, more humid, and more equable than the climates of today. The climate became increasingly colder near the end of the period, signaling the beginning of the Great Ice Age of Pleistocene time.

Because of the marked similarity between many types of Tertiary and Quaternary organisms, the life forms of these two periods will be treated in a single discussion later.

Tertiary economic products are varied and of considerable importance. Some of the world's greatest oil fields produce from Tertiary rocks, especially in California and the Gulf Coast region of Texas and Louisiana. Much of the foreign oil production in the East Indies, Middle West, Russia, and parts of South America is also associated with Tertiary rocks. Much salt is produced from the salt domes located along the Gulf coast of Texas and Louisiana, and although the salt may be older than Tertiary, it is intruded into rocks of Tertiary age. Much petroleum is also associated with these great masses of salt, and one of the earliest major oil discoveries was made in 1901 in such a dome at Spindletop in Beaumont, Texas.

Coal of Tertiary age is mined in Wyoming, Montana, Washington, and Oregon. Lignite (see Chapter 5) occurs in the Gulf Coast region and in South Dakota. Diatomaceous earth is found in California, Virginia, and Maryland. This material, known also as diatomite, is composed of countless numbers of diatom (simple one-celled plants) remains. A white porous rock, diatomite is used as a filtering medium, as an insulating agent, and in the manufacture of paper, paint, polishing powders, plastics, and soap.

Many important metallic minerals have been found in rocks of Tertiary age, and most of them are associated with Tertiary igneous intrusions. These include the vast copper, gold, and silver deposits of the Rocky Mountains, Mexico, Bolivia, and Peru.

THE QUATERNARY PERIOD

The Quaternary, like the Tertiary, derives its name from an early, outdated rock classification. A relatively short geologic period (about one million years), the Quaternary is divided into the Pleistocene Epoch and the Holocene Epoch.

The Pleistocene, known also as the Great Ice Age, is characterized by four major glacial periods and three intervening warmer periods during which the ice melted. Great sheets of ice located in northern Europe, Siberia, and North America, brought about colder climates which hastened the extinction of many Tertiary plants and animals. These great glaciers covered most of Canada and spread as far south as southern Illinois.

Such great masses of ice had a marked effect on the earth and were responsible for fluctuations of the sea level, depression of the land, and considerable change in the drainage pattern of many streams. As the glaciers moved over the surface, they removed tons of soil and scoured the surface of the bedrock. In addition, Pleistocene glaciation is largely responsible for the formation of countless lakes in Canada and the northern United States. These include the Great Lakes and the Finger Lakes of New York.

Although not very definite, the boundary between the Pleistocene and Holocene is usually considered as the time when the last ice sheet retreated from Europe and North America— sometime between 12,000 and 15,000 years ago.

Cenozoic life is characterized by faunas and floras which in many respects were quite similar to those of the present day. The marine life closely resembled that of today, and the mammals had so expanded that they literally ruled the land.

Cenozoic plants were essentially modern in appearance, and forests of hardwoods and grassy plains provided suitable environments for the mammalian expansion that was taking place.

Invertebrate faunas, though resembling their Cretaceous forebears, were decidedly modern in aspect. Foraminifera, which were present in great numbers, are valuable guide fossils of the Tertiary—especially for the petroleum geologist. Corals, bryozoans, echinoderms (particularly echinoids), and arthropods were also abundant. Brachiopods, which had so successfully dominated early Paleozoic seas, were now greatly diminished in numbers and variety. The mollusks were the dominant Cenozoic marine invertebrates. The multitude of ammonoids, so common throughout Mesozoic time, were replaced by an unprecedented number and species of pelecypods and gastropods. Many of these species were quite similar to the clams, oysters, and snails of today.

Tertiary vertebrates are also well known, for there are fossilized remains of fishes, amphibians, reptiles, birds, and, to a greater extent, mammals.

Fishes of the Tertiary were plentiful and consisted of many bony fishes as well as large numbers of sharks. Some of the latter were sixty to eighty feet long and had six-inch teeth. The amphibians were represented by salamanders, toads, and frogs. The reptilian hordes of the Mesozoic had dwindled to representative snakes, lizards, crocodiles, and turtles, which were present in about the same numbers as today.

The majority of Tertiary birds were much like those of today. Unfortunately, however, because of the fragile nature of their bodies they are not often found as fossils. Of particular interest are the so-called "giant" birds of Tertiary. Some of these great ostrich-like flightless creatures were as much as ten feet tall and laid eggs over a foot long. *Dinornis* and *Diatryma* (Fig. 168) are typical of these unusual birds.

The greatest development was, of course, among the mammals. Mammals of the Paleocene Epoch were primitive and small, and were not too similar to those of today. Eocene forms were somewhat larger and included the earliest rodents, camels, and rhinoceroses. *Hyracotherium* (also called *Eohippus,* the "dawn horse"; see Fig. 169) the earliest known horse, also made its appearance during the Paleocene. Another group introduced during the Eocene was the creodonts, forerunners of the carnivores.

Fig. 168. Diatryma, *a large flightless Eocene bird that was seven feet tall.*

Fig. 169. Hyracotherium (*or* Eohippus), *an early Paleocene horse about the size of a fox.*

During Oligocene time, the mammals took on a more modern appearance than preceding Paleocene and Eocene forms. These more advanced types included dogs, cats, camels, horses, rhinoceroses, pigs, rabbits, squirrels, and (in Africa) small elephants.

Also living during the Eocene and Oligocene were certain strange mammals quite unlike any that are living today. These included the *Dinocerata* or uintatheres, great rhinoceros-like beasts, some of which stood seven feet tall at the shoulder. *Uintatherium* (Fig. 170a) is typical of this group. The titanotheres, another group of gigantic early Cenozoic mammals, appeared first in the Eocene. Although originally about the size of sheep, they had increased to titanic proportions by Middle Oligocence time. *Brontotherium* (Fig.

170b) the largest land mammal whose fossil remains have been collected in North America, had an elephant-like body and was as much as eight feet tall at the shoulders. A large bony growth protruded from the massive skull and was extended into a flattened horn which was divided at the top.

Fig. 170. Unusual Tertiary mammals.
      a–Uintatherium   *b*–Brontotherium.
(*By permission from* Fossils *by W. H. Matthews III, Barnes & Noble, Inc., New York.*)

Mammals became even more varied and abundant in the Miocene—so much so that this epoch has been called the "Golden Age of Mammals." This accelerated mammalian development was due in no small part to the expansion of the grasses which blanketed Miocene plains and prairies. Horses, camels, deer, pigs, rhinoceroses, and other familiar mammals were present in North America. The Pleistocene also had its share of strange, now extinct, mammals. Especially worthy of mention was the giant hornless rhinoceros called *Baluchitherium*. This tremendous creature, the largest land-dwelling mammal of all time, was as much as thirty feet long and stood eighteen feet high at the shoulders. The baluchitheres first appeared in the Oligocene and became extinct during Miocene time. These great beasts must have been restricted to Asia, for their remains have not been found elsewhere. Another interesting Oligocene-Miocene form were the entelodonts, or giant swine. Some of these peculiar creatures (Fig. 171) were as much as six feet high at the shoulders.

Fig. 171. An entelodont, a type of giant swine.

Pliocene mammals were even more highly developed than those of the early Tertiary Epochs. Giant ground sloths, such as *Mylodon*, were common in the southern United States during Pliocene and Pleistocene time. Some were as much as fifteen feet tall and weighed thousands of pounds. Present also were the glyptodonts (Fig. 172), distant relatives of the armadillos.

During the Pleistocene the proboscideans (elephants and their kin) underwent considerable development. The mastodon and woolly mammoths were quite common in North America, as was the woolly rhinoceros. Carnivores were well represented by *Smilodon*, the saber-tooth cat, and *Canis dirus*, the dire wolf (Fig. 173). *Smilodon*, which was about the size of a lion, had powerful jaws and highly developed, dagger-like upper canine teeth. The dire wolf was much larger than any living canine, and (along with *Smilodon*) was apparently quite common in southern California in Pleistocene time. The remains of both of these extinct carnivores have been found in great numbers in the La Brea tar pits in Los Angeles.

Probably the most noteworthy of all Pleistocene events was the introduction of the earliest known humans. The evolution of the primates and the geologic history of humans is the topic of the next chapter.

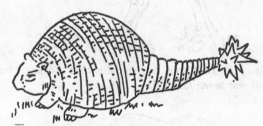

Fig. 172. A glyptodont, a Cenozoic mammal.

Fig. 173. Canis dirus, the dire wolf.

CHAPTER 23

THE GEOLOGIC HISTORY OF HUMANS

Humans are relative newcomers on the geologic scene, having appeared during the Pleistocene Epoch, or Great Ice Age. Although a detailed study of human evolution is beyond the scope of this book, we will briefly review some of the more important events in the evolution of our own species.

The Primates, the mammalian order to which we belong, have well-developed brains, elongated limbs, and cupped or flattened nails on their flexible fingers and toes. Other members of this rather highly developed order are the lemurs, tarsiers, monkeys, and apes. Humans, along with the monkeys and apes, have been assigned to the suborder Anthropoidea (Greek *anthropos,* meaning "man," plus *eidos,* "resemblance"). Anthropoids possess large eyes that face forward, relatively specialized teeth, and large brains. Most are able to sit in an upright position, leaving the hands free for manipulation of objects. Because of the obvious similarities between them, apes and men have been assigned to the superfamily Hominoidea (the **hominoids**). But man is separated from the apes by being placed in the family Hominidae (the **hominids**).

The fossil record of the Primates is not, unfortunately, as complete as the paleontologist would like it to be. Nevertheless, with the aid of increased paleontological and anthropological research, the geologic history of humans is slowly being pieced together.

THE FIRST PRIMATES

The remains of what is reputedly the first primate were found in Upper Cretaceous rocks in Montana. Named *Purgatorius,* this early primate was probably derived from primitive Cretaceous insect-eating mammals. *Plesiadapis,* a Paleocene species, was a rather specialized primate that lived on seeds and insects. It had small ears, a long, pointed muzzle, and flexible digits suitable for grasping.

In Eocene time, primate evolution resulted in an increase in brain size and shifting of the eye orbits to a more forward position. These features are well displayed in *Notharctus,* whose remains have been found in certain Eocene formations of the western United States. *Notharctus* was a long-tailed, small-faced, tree-dwelling animal not unlike our modern lemurs. However, the present-day lemurs no longer inhabit North America, being found largely in Madagascar. A few are found in Africa and Indonesia.

The tarsiers, rather delicate, wide-eyed creatures about the size of rat, also appeared during the Eocene. These animals live in the jungles of Indonesia and the Philippines today, but their fossil record indicates that they inhabited North America and Europe during Eocene time.

The monkeys and apes made their initial appearance in early Oligocene time. Remains of the earliest monkey, *Parapithecus,* were collected in Egypt, as were the bones of *Propliopithecus,* the oldest known ape. Another important fossil ape was found in the Miocene of Africa. This ape, called *Dryopithecus* (formerly named *Proconsul*), has certain anatomical characteristics which suggest that it may have been ancestral to the chimpanzee, gorilla, and humans.

EARLY HOMINIDS

Dryopithecus is believed to have given rise to the gorillas, chimpanzees, orangutans, and the oldest known hominid, *Ramapithecus*. The latter is believed to be the ancestor of all fossil humans.

Ramapithecus is known from teeth and jaw fragments found in Miocene and Pliocene strata in India, East Africa, China, and southern Europe. Reconstruction of the remains suggests a small, bipedal creature, between three and four feet tall, with a short face and humanlike teeth. Another hominid, *Australopithecus africanus*, appeared in Late Pliocene or Early Pleistocene time; its remains were first found in South Africa in 1924. The australopithecines (or "southern apes") had apelike skulls, were bipedal, were probably less than five feet tall, and stood and walked erect. Although their brains were only half the size of those of modern humans, they were hunters who used sticks and stones as weapons and probably fashioned crude tools. Another species, *Australopithecus boisei* (formerly *Zinjanthropus boisei*), was described from remains found in Tanzania's Olduvai Gorge in 1959. Discovered by Louis S. B. Leakey, this specimen has been assigned an age of at least 1.75 million years. However, recent findings suggest that these hominids may date back as much as 2.5 million years. Although the australopithecines became extinct in about Middle Pleistocene time, they were widespread, for their remains have also been found in Java, northern Israel, and mainland China.

Australopithecus was succeeded by *Homo erectus*, the well-known "Java man" (Fig. 174a), whose remains were first discovered on the banks of the Solo River, near Trinil, Java, in 1891. Originally described as *Pithecanthropus erectus*, this creature appeared in the Early Pleistocene (perhaps during an interglacial stage) and became extinct near the end of Middle Pleistocene time. The skull of *Homo erectus* is apelike, the forehead slopes or is flat, and the lower jaw lacks a chin. But the teeth are near-human and the brain size begins to approach modern human brain capacities. In addition, a cast of the inside of the skullcap provides evidence of a near-human level of brain development, especially in relation to its

speech area. Muscle attachments on the femurs indicate that *Homo erectus* probably had an upright posture.

Between 1927 and 1937 scientists recovered fossilized remains of more than forty prehistoric people in the vicinity of Peking, China. This fossil, originally named *Sinanthropus pekinensis*, has also been called "Peking man." The skeletons were collected from cave deposits that also contained the remains of extinct Middle Pleistocene mammals. Because the brain case and certain other bones of *Sinanthropus* closely resemble similar skeletal parts of *Homo erectus*, Peking man and Java man have now been placed in the same species. The Chinese skulls have a larger brain capacity; Peking man apparently possessed cutting tools of stone and knew how to use and control fire. These Chinese hominids were probably cannibals, for the basal parts of most skulls had been broken open so that the brains could be removed. Furthermore, many of the long bones had been split to expose the marrow.

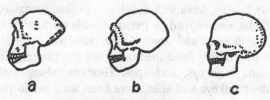

Fig. 174. Skulls of fossil men.
a–Java man   b–Neanderthal man
c–Cro-Magnon man

THE FIRST HUMANS

Homo sapiens, the single species that includes all present-day humans, evolved from *Homo erectus* and appeared near the middle of the Pleistocene Epoch, perhaps as much as 1 million years ago. An early member of this species was *Homo sapiens neanderthalensis*, who inhabited Europe, Africa, China, and the Near East from about 110,000 to 35,000 years ago. Among the best known fossil humans, "Neanderthal man" was first described from a skullcap and some leg bones dug up from the floor of a limestone cave in the Neanderthal Valley near Düsseldorf, Germany. These particular fossils were discovered in 1856 but were not recognized as a distinct human species until 1864. Meanwhile, the bones were variously regarded as those of a pathologically deformed person, the skull of an idiot, or perhaps belonging to primitive savages. Another skull, that of a young female, had been found in a quarry on the Rock of Gibraltar as early as 1848. However, it was not recognized as a Neanderthal until 1906. Since the original 1848 discovery, several complete skeletons and many incomplete skeletons of men, women, and children have been collected. These abundant remains suggest that the Neanderthals were widespread and prolific during Late Pleistocene time.

The Neanderthals were short, stocky individuals, typically about five feet in height. The head was thrust forward and the shoulders were stooped, giving the body a slouched appearance; hands and feet were large and the knees were slightly bent. The head of Neanderthal man was large and marked by a low forehead, flat nose, receding chin and heavy brow ridges (Fig. 174b). In spite of their primitive appearance, Neanderthals had a brain capacity approximately equal to that of modern humans. They were apparently cave dwellers and hunters, for their skeletons are often accompanied by stone implements such as scrapers, spearheads, and axes. Their remains are also found associated with the bones of the animals they hunted. These include the woolly mammoth, giant cave bear, bison, horse, and woolly rhinoceros. Neanderthals appear to have developed a primitive culture and are known to have used fire. The positions in which certain of their skeletons were found, and the arrangement of food, stone implements, and other artifacts with the bones indicates that the Neanderthals buried their dead. It also suggests that they may have had some type of religion or burial ritual.

Homo sapiens neanderthalensis was replaced by modern humans—*Homo sapiens sapiens*—some 35,000 to 40,000 years ago. The first of these was "Cro-Magnon man," whose remains were initially discovered in 1868 at the rock shelter of Cro-Magnon, near the village of Les Eyzies-de-Tayac in the Dordogne valley of France. The Cro-Magnons are well known from a large number of skeletons collected in western and central Europe and appear to be modern in all respects. They were far advanced over the Neanderthal people, were tall (many skeletons exceeded six feet in height), walked erect, and had relatively long legs with straight thigh bones. The head (Fig. 174c) was long, with a high forehead, long nose, and pointed chin. Cro-Magnons were highly developed mentally as well as physically, for their brain capacity equalled that of present-day people. They fashioned many well-formed tools from flint and bone, and possessed considerable artistic ability, as evidenced by the large number of paintings and sculptured bones found in certain caves.

The early development of modern humans probably took place in the Old World. Although recent finds in New Mexico suggest that *Homo sapiens sapiens* may already have been living in the New World many thousands of years ago, most scientists consider the species relatively late in arriving in the Western Hemisphere. It is generally agreed that the early inhabitants of both North and South America belong to the Mongoloid division of *Homo sapiens sapiens*. The ancestors of these early Americans apparently migrated from northeastern Asia (Siberia) to Alaska by way of the Bering Strait area. There were probably many such migrations, the first known occurring after the last Pleistocene glaciation about 10,000 years ago. Remains have been found in such widely separated places as Texas, Florida, Washington, Mexico, and Peru. It is evident that the first humans reached the New World before the extinction of such typical Pleistocene mammals as the mammoth, mastodon, ground sloth, and various extinct horses and bison. In fact, there is evidence to suggest that the extinction of some of these species (especially the mastodons and mammoths) was hastened by the hunting activities of early people.

The foregoing is but a very brief review of primate evolution in general and human development in particular. These are exciting times in the field of human paleontology and new finds are continually being reported. Consequently, the names and ages of some of the early people discussed above may have changed since these words were written. As a result of this accelerated research, many new books have been written in order to report the latest findings. Several of these are listed in Appendix C.

APPENDIX A

WHERE AND HOW TO COLLECT ROCKS, MINERALS, AND FOSSILS

In rock and mineral collecting, as in most "collecting" hobbies, the key to success lies in knowing where to look, what equipment to use, and the most effective methods of collecting.

COLLECTING EQUIPMENT

Rock collecting is a relatively inexpensive hobby because it requires a minimum of supplies and equipment. However, as in most other hobbies, there are certain basic items of equipment that must be acquired.

Hammer. The hammer is the basic tool in the collector's kit. Almost any type of hammer is satisfactory, but as collecting experience is gained you will probably want to get a geologist's hammer. These hammers, also called mineralogist's or prospector's picks, are of two types. One type has a square head on one end and a pick on the other; the second type is similar to a stonemason's or bricklayer's hammer and has a chisel end instead of the pointed pick end. The square head of the hammer is useful in breaking or chipping harder rocks and in trimming large rock specimens. The chisel or pick end is good for digging, prying, and splitting softer rocks.

Collecting Bag. It will be necessary to have some type of bag in which to carry collecting equipment, rocks and minerals, and other supplies. A Boy Scout knapsack, musette bag, hunting bag, or similar canvas or leather bag is suitable.

Chisels. A pair of chisels are useful when specimens must be chipped out of the surrounding rock. Two sizes, preferably one-half-inch and one-inch, will usually suffice. A small sharp punch or awl is effective in removing smaller specimens from the softer rocks.

Wrapping Materials. Some specimens are more fragile than others, and these should be handled with special care. Always keep several sheets of newspapers in the collecting bag, and wrap each specimen individually as it is collected. Precautions taken in the field will usually prevent prized specimens from being broken or otherwise damaged. In addition to newspaper, it is wise to carry a supply of tissue paper and cotton in which to wrap the more fragile specimens. Small plastic or glass vials filled with cotton can be used for the more delicate crystals.

Map, Notebook, and Pencil. It is most important to have some method of recording where your specimens were found. It is very easy to forget where the material was collected, and one should never rely on memory. A small pocket-sized notebook is inexpensive and just the right size to carry in the field.

A highway or county map should be used to find the geographic location of each collecting locality. Maps of the counties in your state can probably be obtained from the State Highway Department in your state capital. These maps usually come in different sizes, but for most purposes the 18 × 25-inch sheets, with a scale of ½ inch = 1 mile will be satisfactory.

Magnifying Glass. A magnifying glass or hand lens is useful in looking at small specimens. It will also prove helpful in examining larger rocks for small mineral inclusions. A 10-power magnification is satisfactory for most purposes, and several inexpensive models are available.

Paper or Cloth Bags. Small bags are useful in separating specimens from different localities. Use heavy-duty hardware bags for large rough material (such as blocks of lava, granite, etc.), and medium-weight grocery bags for smaller specimens. Locality data may be written directly on the bag, or on a label placed inside with the specimens. As an added precaution some collectors do both.

Other Useful Items. The items described above are those that are most needed, and constitute the basic equipment of the "rockhound." The more serious amateur may wish to include certain additional items which will place his collecting on a more professional basis. Some of these accessory items are:

A **topographic map** of the collecting area. These are available for many parts of the United States, and can be purchased from the United States Geological Survey, Washington, D.C. 20402. The Survey will send you (free) a key sheet showing all of the maps available for your state.

A **geologic map** of the collecting area if one is available. Consult the Publication List of your state geological survey to see if a geologic report or map of the area has been published. The state geological survey is usually located in your state capital, or it may be associated with one of the state universities.

A **compass** for more accurate location of collecting localities.

Adhesive or **masking tape.** The locality information can be written on the tape and applied directly to the specimen.

Paper labels (about 3 × 5 inches). Place a properly filled-in label with each bag of material.

A **pocket knife** is useful in testing the hardness of rocks and minerals. A knife is also handy to dig fossils or mineral crystals out of soft rocks.

Acid (*it must be carefully handled*) is needed to test certain rocks to see if they are calcareous. Dilute hydrochloric acid (HCl) can be purchased at most drugstores. It can be carried in one- or two-ounce dropper bottles which may also be purchased from the druggist. A single drop of acid is all that is necessary to test for the presence of lime. If the specimen is calcareous, it will effervesce. (NOTE: Mark the acid bottle POISON and keep it well out of the reach of children. If you should get acid on your clothes or skin, rinse it off with clean water as soon as possible.)

WHERE TO LOOK

Knowing where to look for specimens is a very important part of rock and mineral collecting. We have already noted that rocks and minerals are all around us, but this does not mean that all of these rocks are the types that will be suitable for your collection.

Try to take your rock samples from cuts along highways, railroads, creeks, gullies, etc. Each bank, cliff, or excavation may yield interesting specimens of many different types. If the rock has undergone some degree of weathering, it will make the job of recovering the specimens a bit easier. Weathering will also remove some of the loose surface material that might be covering the rock outcrop.

Mine dumps, rock pits, and quarries are also good places to collect. Be sure to obtain permission to enter these localities (and all other private property), and work with extreme care as such places may be quite dangerous. Be especially cautious of falling rocks and blasting.

Lava flows are good places to look for volcanic rocks. Many of the gas cavities (amygdules) are lined with quartz crystals, calcite, agate, and other minerals.

Igneous rocks can be found in many parts of the country—especially in such regions as the Rocky Mountains, Appalachians, and other mountainous areas. Such intrusive bodies as granite or pegmatite dikes or sills often yield many fine mineral crystals.

Look also in stream beds. Remember, however, that many of the rocks found here have been transported for great distances, and the specimens may not be native to the area in which they were collected.

Fossils are found under somewhat different conditions. We have already learned that igneous and metamorphic rocks are not likely to be fossiliferous, and that most fossils are found in marine sedimentary rocks. These sediments were deposited under conditions that were favorable for organisms during life, and which facilitated preservation after death. Limestones, limy shales, and certain types of sandstones are typically deposited under such conditions.

Look particularly for areas where marine sediments have not been greatly disturbed by heat, pressure, and other physical and chemical change. Try also to find places where the rocks have been exposed to weathering—this helps greatly to release the fossils from the enclosing rock material.

Quarries are good places to look, but—and this bears repeating—be sure to obtain permission before entering. Rock exposures in quarries are rather fresh, but have still undergone some weathering. Bones and petrified wood are commonly found in sand and gravel pits associated with river terraces.

Pay particular attention to all railroad and highway cuts. Rocks exposed in this way are usually still in their original position and are fairly well weathered. Cuts made by recent construction are usually more productive after they have undergone a period of weathering, as this helps to separate the fossils from the surrounding rock.

Gullies, canyons, and stream beds are also good places to look. These areas are continually subjected to the processes of erosion or stream action, and new material is uncovered year after year.

If there are abandoned coal mines nearby, check the dumps of waste rocks around the mine shafts. A careful examination of the waste may reveal specimens of well-preserved plant fossils.

HOW TO COLLECT

When a likely collecting spot has been located, examine the ground very carefully. See if there are any rock fragments which contain pieces of minerals, fossils, or interesting types of rocks.

If the specimens have been freed by weathering, they can be easily picked up and placed in the bag. Many times, however, it will be necessary to take the hammer and very carefully remove the surrounding rock. Smaller specimens may be more safely freed with the careful use of the proper size chisel. Gently tap the chisel and gradually chip away the matrix—the rock that is holding the specimen. After most of the matrix has been removed, the specimen should be carefully wrapped and placed in the collecting bag.

Before leaving a collecting locality, be sure to record its geographic location in the field notebook.

Locate the place on the map, then enter it in the notebook in such a manner that you, or another collector, could easily return to the same locality. If a county or topographic map is available, it is wise to mark the locality on the map. Next, write the geographic data on a label and drop it into the bag of material collected at that particular locality. In addition, many collectors find it helpful to write the locality on the outside of each bag of rocks, minerals, or fossils.

Material from separate localities should be kept in individual cloth or paper bags. Take every precaution to keep the labels with their respective specimens, and always remember that *a specimen without a locality is greatly reduced in value*. This is especially true if you have discovered a rare or valuable mineral.

The collector should *always* ask the owner's permission before entering or collecting on private property. You should respect his property, especially livestock and fences, and leave the area cleaner than you found it.

One of the best ways to learn how to collect is to take a field trip with an organized group, such as a museum class or a rock and mineral club. Here you will be seeing and working with competent collectors who can acquaint you with the fundamentals of field collecting. Contact with members of rock and mineral societies also provides an opportunity for collectors to exchange rocks, minerals, and fossils, collecting and preparation tips, and good collecting localities. If you are interested in rocks and minerals and there is a mineral club in your community, by all means join it.

APPENDIX B

GLOSSARY

Aa—Blocky basaltic lava flow.

Abrasion—The process of wearing away by friction.

Absolute Time—Geologic time measured in years (compare with **Relative Time**).

Acidic Rocks—General term used in referring to quartz-containing igneous rocks; for example, granite.

Aeolian—In geology, refers to material deposited by wind which has transported particles from elsewhere; for example, loess, sand dunes.

Aftershock—Earthquake that follows a large earthquake and originates at or near focus of larger earthquake (compare with **Foreshock**).

Alluvial Fan—Deposit formed where stream emerges from a steep mountain valley upon open, relatively level land.

Alluvium—Sediment deposited by running water.

Alpine Glacier—A stream of ice occupying a depression in mountainous terrain and moving toward a lower level; also called **Mountain Glacier** or **Valley Glacier**.

Altitude—Height above sea level.

Amber—A hard, yellowish, translucent, fossilized plant resin.

Ammonite—Ammonoid cephalopod with complexly wrinkled suture pattern; member of subclass Ammonoidea.

Amorphous—Without definite molecular structure; not crystalline.

Amphibian—Animals living on both land and water; for example, frogs and salamanders.

Amygdule—Gas cavities or vesicles in igneous rocks which have become filled with secondary minerals.

Angular Unconformity—See **Unconformity**.

Anhydrite—Calcium sulfate ($CaSO_4$).

Anthracite Coal—Hard, very pure coal.

Anticline—An upfold or arch in the rocks.

Aperture—The opening of shells, cells, etc.

Aphanitic—Refers to rocks of such fine texture that the crystals cannot be seen with the naked eye.

Aquifer—A porous, water-bearing rock formation.

Aragonite—Calcium carbonate ($CaCO_3$) crystallizing in the orthorhombic system. In shells it is chalky and opaque; is less stable than calcite.

Archeo-—Prefix or combining form meaning ancient; from the Greek word, *archaios* ("ancient").

Archeozoic—The oldest known geological era; early Precambrian time.

Arenaceous—Of the texture or character of sand.

Arête—A narrow sharp divide separating two cirques or glacial valleys.

Argillaceous—Clayey.

Artesian Well—A well in which water is derived from an aquifer overlain by impervious strata.

Articulated—Joined by interlocking processes, or by teeth and sockets.

Artifacts—Implements or objects made by man.

Asteroid—One of the many small planets between the orbits of Jupiter and Mars; known also as **planetoid**.

Asthenosphere—Zone within the earth's mantle where plastic movements occur to permit isostatic adjustments.

Astrogeology—Geology of celestial bodies other than Earth.

Asymmetrical—Without or lacking symmetry.

Asymmetrical Fold—A fold in which the limbs dip at different angles; compare with **Symmetrical Fold**.

Atmosphere—The air surrounding the earth.

Attitude—The position of a segment of rock stratum with respect to a horizontal plane (attitude is determined by dip and strike).

Axis—One of the imaginary lines in a crystal.

Axis of Fold—An imaginary line passing through the crest of an anticline or the trough of a syncline.

Barchan—A crescent-shaped sand dune.

Barrier Beach—A low sandy beach separated from the mainland by a marsh or lagoon.

Basalt—A fine-grained igneous rock.

Base Level—Level of the body of water into which a stream flows.

Basic Rock—Igneous rock containing a low percentage of silica; for example, basalt.

Batholith—A huge mass of intrusive igneous rock with no known floor, more than forty miles in diameter.

Bauxite—The chief ore of aluminum; hydrous aluminum oxide.

Bedding Plane—The surface of demarcation between two individual rock layers or strata.

Bedrock—Solid unweathered rock underlying mantle rock.

Belemnite—An extinct cephalopod related to the present-day squid.

Benioff Zone—A seismic zone dipping beneath a continental margin and having a deep-sea trench as a surface expression.

Bilateral—Pertaining to the two halves of a body as symmetrical mirror images of each other.

Binomial Nomenclature—System of scientific nomenclature requiring two names: the generic and trivial names.

Biotite—A type of mica forming dark, usually black, crystals.

Bituminous Coal—Soft coal.

Blastoid—Stalked echinoderm with a budlike calyx, usually consisting of thirteen plates; member of class Blastoidea.

Block Diagram—A three-dimensional sketch combining the surface geology and the front and side structure of an area.

Block Mountains—Mountains formed by faulting.

Blowout—A relatively small, basin-shaped depression caused by wind erosion.

Boulder—A more or less rounded rock with a diameter in excess of ten inches.

Brachiopod—Bivalved marine invertebrate; member of phylum Brachiopoda.

Brackish—A mixture of salt and fresh waters.

Breccia—Rock composed of angular or broken fragments.

Bryozoan—Small, colonial, aquatic animal, usually secreting a calcareous skeleton; member of phylum Bryozoa.

Calcareous—Composed of, or containing, calcium carbonate; limy.

Calcite—Calcium carbonate ($CaCO_3$) crystallizing in the hexagonal system. In shells it is translucent and more stable than aragonite.

Caldera—A great basin-like depression formed by the destruction of a volcanic cone.

Calyx—In corals, the bowl-shaped depression in the upper part of the skeleton; in stalked echinoderms, that part of the body which contains most of the soft parts.

Cambrian—The first (oldest) period of the Paleozoic Era.

Carbonaceous—Containing carbon.

Carbonate—Rock or mineral composed of carbon, oxygen, and other elements.

Carboniferous—The fifth geologic period of the Paleozoic Era as recognized in Europe; comprises the Mississippian and Pennsylvanian periods of North America.

Carbonization—The process of fossilization whereby organic remains are reduced to carbon or coal.

Carnivore—A flesh-eating animal.

Cast—The impression taken from a mold.

Cement—Material binding together particles of sedimentary rocks.

Cementation—Deposition of mineral material between rock fragments.

-cene—Combining form meaning recent; from the Greek *kainos* ("new").

Ceno- —Combining form meaning recent; from the Greek *kainos* ("new").

Cenozoic—The latest era of geologic time, following the Mesozoic Era and extending to the present.

Cephalopod—Marine invertebrate with well-defined head and eyes and with tentacles around the mouth; member of class Cephalopoda, phylum Mollusca; includes squids, octopuses, pearly nautilus.

Ceratite—An ammonoid cephalopod with suture composed of rounded saddles and jagged lobes; member of subclass Ammonoidea.

Chalk—A soft white limestone.

Chemical Weathering—Weathering which results in a change in chemical composition; known also as **Decomposition.**

Chert—A compact, cryptocrystalline, flintlike variety of silica.

Chitin—A hornlike substance, found in the hard parts of all articulated animals, such as beetles and crabs.

Chitinous—Composed of chitin.

Chlorite—A greenish mineral chemically related to the micas.

Chromosome—In organic cells the bodies of tissue which carry the genes or hereditary determiners; there is a pair of chromosomes in each somatic cell and in each zygote; there is one chromosome in each gamete.

Cinder Cone—A steep-sided cone composed primarily of ash and cinders and formed by volcanic action.

Cirque—A large, deep, amphitheater-shaped depression at the head of a glacial valley.

Class—Subdivision of a phylum; a unit of biological classification.

Clastic Rock—Rock composed primarily of rock fragments transported to their place of deposition.

Cleavage—The tendency of certain minerals to split in particular directions, yielding relatively smooth plane surfaces.

Coastal Plain—A level plain composed of gently dipping wave- or stream-deposited sediments, with its margin on the shore of a large body of water; commonly represents an exposed part of the recently elevated sea floor.

Coelenterate—Invertebrates characterized by a hollow body cavity, radial symmetry, and stinging cells; a member of phylum Coelenterata includes jellyfishes, corals, sea anemones.

Col—A saddle-like gap across a ridge or between two peaks.

Colonial—In biology, refers to the way in which some invertebrates live in close association with, and are more or less interdependent upon, each other; colonial corals, hydroids, etc.

Columnar Section—A diagram, drawn to scale, that illustrates the character of the formations by means of geologic symbols, the thickness of strata, and their order of accumulation.

Columnar Structure—Parallel rodlike structure in igneous rocks.

Compact—Closely packed.

Compaction—In geology, the process whereby loose sediments are consolidated into firm hard rocks.

Composite Cone—A volcanic cone composed of alternate layers of lava and cinders; known also as a **Stratovolcano.**

Concentric—Having a common center, as circles; refers to shell markings that are parallel to shell margin.

Conchoidal—A type of fracture having curved concavities or the approximate shape of one-half of a bivalve shell. Glass has excellent conchoidal fracture.

Concretion—An aggregate of nodular or irregular masses in sedimentary rocks and usually formed around a central core, which is often a fossil.

Conglomerate—The rock produced by consolidation of gravel; constituent rock and mineral fragments are usually varied in composition and size.

Conifers—Cone-bearing shrubs or trees.

Connate Water—Water trapped in a sedimentary rock at the time of deposition.

Conodont—Minute toothlike fossils found in certain Paleozoic rocks; their origin is not definitely known, but they may have been part of some type of extinct fish.

Consolidation—Process whereby sediment is changed into solid rock.

Contact—The surface which marks the junction of two bodies of rock.

Contact Metamorphism—Metamorphism brought about as a result of the intrusion or extrusion of igneous rock materials, and taking place in rocks at or near their contact with a body of igneous rock.

Continental Drift—Slow, lateral movement of continents (involves rigid plates that may transport continental and oceanic crust as they move).

Continental Shelf—The relatively shallow ocean floor bordering a continental landmass.

Continental Slope—The relatively steep slope between the edge of continental shelf and the ocean deeps.

Contour Interval—The difference in elevation between two consecutive contour lines.

Contour Line—Line drawn on a map to join points at the same height above sea level.

Convection—Mechanism by which material moves because its density differs from that of the surrounding material.

Convection Cell—A pair of convection currents adjacent to each other.

Convection Current—Closed circulation of material sometimes developed during convection.

Convergent Plate Boundary—Boundary between two plates that are moving toward each other (compare with **Divergent Plate Boundary).**

Coprolite—The fossil excrement of animals.

Coquina—A porous, coarse-grained limestone composed primarily of broken shell material.

Coral—Bottom-dwelling marine invertebrate that secretes calcareous hard parts; member of class Anthozoa phylum Coelenterata.

Core—The dense innermost zone of the earth.

Correlation—The process of demonstrating that certain strata are closely related to each other or stratigraphic equivalents.

Crater—The funnel-shaped depression in the top of a volcanic cone.

Creep—The slow downward movement of soils and surface rocks.

Cretaceous—Youngest division of the Mesozoic Era.

Crevasse—A deep fissure or crack in a glacier.

Cross-cutting Relationships, Law of—A rock is younger than any rock across which it cuts.

Crust—In geology, the outer layer of the earth.

Cryptocrystalline—Composed of very fine or microscopic crystals.

Crystal—The regular polyhedral form, bounded by plane surfaces, that is assumed by a mineral under suitable conditions. Crystals have definite external symmetry and internal structure.

Crystalline—Possessing definite internal structure; not amorphous.

Crystal Symmetry—The number, location, and balanced arrangement of crystal faces in reference to the crystallographic axes or other crystallographic planes or directions.

Cube—Crystal form in isometric system; has six faces, each of which is perpendicular to an axis.

Cubic—In the general shape of a cube, the isometric crystal system is often called the cubic system.

Cystoid—An extinct stemmed echinoderm with calyx composed of numerous irregularly arranged plates; member of class Cystoidea.

Decomposition—Chemical decay or breakdown of a rock; see also **Chemical Weathering**.

Deep-focus Earthquake—An earthquake whose focus is at a depth of 186 to 435 miles (compare with **Shallow-focus Earthquake**).

Deep-sea Trenches—Arcuate trenches bordering certain continents; some are as much as 29,530 feet below the ocean surface.

Deflation—The removal of loose rock and soil particles by wind.

Deformation of Rocks—Any change from the original form of the rocks, for example, by folding or faulting.

Delta—A roughly triangular, level deposit formed where a stream enters a body of standing water.

Dendrite—A branching or treelike figure produced on or in a rock or mineral, usually formed by crystallization of an oxide of manganese.

Dendritic—Branching or treelike in form.

Deposit—Anything laid down, as sediment from a stream.

Deposition—The act of depositing or dropping rock material.

Desiccation—The loss of water from sediments.

Detrital—Composed of mineral or rock fragments.

Detrital Rock—Sedimentary rock derived from fragmental material of other rocks; sand, mud, gravel, etc.

Devonian—The fourth oldest period of the Paleozoic Era, follows the Silurian, precedes the Mississippian.

Diagonal—Two-angled.

Diamond—Crystalline carbon, the hardest known substance.

Diastrophism—Movements within the rocky crust of the earth.

Diatomite—A siliceous deposit composed of the remains of microscopic plants called diatoms.

Dike—A tabular rock body, usually igneous in origin, which cuts across the surrounding rock strata.

Dilatancy—Tendency of rocks to expand along tiny fractures immediately prior to rupture.

Dinosaur—Any of a large group of extinct reptiles which lived only during the Mesozoic Era.

Dip—The angle of inclination which the bedding plane of rocks makes with a real or imaginary horizontal plane.

Disconformity—See **Unconformity**.

Disintegration—Breakdown of a rock by mechanical means; known also as **Physical Weathering** or **Mechanical Weathering**.

Dissected—Cut into hills and valleys by erosion.

Distillation—In fossils that process by which volatile organic matter is removed, leaving a carbon residue as evidence of their existence.

Divergent Plate Boundary—Boundary between two plates moving apart. New oceanic crust is created at the opening formed between the two spreading plates (compare with **Convergent Plate Boundary**).

Divide—A ridge or high area separating adjoining drainage basins.

Dolomite—A mineral composed of calcium magnesium carbonate [$CaMg(CO_3)_2$].

Dome—A folded structure in which the beds dip outward in all directions from a central area; it is the opposite of a basin.

Drift—Material deposited by a glacier.

Drumlin—Rounded streamlined mounds of till.

Dune—A hill or ridge of sand formed by the wind.

Earthquake—A shaking of the earth's crust caused by the fracture and movement of rocks or by volcanic shocks.

Echinoderm—A marine invertebrate with calcareous exoskeleton and usually exhibiting a fivefold radial symmetry; member of phylum Echinodermata; includes cystoids, blastoids, crinoids, starfishes, and sea urchins.

Echinoid—Bottom-dwelling, unattached marine invertebrate with exoskeleton of calcareous plates covered by movable spines; member of class Echinoidea; sea urchins, heart urchins, biscuit urchins.

Elastic Rebound—Recovery of elastic strain when material breaks or stress is removed.

Embryology—That division of biology which deals with the formation and development of embryos.

Embryonic—Referring to the earliest undeveloped stage of an animal after the egg stage.

End Moraine—See **Terminal Moraine**.

Endoskeleton—The internal supporting structure of an animal.

Environment—The surroundings, physical, chemical, and organic, of an organism.

Eocene—A division of geologic time, estimated to be the time from 50 to 40 million years ago; one of the older divisions of the Cenozoic Era.

Epicenter—A point or line directly above the focus or point at which an earthquake occurs.

Epoch—A division of geologic time, subdivision of a period.

Era—A division of geologic time, includes one or more periods.

Erathem—In stratigraphy: the rocks formed during an era of geologic time.

Erosion—The wearing away and removal of soil and rock fragments by wind, water, or ice.

Erratic—A boulder, transported by glacial action, which differs from the bedrock on which it rests.

Eskers—Winding ridges of stratified sand and gravel deposited by streams running through or under a glacier.

Estuary—A drowned river valley where tidal effects are evident.

Evaporation—The process whereby a liquid becomes a vapor.

Evaporite—A sediment derived by chemical precipitation as salt-saturated water evaporates.

Evolution—A term applied to those methods or processes and to the sum of those processes whereby organisms change through successive generations.

Exfoliation—The splitting off of scales or flakes from a rock surface as a result of weathering.

Exoskeleton—An external skeleton, or hard covering for the protection of soft parts, particularly among invertebrates.

Exposure—An unobscured outcrop of rock appearing at the surface; see **Outcrop**.

Extrusive Rock—Igneous rock that has been extruded or forced out onto the earth's surface.

Face—The outer surface of a crystal.

Facies—An assemblage of mineral, rock, or fossil features reflecting an environment in which rock was formed (see **Sedimentary Facies**).

Fault—The displacement of rocks along a zone of fracture.

Fault Breccia—Breccia formed along the plane of a fault.

Fault Line—The line along which the fault plane meets the earth's surface.

Fault Plane—A fracture in a rock along which movement has taken place.

Fault Scarp—A small cliff formed at the surface along a fault line.

Fauna—An assemblage of animals (living or fossil) living in a given place at a given time.

Feldspar—A group of closely related silicate minerals, including orthoclase, microcline, sanidine, plagioclase, labradorite, and others.

Fiord—A deep, narrow, steep-walled inlet of the sea; formed by the flooding of a glaciated valley.

Firn—See Névé.

Fission—Process in which atomic nucleus breaks down to form nuclei of lighter atoms (compare with **Fusion**).

Flint—An amorphous siliceous rock, usually dark and dull.

Flood Plain—A low area bordering a river which is covered by water when the stream is in flood stage.

Flora—An assemblage of plants (living or fossil) living in a given place at a given time.

Fluvial Deposit—Sediment deposited by streams.

Focus—The point within the earth where an earthquake originates.

Fold—A flexure or bend produced when rocks were in a plastic condition.

Fold Mountains—Mountains formed from folding of the rocks.

Foliated—Made up of thin leaves, as in mica.

Foliation—The foliated (layered) structure in metamorphic rock.

Footwall—The rock beneath the hanging wall in an inclined fault.

Foramen—A small opening, pore, or perforation.

Foraminifera—One-celled, generally microscopic animals which aid in the deposition of limestone; an order of class Sarcodina, phylum Protozoa.

Foreshock—Relatively small earthquake that precedes larger earthquake by a few days or weeks and originates at or near focus of the larger earthquake (compare with **Aftershock**).

Formation—A rock unit useful for mapping and distinguishing primarily on the basis of lithologic characters.

Fossil—The remains or traces of organisms buried by natural causes and preserved in the earth's crust.

> *Guide Fossil*—A fossil which, because of its limited vertical but wide horizontal distribution, is of value as a guide or index to the age of the rocks in which it is found; known also as **Index Fossil**.

Fossil Fuels—Organic remains used to produce heat or energy by combustion. Includes coal, oil, and natural gas.

Fossiliferous—Containing fossilized organic remains.

Fracture—The texture of a freshly broken surface other than a cleavage surface, described as conchoidal, even, splintery, etc.

Fragmental Rock—Rock composed of pieces of minerals or pre-existing rocks cemented together.

Fumarole—Vents or holes in volcanic regions from which gases issue.

Fusion—Process by which nuclei of lighter atoms join to form nuclei of heavier atoms (compare with **Fission**).

Gabbro—Coarse-grained igneous rock consisting primarily of plagioclase, feldspar, and pyroxene.

Galaxy—An astronomical system consisting of billions of stars, for example, the Milky Way.

Gangue—The worthless minerals associated with the valuable minerals in an ore.

Garnets—A group of complex silicates characteristic of certain metamorphic rocks; may form perfect red glassy crystals.

Gastroliths—Highly polished well-rounded pebbles found associated with certain reptilian fossils; "stomach stones."

Gastropod—A terrestrial or aquatic invertebrate, typically possessing a single-valved, calcareous, coiled shell; member of class Gastropoda, phylum Mollusca; snails and slugs.

Geanticline—A broad upwarp of the earth's crust, covers hundreds of miles.

Geiger Counter—An instrument used to detect radioactivity.

Gem—A cut and polished gemstone.

Gemology—The science dealing with the study of gemstones.

Gemstone—A mineral suitable for cutting into a gem; the term gemstones is frequently used collectively to include both cut and polished stones and rough stones.

Gene—The basic building unit of heredity, a hereditary determiner.

Genetic—Pertaining to origin.

Genetics—That division of biology which deals with heredity and variation among related organisms.

Genus (genera, plural)—A group of closely related species of organisms.

Geochronology—The study of time in relation to the history of the earth.

Geode—A rounded or spherical rock cavity; commonly lined with crystals.

Geologic Age—The age of an object as stated in terms of geologic time; for example, a Pennsylvanian fern, Cretaceous dinosaur.

Geologic Map—Map showing distribution of rock outcrops, structural features, mineral deposits.

Geologic Range—The known duration of an organism's existence throughout geologic time, for example, Cambrian to Holocene for brachiopods.

Geologic Time Scale—Tabular record of the divisions of earth history.

Geomorphology—That branch of geology dealing with the earth's form; a study of landscape development.

Geophysical Prospecting—Mapping rock structures by means of experimental physics.

Geosyncline—A great downward flexure of the earth's crust, usually tens of miles wide and hundreds of miles long.

Geothermal Energy—Energy derived from the earth's natural heat; found in hot water, hot brines, and hot rocks.

Geyser—A hot spring which erupts periodically, throwing out steam and hot water.

Geyserite—Siliceous deposits formed around the openings of geysers and hot springs.

Glacier—A slowly moving mass of recrystallized ice flowing forward as a result of gravitational attraction.

Glass—In geology, a brittle noncrystalline rock that has cooled rapidly.

Gneiss—A coarse-grained metamorphic rock having segregations of granular and platy minerals that give it a more or less banded appearance without well-developed schistosity.

Gondwanaland—Hypothetical continent of Southern Hemisphere thought to have broken up during Mesozoic time. Present-day Africa, Antarctica, Australia, India, and South America are believed to have formed from resulting fragments.

Goniatite—An ammonoid cephalopod with suture composed of rounded saddles and angular lobes; member of subclass Ammonoidea.

Graben—A long narrow block that has been dropped down between two faults.

Gradient—The slope of a stream bed, usually expressed in feet per mile.

Granite—A granular igneous rock composed mostly of quartz, feldspar, and commonly mica or hornblende.

Granitic Texture—Coarse-grained texture; characteristic of intrusive rocks.

Granitization—An essentially metamorphic process by which solid rock is changed into a granitic rock without passing through a magmatic stage.

Granular Texture—Texture marked by interlocking grains of similar size, as in granite.

Graptolite—An extinct marine colonial organism with chitinous hard parts; believed to belong to subphylum Hemichordata of phylum Chordata.

Gravity Fault—See **Normal Fault.**

Groundmass—Glassy or crystalline background material for the phenocrysts (larger crystals) in a porphyritic rock.

Ground Water—Underground water within the zone of saturation in the lower part of the mantle rock;

known also as subsurface water, underground water, and subterranean water.

Guide Fossil—See Fossil.

Gypsum—Hydrated calcium sulfate ($CaSO_4 \cdot 2H_2O$).

Habit—The characteristic crystal form of a mineral.

Halite—Common rock salt ($NaCl$).

Hanging Valley—A tributary valley which enters the main valley at a greater elevation than the main valley floor.

Hanging Wall—The rock above the footwall in an inclined fault.

Hardness—The resistance of a rock to being scratched.

Hardness Scale—A standard scale used to determine the relative hardness of minerals; Mohs Scale.

Hematite—Iron oxide (Fe_2O_3); the principal ore mineral for most of the United States iron production.

Herbivore—A plant-eating animal.

Hexa-—A prefix meaning six.

Hexagonal—Having six angles and six sides; a crystal system in which the crystal faces are referred to four intersecting axes; three of these axes are equal, lie in the same plane, and intersect at angles of 120 degrees; the fourth axis is perpendicular to the other three and is either longer or shorter.

Hinge Line—In brachiopods the edge of the shell where the two valves articulate; in pelecypods the dorsal margin of the valve which is in continual contact with the opposite valve.

Historical Geology—Study of the geologic history of the earth.

Holocene—The latest epoch of the Quaternary Period of the Cenozoic Era; known also as the Recent.

Homologous Structure—Structures or organs in different animals that have the same fundamental structure, but that are used for different purposes.

Hook—A curved spit.

Hornblende—A rock-forming mineral belonging to the amphibole group.

Horst—A block that has been raised between two faults.

Hot Spot—Localized zone of melting in mantle near base of lithosphere.

Hot Springs—A spring that brings hot water to the surface.

Hydrocarbon—Compound of hydrogen and carbon that burns in open air to form water and oxides of carbon.

Hydrologic Cycle—The continuous process whereby water evaporates from the sea, is precipitated to the land, and eventually moves back to the sea.

Hydrosphere—All of the water upon the earth's surface or in the open spaces below the surface.

Ice Age—The Pleistocene Epoch of the Quaternary Period, Cenozoic Era; a time of great glaciation.

Ice Cap—A localized ice sheet.

Ice Sheet—A large moundlike mass of glacier ice spreading in several or all directions from a center.

Ichthyosaur—A porpoise-like marine reptile of Mesozoic time.

Igneous Rock—Rock which has solidified from lava or molten rock called magma.

Inclusion—Rock or mineral fragment surrounded by other rock.

Index Fossil—See Fossil.

Intensity—A measure of the effects of an earthquake at a particular place (compare with Magnitude).

Intermittent Stream—A stream whose bed is dry part of the time.

Intrusion—Igneous rock which, while in a molten condition, has forced its way into other rock.

Intrusive Rock—Rock that has been pushed (usually in a molten state) among pre-existing rock strata, commonly along faults or fissures; intrusive rocks do not reach the earth's surface but are commonly exposed at the surface by later erosion; known also as Plutonic Rock.

Invertebrate—An animal without a backbone or spinal column.

Isometric—A crystal system in which the crystal forms are referred to three equal axes intersecting at right angles to each other.

Isoseismal—An imaginary line connecting equal points of earthquake wave intensity, known also as isoseismic lines.

Isostasy—The state of general equilibrium within the earth's crust.

Isotopes—Elements having the same atomic numbers, but differing in atomic weights and some properties.

Joint—A fracture in a rock along which there has been no displacement on opposite sides of the break.

Jurassic—The middle period of the Mesozoic Era.

Kame—A small cone-shaped mound of stratified sand and gravel deposited by a glacial stream.

Kaolin—A white or nearly white clay resulting from the decomposition of rocks containing large amounts of feldspar.

Karst Topography—Irregular topography marked by sinkholes, streamless valleys, caverns, and underground streams.

Kettle—A basin-shaped depression in glacial drift, formed when buried blocks of glacial ice melt.

Laccolith—A large lens-shaped mass of igneous intrusive rock.

Lacustrine Deposits—Deposits formed on the bottom of lakes.

Landslide—The relatively rapid movement of large masses of rock and earth down the slope of a hill or mountain.

Lapilli—Small rounded or irregular fragments of volcanic rock thrown out during an eruption.

Lateral—Side, or to the side.

Lateral Moraine—An elongated ridge of till along the lateral margins of an alpine glacier; derived largely from superficial debris falling on the glacier from the valley walls.

Laterite—Tropical soil rich in hydroxides of aluminum and iron.

Laurasia—Hypothetical continent of Northern Hemisphere which is thought to have broken up during Mesozoic time. Present-day North America, Greenland, and most of Eurasia (except India) believed to have formed from resulting fragments.

Lava—Molten rock upon the surface.

Lava Dome—See **Shield Volcano**.

Lava Plateau—See **Plateau Basalts**.

Lignite—Low-grade soft brown coal.

Limestone—A sedimentary rock composed mostly of calcium carbonate.

Limonite—Amorphous hydrated iron oxide.

Lithification—The process whereby sediments are changed into solid rock.

Lithology—The study and description of rocks based on the megascopic (with the naked eye) examination of samples; used also to refer to the texture and composition of any given rock sample.

Lithosphere—Rigid outer layer of the earth as compared to the atmosphere and hydrosphere. Includes crust and upper part of mantle and is relatively strong in contrast to the underlying asthenosphere.

Load—The amount of material that can be transported by an eroding agent (such as a stream, glacier, or the wind) at a given time.

Lode—An unusually thick ore vein or a group of ore veins that can be mined as a unit.

Loess—A deposit of wind-blown silt.

Longitudinal—In a direction parallel with the length.

Luster—The appearance of the freshly broken or unweathered surface of a mineral in reflected light.

Macrofossils—Fossils whose average representatives are readily visible to the naked eye; known also as **Megafossils**.

Magma—Molten rock material beneath the earth's surface and from which igneous rocks are formed.

Magnitude—Measure of total energy released by an earthquake (compare with **Intensity**).

Mantle—The thick dense part of the lithosphere beneath the earth's crust extending to a depth of about 1800 miles below the surface.

Mantle Rock—Layer of loose soil, earth, or rock which covers bedrock.

Marble—Recrystallized carbonate rock which, prior to being metamorphosed, was limestone or dolomite.

Marine—Of, or pertaining to, the sea.

Mass Movement—Surface movements of earth materials caused primarily by gravity; known also as **Mass Wasting**.

Mass Wasting—See **Mass Movement**.

Matrix—The material in which a specific mineral is embedded; also the rock to which one end of a crystal is attached.

Meanders—A series of wide, looping curves in the course of a well-developed stream.

Mechanical Weathering—See **Disintegration**; **Physical Weathering**.

Medial Moraine—An elongated ridgelike body of till formed by the junction of two lateral moraines.

Megafossils—See **Macrofossils**.

Meso-—A prefix signifying middle.

Mesozoic Era—Consists of Triassic, Jurassic, and Cretaceous periods.

Metamorphic Rock—Rock formed from igneous or sedimentary rocks that have been subjected to great changes in temperature, pressure, and chemical environment.

Metamorphism—Extensive change of rocks or minerals.

Meteoric Water—Ground water derived primarily from precipitation.

Meteorology—The science which deals with the atmosphere.

Micas—A group of rock-forming silicates.

Microfossil—A fossil which is, typically, microscopic in size.

Mid-oceanic Ridge—Continuous, seismically active median mountain range extending through the Indian, South Pacific, and North and South Atlantic oceans.

Milky Way—The galaxy to which the earth belongs.

Mineral—A naturally occurring inorganic substance possessing definite chemical and physical properties.

Mineralogy—The science concerned with the study of minerals, including their occurrence, composition, forms, properties, and structure.

Miocene—The fourth epoch of the Tertiary Period of the Cenozoic Era, it lasted about 12 million

years, follows the Oligocene, precedes the Pliocene.

Mississippian—The fifth period of the Paleozoic
Era.

Mohorovicic Discontinuity—The zone of contact between the rocky crust and the mantle; known also
as the Moho.

Mohs Scale—Scale developed for determining the
relative hardness of minerals; **Hardness Scale.**

Monadnock—An isolated hill left as an erosional
remnant standing above the surface of a peneplane.

Monoclinic—A crystal system in which the crystal
faces are described in relation to three intersecting
unequal axes, two of which are at right angles and
the third inclined.

Moon—A celestial body that revolves around a
planet; a satellite.

Moraine—An accumulation of rock materials carried and deposited by a glacier.

Morphology—The study of structure or form.

Mountain—Any part of the land that rises conspicuously above the surrounding terrain; usually
steep-sided and possessing a relatively small summit area.

Mountain Glacier—See **Alpine Glacier** or **Valley
Glacier.**

Mountain Glacier—See **Alpine Glacier.**

Mudflow—The movement of a large mass of mud,
rock, and water down a valley or stream course.

Mud Volcano—Bubbling springs of mud, often
brightly colored; also called **paint pots.**

Multicellular—Composed of more than one cell.

Muscovite—"White mica"; characterized by silvery
white crystals.

Mutation—An inherited change transmitted as a result of changes within the germ plasm.

Natural Gas—Gaseous hydrocarbons (essentially
methane) that occur in rocks.

Natural Resources—Energy and materials produced
by geologic processes.

Natural Selection—Survival of organisms by reason
of their ability to adapt to their surroundings and
to changing environmental conditions.

Nebula—A blurred, hazy mass of gases or dust in
space.

Névé—Granular snow and ice which later becomes
glacial ice; also called **firn.**

Nodule—Rounded lump of rock or mineral.

Nonconformity—See **Unconformity.**

Normal Fault—A fault in which the hanging wall
has moved downward with respect to the footwall;
known also as a **Gravity Fault.**

Oblate—Flattened at the poles.

Obsidian—Glassy volcanic rock.

Oceanography—The study of the sea and its characteristics.

Octo-—A prefix meaning eight.

Oil Shale—A highly organic shale from which petroleum can be extracted.

Oligocene—A division of geologic time, estimated to
be the time from 40 to 28 million years ago; part
of the Cenozoic Era.

Olivine—A dark green, rock-forming silicate mineral.

Oölitic—Term applied to rock consisting of small
rounded particles called oölites.

Ordovician—The second period of the Paleozoic
Era.

Ore—A metalliferous mineral deposit.

Organ—A part of a plant or animal that functions
as a unit—the heart, stomach, eye.

Organic—Pertaining to, or derived from, life.

Organism—Any living being.

Orogeny—The process by which mountain structures are developed.

Orthoclase—A feldspar characteristic of acidic igneous rocks; potash feldspar.

Orthorhombic—A crystal system in which crystal
faces are referred to three unequal axes intersecting at right angles.

Outcrop—Place where bedrock is exposed at the
surface; see **Exposure.**

Outwash Plain—A broad plain formed of deposits
laid down by streams of a melting glacier.

Oxbow Lake—A crescent-shaped lake formed by the
isolation of a meander from the main part of the
stream.

Oxidation—The chemical union of oxygen with
other substances.

Pahoehoe—A type of solidified lava characterized
by a smooth, ropy, or billowy surface.

Paint Pot—See **Mud Volcano.**

Paleocene—The first epoch of the Tertiary Period.

Paleoecology—The study of the relationship between
ancient organisms and their environment.

Paleogeography—The study of ancient geography.

Paleomagnetism—Study of the earth's magnetic field
as it has existed throughout geologic time.

Paleontology—The science that deals with the study
of fossils.

Paleozoic—That era of geologic time containing the
Cambrian, Ordovician, Silurian, Devonian, Mississippian, Pennsylvanian, and Permian periods.

Pangaea—Hypothetical continent from which all
others are thought to have originated through the
process of fragmentation and drifting; also spelled
Pangea.

Peat—An accumulation of dark brown partially decomposed plant material; the first stage in coal formation.

Pedicle Opening (pedicle foramen)—See **Foramen.**

Pegmatite—A body of coarse-grained intrusive igneous rock, commonly lens- or dike-shaped.

Pelecypod—A bivalved aquatic invertebrate; member of class Pelecypoda, phylum Mollusca.

Peneplain (peneplane)—An extensive, low, nearly flat region produced by continued erosion.

Pennsylvanian—The sixth oldest period of the Paleozoic Era, follows the Mississippian, precedes the Permian.

Pentamerous Symmetry—Symmetry arranged in a pattern of fives. See **Symmetry.**

Peridotite—Coarse-grained basic igneous rock consisting primarily of olivine and pyroxene.

Period—The division of geologic time which is next lower in rank than an era, and next above an epoch.

Permeable—Capable of transmitting fluids.

Permian—The last period of the Paleozoic Era.

Permineralization—In some fossils that process by which mineral matter has been added to the original shell material by precipitation in the interstices rather than by replacing the original shell material.

Petrography—The descriptive study of rocks.

Petroleum—Oil, a complex mixture of hydrocarbons occurring in the earth's crust.

Petrology—The study, by all possible methods, of the natural history of rocks.

Phenocryst—A crystal that is considerably larger than the crystals of the surrounding material.

Phosphatic—Containing or pertaining to phosphate minerals.

Phylum—One of the primary divisions of the animal or vegetable kingdoms.

Physical Geology—The study of earth materials, their composition and distribution, and the forces which affect them.

Physical Weathering—The process of breaking rock down by physical forces, known also as **Mechanical Weathering** or **Disintegration.**

Physiography—A description of the natural features of the surface of the earth.

Piedmont Glacier—A glacier formed by the union of several alpine glaciers at the foot of the mountains from which the alpine glaciers originated.

Pitch—The angle between the axis of a fold and the horizontal plane.

Plagioclase—A mixture of feldspars containing sodium and calcium; occurs in both acidic and basic igneous rocks.

Plain—An area of low relief and low elevation underlain by essentially horizontal strata.

Planet—An astronomical body that revolves around the sun in a regular orbit.

Planetoid—See **Asteroid.**

Plate—Segment of crustal lithosphere including part of the upper mantle above the lithosphere.

Plate Tectonics—Theory of global tectonics in which the lithosphere is divided into a number of plates which move horizontally, causing seismic and tectonic activities as the plates interact along their boundaries.

Plateau—A relatively flat area of high elevation underlain by essentially horizontal strata.

Plateau Basalts—Great sheets of basalt which have flowed out of fissures in the earth's crust, known also as lava plateaus or flood basalts.

Playa—The dried floors of intermittent lakes found in desert areas.

Pleistocene—Earliest epoch of Quaternary Period Cenozoic Era, follows Pliocene Epoch of Tertiary Period, precedes Holocene Epoch of Quaternary.

Pliocene—Latest epoch of Tertiary Period of Cenozoic Era, follows Miocene Epoch and precedes Pleistocene Epoch of Quaternary Period, lasted about 13 million years.

Pluton—Igneous rock bodies that solidified from magma at depth.

Plutonic Rock—See **Intrusive Rock.**

Polar Wandering, or Migration—Movement of the position of the magnetic poles during past time in relation to their present position.

Polygonal—Having more than four angles.

Polyp—A many-tentacled aquatic coelenterate animal, typically cylindrical or cup-shaped as in corals.

Porosity—The percentage of porous rock that consists of open space.

Porous—Containing pores or void spaces.

Porphyry—An igneous rock containing conspicuous phenocrysts in a glassy or fine-grained groundmass.

Pothole—A rounded hole ground in the rock of a stream channel.

Precambrian—That portion of geologic time before the Cambrian; divided into Archeozoic Era (Early Precambrian) and Proterozoic Era (Late Precambrian).

Predator—A beast of prey.

Prehistoric Time—That portion of time which precedes time of recent history.

Proterozoic—Youngest era of the Precambrian, follows the Archeozoic Era and precedes the Cambrian Period of the Paleozoic Era.

Protista—The organic kingdom including the simplest of all one-celled organisms which possess various characters of both plants and animals; bacteria, algae, foraminifers, radiolarians.

Pseudofossils—Objects of nonorganic origin which resemble fossils, for example, dendrites, concretions.

Pseudomorph—A mineral which has assumed the shape of the mineral it replaced.

Pterosaur—A flying reptile of the Mesozoic Era.

Pyrite—A hard, brass-yellow mineral composed of iron sulfide; "fool's gold"; (FeS_2).

Pyroclastic—Fragmental rock formed of rock fragments thrown out of volcanoes, for example, cinders, volcanic bombs, etc.; known also as **tephra.**

Quartz—A silicate mineral (SiO_2); the hardest common mineral.

Quartzite—Metamorphic rock that, prior to metamorphism, was sandstone.

Quaternary—The youngest period of the Cenozoic Era, follows the Tertiary Period.

Radial Symmetry—The symmetrical repetition of parts around a common dorso-ventrally disposed axis.

Radioactivity—Spontaneous disintegration of atomic nucleus, with release of energy.

Recent—See **Holocene.**

Recessional Moraine—Ridges of till formed by the recession or temporary delays in the advance of glaciers.

Recrystallization—Growth of small grains into large ones.

Recumbent Fold—A fold in which the axis of folding is more or less horizontal.

Red Beds—Red sedimentary rocks.

Reef—A moundlike or ridgelike elevation of the sea bottom which almost reaches the surface of the water; composed primarily of organic material.

Rejuvenation—Changes which tend to increase the gradient of a stream.

Relative Time—The dating of events in chronologic order of occurrence rather than in years (compare with **Absolute Time**).

Relief—The irregularity of a land surface; the difference in elevation between the highest and lowest points in an area.

Replacement—Type of fossilization whereby organic hard parts are removed by solution accompanied by almost simultaneous deposition of other substances in the resulting voids; mineralization.

Reverse Fault—See **Thrust Fault.**

Rhyolite—A fine-grained extrusive or shallow intrusive igneous rock of approximately the same composition as granite.

Rift Valley—See **Graben.**

Rift Zone—System of fractures in the earth's crust; often associated with the extrusion of lava.

Ripple Marks—Wavelike corrugations produced in unconsolidated materials by wind or water.

Rock—Any naturally formed mass of mineral matter forming an essential part of the earth's crust.

Rock Cycle—The concept of a sequence of events through which earth materials may pass when subjected to geological processes.

Rock-forming Minerals—Common minerals which compose large percentages of the rocks of the lithosphere.

Rock Glacier—Lobate tongues of rock debris slowly moving downslope in the manner of a glacier.

Rock Salt—Common salt (NaCl) or **halite.**

Rockslide—The relatively rapid downward movement of recently detached rock material sliding along zones of separation.

Rock-unit—Divisions of rocks based on definite physical and lithologic characteristics and not defined on the basis of geologic time; groups, formations, members.

Runoff—Water that flows off the surface of the land.

Salt—See **Halite** or **Rock Salt.**

Salt Plug—Vertical pipelike bodies of salt or gypsum formed by the upward flowage of salt under pressure; they have pushed up through the surrounding sediments in order to attain their present position.

Sand—Small mineral grains, usually quartz.

Sand Dune—A ridge or hill of sand caused by the wind.

Sandstone—Sedimentary rock consisting of consolidated sand.

Satellite—See **Moon.**

Schist—A metamorphic rock that contains an abundance of oriented platy minerals that enable the rock to be split with relative ease parallel to the flat surfaces of the platy minerals.

Sea Cave—Cave formed as a result of erosion by sea waves.

Sea Cliff—Cliff formed by marine erosion.

Sea-floor Spreading—Process by which ocean floors spread laterally from crests of mid-oceanic ridges.

Sediment—Material that has been deposited by settling from a transportation agent such as water or air.

Sedimentary Facies—An accumulation of deposits, that displays specific characteristics and grades laterally (horizontally) into other sedimentary deposits that were formed at the same time but exhibit different characteristics. See **Facies.**

Sedimentary Rock—Rocks formed by the accumulation of sediments.

Sedimentation—Deposition of the rock particles (sediments) that make up sedimentary rock.

Seismic Sea Wave—See **Tsunami.**

Seismogram—The record made by a seismograph.

Seismograph—An instrument used to record earth tremors.

Seismology—The scientific study of earthquakes and other earth tremors.

Series—The rocks formed during an epoch; the time-stratigraphic term next in rank below a system.

Shale—Thinly layered sedimentary rock composed of consolidated mud, clay, or silt.

Shallow-focus Earthquake—An earthquake whose focus is at a depth of less than 44 miles (compare with deep-focus earthquake).

Shield—A large area of exposed Precambrian rock.

Shield Cone—See **Shield Volcano.**

Shield Volcano—A volcano composed almost exclusively of lava; known also as **shield cone, lava dome,** or **volcanic shield.**

Silica—An oxide of silicon (SiO_2).

Siliceous—Containing or pertaining to silica.

Silicification—The process of combining or impregnating with silica.

Silicified—Replaced by or containing a large amount of quartz or silica.

Sill—Solidified magma forced between layers of sedimentary rock.

Silt—Fine muddy sediment consisting of particles intermediate in size between clay particles and sand grains.

Silurian—The third oldest period of the Paleozoic Era, follows the Ordovician, precedes the Devonian.

Sink—See **Sinkhole.**

Sinkhole—A surface depression in the ground caused by collapse due to solution of the underlying rocks; known also as a **sink.**

Slate—Finely layered, compact metamorphic rock which splits readily into sheets; formed by metamorphism of shale.

Slickensides—Polished and grooved surfaces that are the result of two rock masses sliding past each other as in faulting.

Slump—The relatively small-scale downward slipping of a mass of rock or soil.

Snow Line—The level above which snow exists throughout the year.

Soil—Broken and decomposed rock and decayed organic matter.

Solar System—The sun and the astronomical bodies that revolve about it.

Solifluction—Slow mass movement of soil especially characteristic of arctic or subarctic regions.

Solitary—Living alone; not part of a colony.

Species—One of the smaller natural divisions in classification.

Specific Gravity—The weight in air divided by the loss of weight in water at a given temperature, or the weight of an object in air divided by the weight of an equal volume of water; also called relative density; the most commonly used standard temperature for this measurement is 4° C. or 39.2° F.

Specific Name—The name applied to a species, usually the second of two names applied to a fossil, as *wacoensis* in *Kingena wacoensis*. See **Trivial Name.**

Spheroidal—Pertaining to a spheroid (a distorted sphere).

Spit—A finger-shaped sand bar extending out from the shore.

Spring—Place where ground water reaches the surface through a natural opening.

Stack—An isolated steep-sided column of rock left standing as waves erode a shoreline.

Stalactite—An icicle-shaped deposit formed by evaporation of solutions dripping from the roof of a cavern.

Stalagmite—Icicle-shaped mineral deposit formed by the evaporation of solutions on the floor of a cavern.

Star—A highly heated mass of incandescent gases such as our sun.

Steinkern—An internal mold.

Stock—A circular or oval-shaped igneous body which increases in size with depth, has no known floor and an exposed surface area of less than forty square miles.

Stoping—One of the processes by which intrusive igneous rocks enter the country rock; the magma works its way upward as blocks of country rock break off and fall into the magma where they are incorporated into the molten mass.

Strain—Change in the dimensions of matter in response to stress.

Stratification—Bedding or layering in sedimentary rock.

Stratigraphy—The geologic subscience dealing with the definition and interpretation of stratified rocks; especially their lithology, sequence, distribution, and correlation.

Stratovolcano—A volcano characterized by a cone composed of alternating layers of lava and pyroclastics; known also as **composite cone.**

Stratum (strata, plural)—A single bed or layer of sedimentary rock.

Streak—The color of a mineral when finely powdered; usually determined by rubbing the mineral against a piece of unglazed porcelain.

Streak Plate—A piece of unglazed porcelain or tile used to determine the streak of a mineral.

Stream Capture—See **Stream Piracy.**

Stream Piracy—The diversion of water from one stream channel into that of another; known also as **Capture.**

Striations—Closely spaced fine parallel lines.

Strike—The direction of a real or imaginary line that is formed by the intersection of a bed or stratum with a horizontal plane; strike is perpendicular to the dip.

Strike-slip Fault—A fault in which the movement is essentially in the direction of the fault's strike.

Structural Geology—That branch of geology which deals with the study of the architecture of the earth (the rocks and their relationships to each other).

Structure—The general disposition, arrangement, and relative position of deformed masses of rock.

Subduction—Movement by which one lithospheric plate descends under another.

Subduction Zone—A long narrow belt in which one lithospheric plate descends relative to another lithospheric plate.

Subglacial Stream—Stream flowing in a tunnel beneath a glacier.

Sublimation—The process whereby a substance passes from a solid to a gaseous state and again becomes a solid, without first becoming a liquid.

Subsidence—Sinking of the earth's crust.

Subsurface Water—See **Ground Water.**

Subterranean Water—See **Ground Water.**

Superposition, Law of—In an undisturbed sequence of rocks younger beds will overlie older beds of rocks.

Suspension—The manner in which a stream carries material between the surface and the bottom.

Symmetrical Fold—A fold in which the axial plane is essentially vertical, resulting in limbs which dip at similar angles.

Symmetry—The reversed repetition of parts with reference to an axis:

    Bilateral Symmetry—The symmetrical duplication of parts on each side of a vertical anterior-posterior plane; a median sagittal plane.

    Radial Symmetry—The symmetrical repetition of parts around a common vertical dorso-ventrally disposed axis.

    Pentamerous Symmetry—Symmetry arranged in a pattern of fives.

Syncline—A trough or downfold in the rocks.

System—In stratigraphy: the rocks formed during a period; the time-stratigraphic term next in rank above a series; in mineralogy: one of six divisions into which crystals are classified according to their symmetry.

Tabular—Having a flat, relatively large surface relative to thickness.

Talus—A mass of rock debris which collects at the bottom of a steep hill or cliff.

Tarn—A small mountain lake formed in a cirque after removal of the glacial ice.

Taxonomy—That branch of science which deals with classifications, especially in relation to plants, animals, or fossils.

Tectonic Movements—Movements resulting in deformation of the earth's crust.

Tephra—See **Pyroclastic.**

Terminal Moraine—Moraine formed at the point marking the farthest advance of the glacier; known also as **end moraine.**

Termination—The end of a crystal that is completely enclosed by crystal faces; the crystal end that is not attached to the matrix.

Tertiary—The oldest period of the Cenozoic Era, follows the Cretaceous Period of the Mesozoic and precedes the Quaternary Period of the Cenozoic.

Test—The protective covering of some invertebrate animals.

Tetragonal—One of the six crystal systems.

Texture—Physical appearance of a rock as indicated by the size, shape, and arrangement of the materials comprising the rock.

Thrust Fault—A fault in which the hanging wall has moved up relative to the footwall; known also as a **reverse fault.**

Till—Unstratified glacial deposit.

Tillite—Rock formed from the consolidation of till.

Time-unit—A portion of continuous geologic time, for example, eras, periods, epochs, and ages.

Time-rock Unit—Same as **Time-stratigraphic Unit.**

Time-stratigraphic Unit—Term given to rock units with boundaries established by geologic time; strata deposited during definite portions of geologic time, for example, erathems, systems, series, stages. Same as **Time-rock Unit.**

Tombolo—A strip of sand so deposited as to connect a small island with the mainland or with another island.

Topographic Map—A map showing the physical features of an area, especially the relief and contour of the land.

Topography—The physical features or configuration of a land surface.

Transform Fault—A strike-slip (lateral or horizontal) fault, characteristic of mid-oceanic ridges along which the ridges are offset, presumably by sea-floor spreading.

Transportation—The process by which rock materials are carried.

Trap—See **Traprock.**

Traprock—A general term for certain dark-colored igneous rocks such as diabase and basalt; also called **trap.**

Travertine—A form of calcium carbonate ($CaCO_3$) deposited by ground or surface waters; subterranean formations such as stalactites and stalagmites are composed of travertine; such deposits may also occur around the mouths of certain springs. Known also as **Tufa.**

Triassic—The oldest period of the Mesozoic Era, follows the Permian Period of the Paleozoic and precedes the Jurassic Period of the Mesozoic.

Triclinic—One of the six crystal systems.

Trigonal—Three-angled.

Trilobite—An extinct marine arthropod having a flattened segmented body covered by a hardened dorsal exoskeleton marked into three lobes.

Trivial Name—The Latin name added to a generic name to distinguish the species; same as **Specific Name.**

Tsunami—A giant seismic sea wave generated by submarine earthquakes or other disturbances on the sea floor, known also as "tidal wave."

Tufa—Porous calcareous deposits accumulating around springs; calcareous tufa is sometimes called **travertine.**

Tuff—Rock formed from the lithification of volcanic ash.

Turbidity Currents—Strong currents produced by muds sliding down continental slopes.

Twin Crystals—Two or more crystals which have intergrown in a definite way.

Type Locality—The geographic location at which a formation was first described and from which it was named; or from which the type specimen of a fossil species comes.

Unconformity—A break in sedimentation due to erosion; a place in the earth's crust where eroded bedrock is covered by younger sedimentary rocks:

Angular Unconformity—Unconformity where the beds below the unconformable beds had undergone structural deformation before the overlying beds were deposited.

Disconformity—Unconformity where beds above and below the unconformable contact are parallel.

Nonconformity—Unconformity formed by deposition of sedimentary rocks on rocks of igneous origin.

Underground Water—See **Ground Water.**

Unicellular—Composed of one cell.

Uniformitarianism—The doctrine of the present as the key to the past; that geologic history is best interpreted in the light of what is known about the present.

Unstratified Rocks—Rocks that are not stratified or layered.

Valley—A generally elongated depression of the land surface which commonly contains a stream.

Valley Glacier—See **Alpine Glacier.**

Valley Train—A gently sloping flood plain formed of sediment deposited by water flowing out from the foot of a valley glacier.

Valve—The one or more pieces comprising the shell of animals.

Variety—In mineralogy, a subdivision of a mineral species.

Varves—Paired layers of sediments (one coarse and and one fine) deposited in a glacial lake in a period of one year.

Vein—A more or less sheetlike occurrence of ore which has great length and depth but relatively little thickness.

Vent—The pipe or vertical hole through which magma rises in the center of a volcano.

Ventifact—Stone that has been smoothed or changed in shape by wind action.

Vertebrate—An animal having a backbone or spinal column.

Vesicular Rock—Rock characterized by numerous small cavities caused by gas expansion.

Vestigial Structure—Structure that has been reduced in size or usefulness during the course of evolutionary change.

Volcanic Ash—The finest rock particles emitted during volcanic eruptions.

Volcanic Block—A solid, angular fragment thrown out of an erupting volcano.

Volcanic Bomb—A spindle- or tear-shaped mass of congealed magma blown out during a volcanic eruption.

Volcanic Glass—Noncrystalline rock formed by rapid cooling of lava.

Volcanic Neck—Solidified rock material formed by the cooling and hardening of magma in the central vent of a volcano.

Volcanic Shield—See **Shield Volcano.**

Volcanism—Effects of molten rock and volcanoes or volcanic activity; also known as **Vulcanism.**

Volcano—An opening or vent in the earth's crust through which volcanic materials are erupted; refers also to the landform developed by the accumulation of volcanic materials around the vent.

Vulcanism—See **Volcanism.**

Water Gap—Valley or pass through a mountain ridge through which a stream flows.

Water Table—The surface below which all empty spaces within the rock are filled with water.

Weathering—The natural physical and chemical breakdown of rocks under atmospheric conditions.

Wind Gap—A water gap that has been abandoned by its stream.

-zoic—Combining form meaning life (from the Greek *zoikos*, "life").

APPENDIX C

SUGGESTIONS FOR FURTHER READING

Some readers may want to know more about geology in general, or some particular phase of this interesting science. The following list includes selected references of many types, any one of which will provide additional information on a wide variety of geologic topics. This list is by no means all-inclusive, and many other interesting and informative publications can be found in many public, school, and college libraries. The publications are grouped together according to subject matter. Each listing consists of the author, title, publisher, and date of publication.

GENERAL GEOLOGY

Bates, Robert L.; Sweet, Walter C.; and Utgard, Russell O. *Geology: An Introduction*, 2nd ed. D. C. Heath & Company, Lexington, Massachusetts (1973).

Cailleux, André. *Anatomy of the Earth*. McGraw-Hill Book Company, New York (1968).

Krauskopf, Konrad B. *The Third Planet: An Invitation to Geology*. W. H. Freeman and Company, San Francisco (1974).

Mallory, Bob F., and Cargo, David N. *Physical Geology*. McGraw-Hill Book Company, New York (1979).

Matthews, William H., III. *Invitation to Geology: The Earth Through Time and Space*. Doubleday & Company, Garden City, New York (1971).

————. *Introducing the Earth: Geology, Environment, and Man*. Dodd, Mead & Company, New York (1972).

————. *A Guide to the National Parks: Their Landscape and Geology*. Doubleday/Natural History Press, Garden City, New York (1973).

Mears, Brainerd, Jr. *The Changing Earth: Introduction to Geology*, 2nd ed. D. Van Nostrand Company, New York (1977).

Pearl, Richard M. *Geology: An Introduction to Principles of Physical and Historical Geology*, 4th ed. Barnes & Noble Books, New York (1975).

Scientific American. Readings in the Earth Sciences. W. H. Freeman and Company, San Francisco (1969).

Shelton, John S. *Geology Illustrated*. W. H. Freeman and Company, San Francisco (1966).

Stokes, William Lee; Judson, Sheldon; and Picard, Dane M. *Introduction to Geology: Physical and Historical*. Prentice-Hall, Englewood Cliffs, New Jersey (1978).

PHYSICAL GEOLOGY

Allison, Ira S., and Palmer, Donald F. *Geology: The Science of a Changing Earth*, 7th ed. McGraw-Hill Book Company, New York (1980).

Birkeland, Peter W., and Larson, Edwin E. *Putnam's Geology*, 3rd ed. Oxford University Press, New York (1978).

Davis, Stanley N.; Reitan, Paul H.; and Pestrong, Raymond. *Geology: Our Physical Environment*. McGraw-Hill Book Company, New York (1976).

Flint, Richard F., and Skinner, Brian J. *Physical Geology*, 2nd ed. John Wiley & Sons, New York (1977).

Foster, Robert J. *Geology*, 4th ed. Charles E. Merrill Publishing Company, Columbus, Ohio (1980).

Gilluly, James; Waters, Aron C.; and Woodford, A. O. *Principles of Geology,* 4th ed. W. H. Freeman and Company, San Francisco (1975).

Holmes, Arthur, and Holmes, Doris L. *Holmes Principles of Physical Geology,* 3rd ed. John Wiley & Sons, New York (1978).

Leet, L. Don; Judson, Sheldon; and Kauffman, Marvin E. *Physical Geology,* 5th ed. Prentice-Hall, Englewood Cliffs, New Jersey (1978).

Press, Frank, and Siever, Raymond. *Earth,* 2nd ed. W. H. Freeman and Company, San Francisco (1978).

Sanders, John E.; Anderson, Alan H.; and Carola, Robert. *Physical Geology.* Harper & Row, Publishers, New York (1976).

Sawkins, Frederick J., et al. *The Evolving Earth: A Text in Physical Geology.* Macmillan Publishing Company (1974).

HISTORICAL GEOLOGY

Dott, Robert H., Jr., and Batten, Roger L. *Evolution of the Earth,* 2nd ed. McGraw-Hill Book Company, New York (1976).

Eicher, Don L., and McAlester, A. Lee. *History of the Earth.* Prentice-Hall, Englewood Cliffs, New Jersey (1980).

Levin, Harold L. *Life Through Time.* William C. Brown Company, Dubuque, Iowa (1975).

————. *The Earth Through Time.* W. B. Saunders Company, Philadelphia (1978).

Mintz, Leigh W. *Historical Geology: The Science of a Dynamic Earth,* 2nd ed. Charles E. Merrill Publishing Company, Columbus, Ohio (1977).

Ojakangas, Richard W., and Darby, David G. *The Earth: Past and Present.* McGraw-Hill Book Company, New York (1976).

Petersen, Morris S.; Rigby, J. Keith; and Hintze, Lehi F. *Historical Geology of North America,* 2nd ed. William C. Brown Company, Dubuque, Iowa (1980).

Seyfert, Carl K., and Sirkin, Leslie A. *Earth History and Plate Tectonics.* Harper & Row, Publishers, New York (1973).

Stearn, Colin W.; Carroll, Robert L.; and Clark, Thomas H. *Geological Evolution of North America,* 3rd ed. John Wiley & Sons, New York (1979).

ROCKS AND MINERALS

Desautels, Paul E. *The Mineral Kingdom.* A Ridge Press Book/Grosset & Dunlap, New York (1968).

Ernst, W. G. *Earth Materials.* Prentice-Hall, Englewood Cliffs, New Jersey (1969).

Hamilton, W. R.; Wooley, A. R.; and Bishop, A. C. *The Larousse Guide to Minerals, Rocks and Fossils.* Larousse and Company, New York (1977).

Hurlbut, Cornelius S., Jr. *Minerals and Man.* Random House, New York (1969).

Mason, Anita. *The World of Rocks and Minerals.* Larousse and Company, New York (1976).

Pearl, Richard M. *How to Know the Rocks and Minerals.* Signet, New York (1957).

Pough, Frederick H. *A Field Guide to Rocks and Minerals,* 4th ed. Houghton Mifflin Company, Boston (1976).

Sinkankas, John. *Mineralogy for Amateurs.* D. Van Nostrand Company, New York (1964).

Tennissen, Anthony C. *Nature of Earth Materials.* Prentice-Hall, Englewood Cliffs, New Jersey (1974).

Zim, Herbert S., and Shaffer, Paul R. *Rocks and Minerals.* Golden Press, New York (1957).

VOLCANOES AND EARTHQUAKES

Bolt, Bruce A. *Earthquakes: A Primer.* W. H. Freeman and Company, San Francisco (1978).

———— (compiler). *Earthquakes and Volcanoes: Readings from Scientific American.* W. H. Freeman and Company, San Francisco (1980).

Bullard, Fred M. *Volcanoes of the Earth,* rev. ed. University of Texas Press, Austin (1976).

Francis, Peter. *Volcanoes.* Penguin Books, New York (1976).

Gribbin, John. *This Shaking Earth: Earthquakes, Volcanoes, and Their Impact on the World.* G. P. Putnam's Sons, New York (1978).

Hallacy, D. S., Jr. *Earthquakes: A Natural History.* Bobbs-Merrill Company, Indianapolis, Indiana (1974).

Iacopi, Robert. *Earthquake Country: How, Why, and Where Earthquakes Strike California.* Lane Magazine & Book Company, Menlo Park, California (1964).

Macdonald, Gordon A. *Volcanoes.* Prentice-Hall, Englewood Cliffs, New Jersey (1972).

Oakeshott, Gordon B. *Volcanoes and Earthquakes.* McGraw-Hill Book Company, New York (1976).

Yanev, Peter. *Peace of Mind in Earthquake Country.* San Francisco Chronicle Books, San Francisco (1974).

LANDFORMS AND THE EARTH'S SURFACE

Bloom, Arthur L. *The Surface of the Earth.* Prentice-Hall, Englewood Cliffs, New Jersey (1969).

Dury, G. H. *The Face of the Earth.* Penguin Books, Baltimore, Maryland (1966).

Tuttle, Sherwood D. *Landforms and Landscapes,* 3rd ed. William C. Brown Company, Dubuque, Iowa (1980).

Wykoff, Jerome. *Rock, Time, and Landforms.* Harper & Row, Publishers. New York (1966).

PLATE TECTONICS

Calder, Nigel. *The Restless Earth.* Viking Press, New York (1972).

Colbert, Edwin H. *Wandering Lands and Animals.* E. P. Dutton & Company, New York (1973).

Fodor, Ronald V. *Earth in Motion: The Concept of Plate Tectonics.* William Morrow & Company, New York (1978).

Glen, William. *Continental Drift and Plate Tectonics.* Charles E. Merrill Publishing Company, Columbus, Ohio (1975).

Press, Frank, and Siever, Raymond (compilers). *Planet Earth: Readings from Scientific American.* W. H. Freeman and Company, San Francisco (1974).

Sullivan, Walter. *Continents in Motion.* McGraw-Hill Book Company, New York (1974).

Tarling, Don, and Tarling, Maureen. *Continental Drift, A Study of Earth's Moving Surface.* Anchor Press/Doubleday, Garden City, New York (1971).

Wilson, J. Tuzo (compiler). *Continents Adrift and Continents Aground: Readings from Scientific American.* W. H. Freeman and Company, San Francisco (1976).

EARTH HISTORY, EVOLUTION, AND FOSSILS

Clark, David L. *Fossils, Paleontology and Evolution,* 2nd ed. William C. Brown Company, Dubuque, Iowa (1976).

Cowen, Richard. *History of Life.* McGraw-Hill Book Company, New York (1976).

Eicher, Don L. *Geologic Time,* 2nd ed. Prentice-Hall, Englewood Cliffs, New Jersey (1976).

Flint, Richard F. *The Earth and Its History.* W. W. Norton & Company, New York (1973).

Hotton, Nicholas, III. *The Evidence of Evolution.* D. Van Nostrand Company, New York (1968).

Lane, N. Gary. *Life of the Past.* Charles E. Merrill Publishing Company, Columbus, Ohio (1978).

Laporte, Leo F. *Ancient Environments,* 2nd ed. Prentice-Hall, Englewood Cliffs, New Jersey (1979).

———— (compiler). *Evolution and the Fossil Record: Readings from Scientific American.* W. H. Freeman and Company, San Francisco (1978).

Matthews, William H., III. *Fossils: An Introduction to Prehistoric Life.* Barnes & Noble Books, New York (1962).

McAlester, A. Lee. *The History of Life,* 2nd ed. Prentice-Hall, Englewood Cliffs, New Jersey (1977).

Poirier, Frank E. *Fossil Evidence: The Human Evolutionary Journey,* 2nd ed. C. V. Mosby Company, Saint Louis, Missouri (1977).

Rhodes, Frank H. T. *The Evolution of Life,* 2nd ed. Penguin Books, New York (1976).

Rhodes, Frank H. T.; Zim, Herbert S.; and Shaffer, Paul R. *Fossils: A Guide to Prehistoric Life.* Golden Press, New York (1962).

Sauer, Norman J., and Phenice, Terrill W. *Hominid Fossils,* 2nd ed. William C. Brown Company, Dubuque, Iowa (1977).

Savage, Jay M. *Evolution,* 3rd ed. Holt, Rinehart and Winston, New York (1977).

ENVIRONMENT AND MINERAL RESOURCES

Cargo, David N., and Mallory, Bob F. *Man and His Geologic Environment,* 2nd ed. Addison-Wesley Publishing Company, Reading, Massachusetts (1977).

Flawn, Peter T. *Environmental Geology,* Harper & Row, Publishers, New York (1970).

Harrison, George R. *The Conquest of Energy.* William Morrow & Company, New York (1968).

Keller, Edward A. *Environmental Geology,* 2nd ed. Charles E. Merrill Publishing Company, Columbus, Ohio (1979).

Kesler, Stephen E. *Our Finite Mineral Resources.* McGraw-Hill Book Company, New York (1976).

Laporte, Leo F. *Encounter with the Earth.* Canfield Press/Harper & Row, Publishers, San Francisco (1975).

Menard, H. William. *Geology, Resources, and Society.* W. H. Freeman and Company, San Francisco (1974).

Skinner, Brian J. *Earth Resources,* 2nd ed. Prentice-Hall, Englewood Cliffs, New Jersey (1976).

Young, Keith. *Geology: The Paradox of Earth and Man.* Houghton Mifflin Company, Boston (1975).

MISCELLANEOUS

American Geological Institute. *A Dictionary of Geological Terms,* rev. ed. Anchor Press/Doubleday, Garden City, New York (1976).

Bates, Robert E., and Jackson, Julia A. *Glossary of Geology,* 2nd ed. American Geological Institute, 5205 Leesburg Pike, Falls Church, Virginia 22041 (1980).

Boyer, Robert E., and Snyder, P. B. *Geology Fact Book,* Hubbard Press, Northbrook, Illinois (1973).

Hurlbut, Cornelius S., Jr. (editor). *The Planet We Live On: An Illustrated Encyclopedia of the Earth Sciences.* Harry N. Abrams, New York (1976).

Lapedes, Daniel N. (editor). *McGraw-Hill Encyclopedia of the Geological Sciences.* McGraw-Hill Book Company, New York (1978).

Matthews, William H., III. *Mineral, Fossil, and Rock Exhibits and Where to See Them.* American Geological Institute, 5205 Leesburg Pike, Falls Church, Virginia 22041 (1977).

Pampe, William R. *Maps and Geological Publications of the United States: A Layman's Guide.* American Geological Institute, 5205 Leesburg Pike, Falls Church, Virginia 22041 (1978).

Index

Aa, 46, 193
Abrasion, 75, 89, 95, 193
Abrasives, 37
Absolute time, 193
Abyssal plain, 101–2
Acadian disturbance, 176
Acidic lavas, 45–46
Acidic or sialic rocks, 42, 193
Acid rain, 125
Acquired characteristics, theory of, 170
Actinolite, 31
Actinolite-tremolite, 37
Active volcano, 44
Adamantine luster, 26
Adirondacks, 121
Aeolian material, 193
Africa
    distribution of glacial deposits in, 15
    proposed fit, prior to continental drifting, 12
African plate, 11, 16
Aftershock, 193
Agate, 30
A-horizon, soil profile, 71
Airy, G. B., 62
Alabaster, 32
Alaid Volcano, 45
Alaska
    earthquakes of, 111, 116–17
    oil formations, 21
    volcanoes of, 44
Alaskan earthquake of 1964, 116–17
Albite moonstone, 29
Aleutian Islands
    earthquakes of, 111
    volcanoes of, 44, 50
Alkali flats or salinas, 109
Alkaline lakes, 109
Allegheny Mountains, 122
Alligators, 163
Allosaurus, 180
Alluvial cones, 78
Alluvial fans, 78, 193
Alluvial plains, 119
Alluvium, 78, 193
Alpine glacier (or mountain or valley glacier), 88, 193

Alps, 121
Altitude, 193
Aluminum, 23, 34, 38, 72, 129
    principal source of, 124
Amber, 144, 193
Amblypods, 168
Ambulacral or food grooves, 159
American plate, 11, 16
Amethyst, 30
Ammonites, 179, 180, 193
Ammonitic suture, 157
Ammonoidea (the extinct ammonoids), 156, 157
Amorphous minerals, 29, 193
Amphibians, 162, 176, 177, 178, 179, 180, 193
Amphiboles, 31
Amphineura (chitons or "sea-mice"), 154
Amygdules, 40, 193
Anatosaurus, 165, 181
Andes, 121
Andesite, 42
Angular unconformity, 67, 206
Anhydrite, 32–33, 55, 69, 193
Animal classification, 151–69
Ankylosaurus (ankylosaurs), 165, 166, 181
Annelid worms, 157
Antarctica, proposed fit prior to continental drifting, 12
Antarctic Ocean
    basaltic bottom of, 8
    coal deposits, 20
Antarctic plate, 11, 16
Antarctic Sea, 100
Antecedent stream, 75
Anthracite coal, 20, 60, 193
Anthropoidea, 187
Anticlines, 64, 193
Apatite, hardness of, 25, 26
Aperture, 155, 193
Apex, 155
Aphanitic texture, 42, 193
Aplite, 40
Appalachian coal, 20
Appalachian Geosyncline, 64
Appalachian Highlands, formation of, 64
Appalachian revolution, 178

Aquifers, 82, 193
Aragonite, 32, 193
Archaeopteryx, 166, 180, 181
Archelon, 182
Archeozoic Era, 137, 173
    meaning of, 136
Archimedes, 152, 177
Arctic Ocean, 8, 100
Arenaceous shale, 54, 193
Arêtes, 89, 193
Argentite, 35
Argillaceous shale, 54, 193
Argon, 7, 139
Aristotle, 142
Arkose, 54
Artesian wells, 83, 193
Arthropods, 157–58, 175, 184
Articulate brachiopods, 153
Articulated process, 193
Artifacts, 193
Artificial lakes, 108
Artiodactyls, 169
Asbestos, 31, 37, 129
    luster of, 27
Astartella, 154
Asterism, 28
Asteroids (or planetoids), 5, 6, 193
Asthenosphere, 193
    plate boundaries, 17
Astraeospongium, 151
Astrogeology, 193
Astronomy, 3, 4, 5
Astronomy Made Simple (Degani), 5
Asymmetrical fold, 193
Athabasca tar sands, 128
Atlantic Coastal Plain, 119
Atlantic Ocean
    basaltic bottom of, 8
    size of, 100
    volcanoes of, 44
Atlantic Outer Continental Shelf, 21
Atmosphere, 7, 193
Atoll, 106
Atoms, 22
Attitude, 64, 193
Augite, 31
Australia
    distribution of glacial deposits in, 15